JOURNEY TO THE SOURCE OF THE NILE

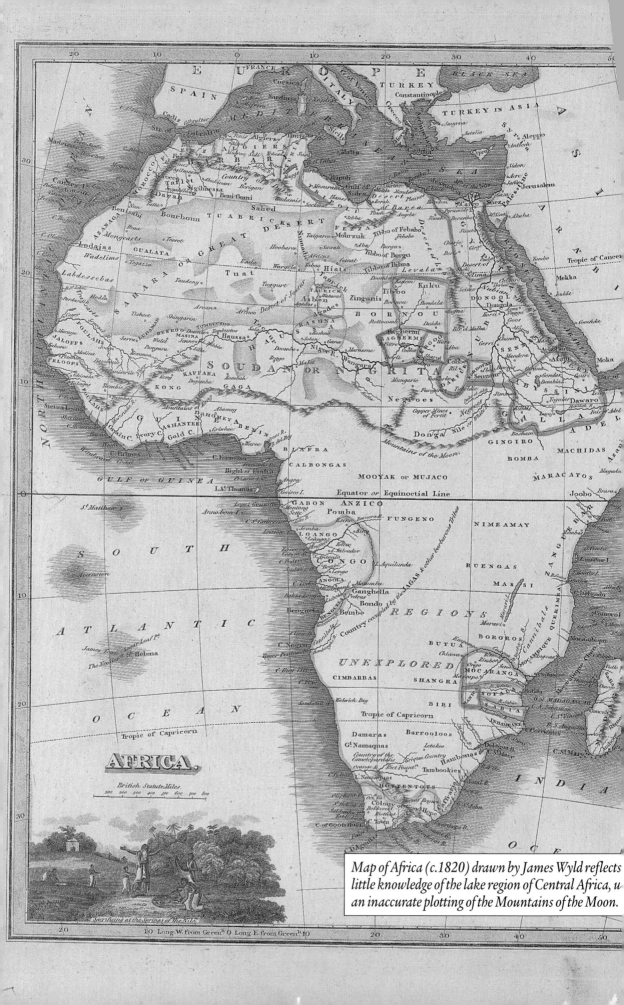

Map of Africa (c.1820) drawn by James Wyld reflects little knowledge of the lake region of Central Africa, u an inaccurate plotting of the Mountains of the Moon.

JOURNEY TO THE SOURCE OF
THE NILE

CHRISTOPHER ONDAATJE

FIREFLY BOOKS

A FIREFLY BOOK

Published by Firefly Books Ltd., 1999.

First Printing

Library of Congress Cataloguing in Publication Data

Ondaatje, Christopher.
    Journey to the source of the Nile / Christopher Ondaatje; special introduction by Lord Selborne, President, Royal Geographical Society
[384] p. : col. ill., maps;   cm.
Originally published: Toronto: HarperCollins, 1998.
Includes bibliographical references (p.   ) and index.
Summary: Story of the author's expedition to the source of the Nile, as he retraces the steps of famous explorers, including Richard Burton and John Hanning Speke
ISBN 1-55209-371-9
1. Nile River Valley— Discovery and exploration. 2. Africa, Central — description and travel. I. Selborne, Lord, President, Royal Geographical Society. II. Title.
916.7/04—dc21   1999   CIP

First published in the United States in 1999 by
Firefly Books (U.S.) Inc.
P.O. Box 1338, Ellicott Station
Buffalo, New York 14205

Book design and project management by Jackie Young/ink
Printing and binding by Transcontinental Printing, Montreal, Quebec
Film separations by Batten Graphics, Toronto, Ontario
Printed and bound in Canada

View of Stone Town from Emerson's House, Zanzibar.

To Valda
who understood the devils

Caravans, called in Kisawahili safári ..., are rarely wanting on the main trunk lines. The favourite seasons for the upward-bound are the months in which the ... tropical rains conclude ... when water and provisions are plentiful.

RICHARD F. BURTON
The Lake Regions of Central Africa

Contents

Shell cleaning on the streets of Zanzibar.

ACKNOWLEDGEMENTS

Both this book and the journey of discovery on which it is based provided unforeseen challenges. It was a search on many levels for the truth about the Nile's sources. I knew, early on, that it was not going to be easy accumulating the material. I simply did not know what was going to be out there.

From the very beginning Rosemary Aubert was invaluable, indeed indispensable. Together we tracked, hacked, and ploughed through mounds of books, magazines, and articles about the nineteenth-century explorers who had sought out the mystery of the world's longest river. We did not know then what we would find. The journey itself provided a whole new set of theories and this required more research.

The next stage of the process needed someone fascinated with both the achievements of the Victorian explorers and the theory of plate tectonics. Geoffrey Ewing helped with the research that made the final edit possible by verifying historical and scientific facts and by checking and finding proof of the theories.

Margaret Allen's editing put it all into perspective. She identified what was essential and allowed the journey's rhythms to shape the story. Joyce Fox met the challenge of preparing the physical manuscript. Elizabeth MacLean provided assistance in the final copy-editing and proofreading stages. Jackie Young brought his discerning eye to the design of the book, including the selection of photographs, illustrations, and maps.

To all these I owe an enormous debt of gratitude. They were patient and tolerant, decisive and understanding. If I have achieved anything in this book, it is because of them.

Preparing charcoal west of Bagamoyo.

INTRODUCTION

The hroughout recorded history there have been times when the urge to explore previously unknown parts of the world has captured the imagination of whole races, to the surprise and often consternation of those on the receiving end of these expeditions. Alexander the Great, Henry the Navigator, Christopher Columbus — each led expeditions which were to have consequences that resonated through the ages. The nineteenth century was another such period when Europeans were stimulated to challenge the frontiers of the world that they knew.

The Royal Geographical Society was founded in London in 1830 by a group of intrepid travellers to "promote that most important and entertaining branch of knowledge ... geography." Geographical knowledge, then as now, was seen as the key to unlocking many of the mysteries relating to this planet.

There were many strands of interest that contributed to this enthusiasm for exploration, of which trade and missionary zeal were but two. The early members of the Royal Geographical Society saw their central role as that of mapping parts of the world unknown to Europe. An expedition was organized to search for the North West Passage, led by the Society's Vice-President Sir John Franklin, and medals were awarded to early explorers of the vast deserts of the Australian Outback. However, even in those early years, the collection of geographical data meant more than mapping unrecorded parts of the world, important though this was. When Captain Robert Fitzroy charted the coast of South America he took with him the young Charles Darwin, who assiduously collected specimens which were ultimately to provide the inspiration for the theory of evolution by natural selection. One of the central figures of this book, Richard Burton, amassed anthropological data of great importance to successive generations during his travels in Asia and Africa.

I am prepared to start alone and if judged necessary disguised as an Arab merchant...
RICHARD F. BURTON
1856 letter to Norton Shaw, Secretary of the Royal Geographical Society

Recently rediscovered portrait of Sir Richard Burton in Afghan dress, by John Phillip, R.A. (1817-1867). Now in the collection of the author.

13

Soon the attention of the Royal Geographical Society turned to Africa, with a particular interest in determining the source of the River Nile. This was a subject which had engaged the interest of men since ancient times, and became in the mid-nineteenth century a subject of fierce debate. Successive expeditions were mounted to resolve once and for all the mystery of the Nile's source. The tribulations of these explorers, of Burton and Speke, then Speke and Grant, of Samuel and Florence Baker, of Livingstone and Stanley, are all astonishing stories of personal sacrifice, tenacity, and courage. They each had different reasons for enduring such hardships, but there is no denying that, with the possible exception of Livingstone, each was driven by a strong competitive instinct to be the first European to be able to claim the distinction of identifying the source of the Nile.

This accolade is now attributed to Speke, who was the first European to see the great body of water that he named Lake Victoria. But it was many years later that the full story of the role of the lakes of Central Africa as reservoirs feeding the Nile and the Congo rivers was finally resolved by Stanley.

The Victorians' fascination for determining the Nile's origins puzzled the Africans, who gave the name *mzungu* (meaning "he who walks around in circles") to the white men who travelled through their land. The suspicion with which these early travellers were received proved all too justified as successive colonies were later established by the British, French, Germans, and Belgians. A long chain of European intervention and influence led to massive changes, culminating in artificial national boundaries which paid little regard to ethnic and geographical realities.

Livingstone was driven by an acute sense of outrage at the cruelty of the slave trade and he was convinced that European influence would bring order out of chaos. Yet, at the end of the twentieth century, Africa seems again to be gripped by political turmoil as waves of refugees move out of their homelands.

Christopher Ondaatje has travelled along the routes of those early explorers, reflecting on his way on the issues that preoccupied these intrepid Victorians and on the nature of the ultimate truth, which the Victorians were so keen to establish. We now understand in precise detail the drainage system of the lakes and we have mapped the Mountains of the Moon, the Ruwenzori Mountains.

Yet now that the Victorians' obsession with one geographical objective, the determination of the source of the Nile, has faded into history we can appreciate the true significance of this part of Africa to humanity. Our first ancestors lived in East Africa. The formation of the Great Rift Valley might have been the evolutionary spur that gave rise to natural selection pressures and to the spread of humanity around the world. As Ondaatje points out, both the Nile and mankind might owe their existence to the creation of these same geological features. If so, then European explorers did not "discover" this part of Africa, they returned to the land of their first ancestors.

Christopher Ondaatje has challenged us to look with a new insight into the significance of the great European expeditions in search of the source of the Nile. Like these Victorian explorers, he has made some unexpected but fascinating discoveries.

Lord Selborne
President, The Royal Geographical Society

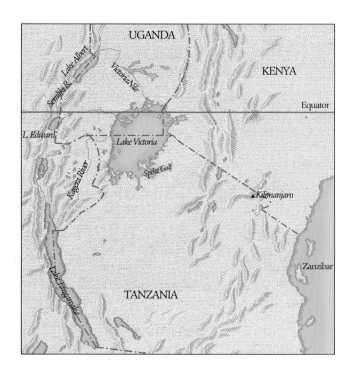

A Song of Africa

I no longer felt any doubt that the lake at my feet gave birth to that interesting River, the source of which has been the subject of much speculation, and the object of so many explorers. The Arab's tale was proved to the letter. This is a far more extensive lake than the Tanganyika; "so broad that you could not see across it, and so long that nobody knew its length."

JOHN HANNING SPEKE
What Led to the Discovery of the Source of the Nile

ON 3RD AUGUST 1858
FROM ISAMILO HILL ONE MILE FROM
THIS POINT SPEKE FIRST SAW
THE MAIN WATERS OF LAKE VICTORIA
WHICH HE AFTERWARDS PROVED TO BE
THE SOURCE OF THE NILE

PROLOGUE:

A SONG OF AFRICA

I stared at the dilapidated plaque inconspicuously placed at the inside edge of a busy roundabout in the centre of Mwanza, a town on the southern shore of Lake Victoria, in the heart of East Africa.

Ours had been a long and tiring journey, almost ten thousand kilometres. We had retraced the routes taken by the greatest of the Victorian explorers of the Nile. We had followed the trail of Richard Burton and John Hanning Speke's 1857 expedition from Zanzibar across Tanzania to Lake Tanganyika. At a time of great political unrest and upheaval in the region, we had skirted the southern and western shores of Lake Victoria, from Mwanza to Uganda. We had re-travelled the route of Speke and James Augustus Grant along the western and northern rim of Lake Victoria to Ripon Falls (now submerged by Owen Falls dam) and the start of the Victoria Nile. We had followed Samuel Baker's journey along the Victoria Nile westward to Murchison Falls and Lake Albert. We had reached the Ruwenzori Mountains, the legendary "Mountains of the Moon." We had seen the Semliki River and Lake Edward and Lake George, as Henry Morton Stanley had. Finally, we had finished circling Lake Victoria through Kenya, travelling southward along the eastern shores to Mwanza for a second time.

Now, it seemed, we had one more mile to go. The plaque read:

> On 3rd August, 1858
> from Isamilo Hill
> one mile from
> this point, Speke first saw
> the main waters of Lake Victoria
> which he afterwards proved to be
> the source of the Nile

Exhausted, filthy, and hungry, my guide Thad Peterson and I stopped for supplies, fixed yet another flat tire, wolfed down some food, and set out on our mile — first through a tract of slum dwellings, then past the luxuriant gardens of much wealthier properties, then past isolated hilltop shacks.

Previous Page: The Wasagara display great varieties of complexion, some being black, whilst the other are chocolate-coloured .... The women are remarkable for a splendid development of limb ....

RICHARD F. BURTON
The Lake Regions of Central Africa

As we approached the top of Isamilo Hill and the spot where Speke had stood on that August morning in 1858, I felt a thrill of anticipation. At last, the long-awaited moment arrived: as we crested the hill I could see below me, to the north, a vast, seemingly endless stretch of glistening, wind-ruffled blue — more like a sea than a lake. Here, on this spot, John Hanning Speke had stared out over the waters and decided — almost on a hunch — that they were the source of the Nile. Although Speke's claims remained controversial for some time, in retrospect we can see that moment as the culmination of centuries of speculation by Europeans about the river's source. It was also the beginning of the next phase in European involvement, providing a new reason to visit Africa, setting in motion a process of "opening" the continent to the rest of the world, and laying the groundwork for a fateful and bitter battle for control of its land, its resources, and its people.

This part of the vast lake had a name when Speke "discovered" it, but its name is different now: Speke Gulf. Houses dot the horizon, making the view different, too — different, but still spectacular. It was a moment of great tranquillity, of brief respite from a feeling of unease I experienced here. This lakeside city seemed to me turbulent, ominous, mysterious, unsettling, and yet apathetic, too. Perhaps because I knew I was an intruder, an uninvited voyeur. Into my mind slipped Karen Blixen's sensitive lament: "If I know a song of Africa ... does Africa know a song of me?"

At the beginning of the nineteenth century, Europeans knew very little about Africa. In a remarkably short space of time, missionaries arrived, introducing Christianity. Then came explorers who located, surveyed, and mapped rivers and mountains, and catalogued flora and fauna. These explorations paved the way for increasing European domination, until, one hundred years later, the enormous continent was ruled by European powers: England, Germany, Belgium, Portugal, and France.

By the end of the twentieth century, Africa seems again a great unknown — a continent gripped by political turmoil, wrestling with huge economic and environmental challenges, and struggling to define itself and emerge from the long shadow cast by colonialism. Today, the boundaries so arbitrarily drawn by Europeans are being blurred by the forces of independence and dictatorship, as well as the re-emergence of tribal influences and the growth of Islam.

I have always found Africa compelling. I had been in Africa, had written about Africa before. Now I was back again, unable to stay away. The intricate origins of the Nile, the greatest of Africa's rivers, still intrigue us, invite study, and compel awe. Very few people understand the complexities of the Nile's discovery. I had wanted to see for myself the now-legendary places where this great life-giving river began its journey north through the vast stretches of Africa. Like John Hanning Speke, I wanted to be able to say for myself, "The Nile is settled."

✳ ✳ ✳

When I set out to trace the labyrinthine network of rivers and lakes that eventually become the Nile, I hoped to achieve several things. I have always been enthralled by the drama of stories about the search for the source of the Nile, savouring the vivid mental pictures they evoke. But the more I travel, the more I realize that mental pictures, however vivid, can never equal the sight of the thing itself. In order to grasp fully why the question of the Nile's origins had been such a difficult puzzle to solve, as well as to appreciate the hazards, the splendours, and the sheer romance of the explorers' stories, I needed to cover the same difficult terrain they had traversed, follow the devious courses of the same waterways. I would have to stand on the banks of those rivers or lakes or waterfalls, see for myself the direction of the current's or the cataract's flow, sense for myself the magnitude of the forces that shaped the mighty river, and fit it all into my own mental jigsaw puzzle.

A second impulse came from my fascination with the men and women explorers who had this obsession before me. I felt that the effort to retrace their steps, to walk — as much as a modern man can — in their shoes, would explain them and their achievements to me in a way written accounts could not.

A third goal, the most elusive of the three, concerned the need I felt to "settle the Nile" in a personal way. Questions about the Nile had occupied my mind for many years; it had come to stand for a large piece of unfinished business. Now, at last, I felt I must — and could — do something about it. It was as though the Nile had cast a powerful spell which I could lift only by having my own "Nile experience" — learning from my own responses and contributing my own story to the lore about this ancient and most fascinating of rivers.

In the nineteenth century, before photographs in mass-circulation magazines, film and television documentaries, and the Internet, there was no way to find out about the wonders of the world except through the accounts of the explorers. But what of today, when we all feel we can learn anything we need to know through our sophisticated communications technology? In Richard Carrington's view, "the writer of travel books today has a less enviable task than his predecessors. When the known world was restricted to the lands bordering the Mediterranean Sea it was sufficient for a traveller who voyaged beyond its confines simply to record what he saw. The facts themselves, by their very novelty and strangeness, had a dramatic or poetic significance which assured him of a readership. Even in more recent times, while much of Africa remained unexplored and men had not yet stood at the poles of the earth or on the summits of its highest mountains, it was still possible for a record of physical achievement alone to capture the imagination."

What this comment does not allow for, however, is the fact that landscapes and peoples are not static. Countless events and forces continually reshape the world. None of us can go back to the landscape exactly as it was in the time of Burton and Speke. Reading their accounts is in a way like looking through an old photograph album. It is wonderful and amazing to

learn how things used to be. It can be even more amazing to revisit historic settings today, delighting in survivals from the past while learning about the way things are now.

The landscape and people of today are at least as interesting as those of yesterday, and I have recorded as much about them as I could. In any age, we hunger for the stories told by explorers who have been to some distant place. It is important for us to record our experiences of that same place today. The past gives us a context for understanding the present and, in turn, our observations provide a context for future travellers.

A man of broad and stalwart frame, with stern countenance, and a quietness of demeanour which usually argues sang-froid and persistency....

RICHARD F. BURTON
The Lake Regions of Central Africa

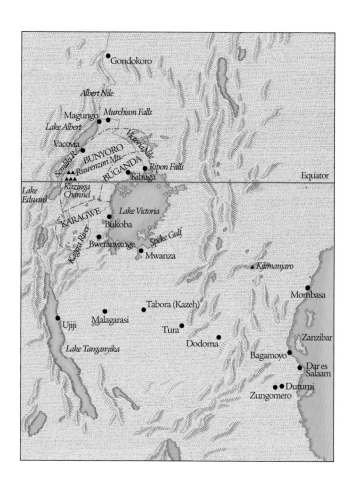

What Led to the Journey
to the Source of the Nile

The very word explorer suggests almost a caricature, a figure, pith helmet firmly on his head, still bravely leading his expedition in spite of exhaustion. Relentlessly hunting big game or elephants, contending with mosquitoes and other nefarious insects, he never abandons his ultimate goal. By turns debonair and commanding, resolute and cautious, enthusiastic and disillusioned, he is the all-round hero, scornful above all else of deceit and irresolution.

ANNE HUGON
The Exploration of Africa: From Cairo to the Cape

1

WHAT LED TO THE JOURNEY TO THE SOURCE OF THE NILE

According to the great Victorian explorer Richard Francis Burton, "it is the explorer's unpleasant duty throughout these lands to doubt everything that has not been subjected to his own eyes."

The urge to see with their own eyes drove Victorian explorers like Burton far into what they considered the dark corners of the Earth. The question of the origin of the Nile was intimately connected with the mysteries of Africa itself. It did not seem to occur to the Victorians that the eyes of others had long gazed on the wonders they "discovered." For an Englishman, seeing for the first time what no European had yet seen was a triumph. And there was no greater triumph than to set eyes on the source of the Nile River.

The search for the source of the Nile both spearheaded and symbolized what nineteenth-century Europeans regarded as the opening of Africa to religion, to exploration, to economic activity — and to civilization. The Victorian explorers never seemed to forget their place as civilized people among those they considered less civilized, and were always ready to impress

I am a little thankful to old Nile for so hiding his head that all "theoretical discoverers" are left out in the cold. With all real explorers I have a hearty sympathy, and I have some regret at being obliged, in a manner compelled, to speak somewhat disparagingly of the opinions formed by my predecessors. The work of Speke and Grant is part of the history of this region, and since the discovery of the sources of the Nile, was asserted so positively it seems necessary to explain, not offensively I hope, wherein their mistake lay, in making a somewhat similar claim. My opinions may yet be shown to be mistaken too, but at present I cannot conceive how.

DAVID LIVINGSTONE
Journal [18 August, 1870]

Eastern shore of Lake Tanganyika, north of Ujiji.

Old Nile played the theorists a pretty prank by having his springs 500 miles south of them all! I call mine a contribution, because it is just a hundred years (1769) since Bruce, a greater traveller than any of us, visited Abyssinia, and having discovered the sources of the Blue Nile, he thought he had then solved the ancient problem.

DAVID LIVINGSTONE
From a paper on the sources of the Nile, December 1868

Previous page: Murchison Falls on the Victoria Nile.

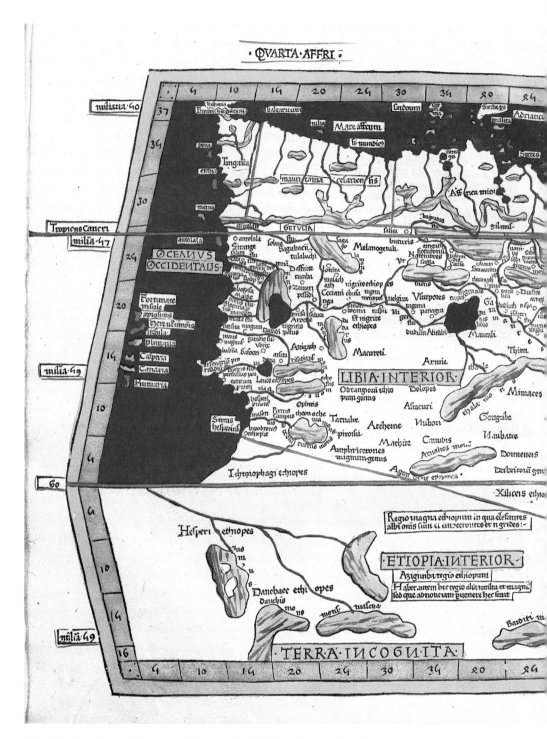

Hand-coloured map, "Quarta Affrice Tabula," based on Ptolemy's second-century Geography.

Map courtesy of the Royal Geographical Society.

They will observe with pleasure that we have not much to boast of; that the ancient travellers, geographers, and authors had a very fair idea whence the Nile issued, that they had heard of the springs which gave birth to the famous river of Egypt.

HENRY MORTON STANLEY
In Darkest Africa

the foreigner with their own superiority. These Victorians were, on the whole, gentlemen (and sometimes lady) adventurers with orderly habits. Even while groping through the unmapped interior of the "dark continent," Burton and his partner in exploration, John Hanning Speke, were used to sitting themselves down "in a bower of leafy branches," as Burton put it, to work on their diaries and sketchbooks, much, I suspect, as I worked with my journal, tape recorder, and camera.

Whatever the peculiarities of the Victorian explorers, in their search for the source of the Nile they were engaged in the solution of a mystery that had puzzled humankind since ancient times. The speculations of the ancients were sometimes remarkably apt. The most accurate were those put forward by Ptolemy, who lived in the second century A.D. He was Graeco-Egyptian, an astronomer who, from accounts of travellers' tales, provided the first correct explanation that the Nile flowed out of two reservoirs located in a great mountain range in the heart of Africa. The early writers followed his example and called this range the "Mountains of the Moon."

Over the centuries, the maps of Europeans showed the Mountains of the Moon clearly, usually with rivers draining from the mountains to a few great lakes, from which issued two or three large rivers that flowed northward and eventually formed the great river Nile.

The ancients of the Western world were not alone in their interest in the Nile and its sources. The Arab slavers and traders had a long tradition of theorizing on the topic. For millennia, they had conducted a thriving trade along the Mediterranean and eastern coasts of Africa, carrying the mined and manufactured goods (especially copper or brass wire, cotton cloth from India and later the United States, and glass or porcelain beads) south from Europe and Asia and returning north with cargoes of gold, ivory, and slaves — and knowledge. After the Sultan of Oman moved his court to Zanzibar in 1832 and consolidated his power along the mainland coast, more Arab and Indian traders were attracted by the improved conditions for their enterprise. Some of them began leading expeditions into the interior instead of just conducting business in the seaports. They reached Lake Tanganyika in the late 1830s, and Lake Victoria in the early 1840s. From the north, the desire of Egypt's ruler, the Albanian-born Mohammed Ali, to expand his territory and power resulted in an 1820–22 expedition which reached the confluence of the Blue and White Niles and founded Khartoum. In the early 1840s, other expeditions penetrated the Sudd and reached Gondokoro. Arab slavers began entering the region but were blocked from reaching the great interior lakes by the hostility of local tribes.

For Europeans, by the early nineteenth century the clear — if sparse — information gleaned from the ancients and from anecdotal accounts had become distorted and confused in the process of transmission. There were conflicting theories. Through his study of historical maps, Henry Morton Stanley came to the conclusion that later map-makers were careless, and that knowledge of the Nile and its sources had begun to decline due to their lack of conscientious skill. "All that we had gathered since the days of old Homer down to the seventeenth century — all the lakes are swept away …. We simply owe our ignorance to the map-makers. We no sooner discover some natural feature than it is removed in a next issue." Victorian explorers felt an intense need to clear up all the confusion.

The search for knowledge that would solve the mystery of the Nile had various motivations. Although the thinkers of the ancient world and the Victorian explorers no doubt saw themselves initially as interested in knowing the truth about the Nile, the focus rapidly shifted to trade and economic and social control of the continent. The Victorian reverence for profits, moral rectitude, and an orderly society shaped the course of events in Africa, as missionaries, entrepreneurs, and administrators followed in the wake of the explorers.

England's interest in Africa had become remarkably complex by the middle of the nineteenth century. Predictably, the burgeoning Industrial Revolution had opened the two-way street between foreign suppliers of raw materials for manufacturing and foreign markets for manufactured goods. The growth of liberal ideas and zeal for moral reform drove the anti-slavery movement, which could be truly effective only if it went to the source. A renewed interest in natural science in Victorian Britain spurred research as never before. The evangelical Christian movement also saw Africa as a new frontier, brimming with souls to be saved. These factors made the "opening" of Africa a compelling idea.

Alan Moorehead provides a brilliant telling of the story of the river in his book *The White Nile*. As he perceptively writes, "until the mystery of the physical nature of the region and its great river was cleared up it was difficult to know precisely how to act." Where did this mighty river — the longest in the world — come from? Solving this mystery would become the great exploration. The stories of the journeys of the explorers, their experiences, findings, battles, claims, and counter-claims, were to fascinate mid-nineteenth-century Europeans and North Americans for several decades. Claims to have discovered the source of the Nile were accepted for reasons that sometimes had as much to do with the mood of the times as with the validity of the information, and debates about the explorers' findings continued until well into the twentieth century. Today there are still questions, and some of these result from a more sophisticated view of the world than was possible then. With all the information available to us today, it requires an effort of imagination to understand the nature of the puzzle that so baffled the early explorers. It was a puzzle with many different pieces, and the topography of the country made it extremely difficult to link those pieces.

To begin with, the single river Nile that flows from Khartoum into the Mediterranean Sea combines the waters from two source rivers, the Blue Nile, which rises in Ethiopia, and the White Nile, which rises in the lake region of Central Africa. The exploration of the Blue Nile is a separate story. It was the source of the White Nile that was regarded as the greater mystery, and the story of its exploration which has always fascinated me.

In his excellent study *The Tears of Isis*, Richard Carrington traces the Nile's course and describes its geological history. The waters of the White Nile come from a cluster of lakes in Central Africa: Lake Victoria in a highland basin, and Lakes Edward, George, and Albert in the western rift valley. The area is a complex of streams and rivers, volcanoes and escarpments, and in the centre is the Ruwenzori range, Ptolemy's Mountains of the Moon. As Rennie Bere tells us in his book *The Way to the Mountains of the Moon*, "for the naturalist this must be one of the most exciting lands on earth. It is the centre of Africa, in biogeographic terms, and is occupied by representative examples of the flora and fauna from many parts of the continent. There are equatorial rain forest and arid lands not far removed from desert. There is the wide sweep of the African savanna — wet or dry, woodland and open grassland. There are high mountain communities some of which are quite unique. Each type of country supports its own particular range of animals."

The Nile, 6,695 kilometres in length, stretches from the lush forests of the equatorial region to — and through — the arid desert region of North Africa. When the river leaves the region of the lakes, it becomes for a time the Bahr el Jebel (Mountain River), navigable for only a few stretches as far as Juba, across the river from what was once Gondokoro. A little north of Juba, the Nile is swallowed by the Sudd, thousands of square kilometres of nearly impenetrable marsh, where half of the water provided by the great lakes evaporates. This was the most intractable obstacle to explorers seeking to follow the White Nile upstream to its source. The Bahr el Jebel manages to struggle northward through the middle of the Sudd. From the west, the Bahr el Ghazal (River of Gazelles) flows into the northern section of the giant marsh and joins the main stream in Lake No, out of which issues the Bahr el Abiad (White River or White Nile) flowing to the east. Just downstream from Lake No, the Bahr el Zeraf (River of Giraffes) flows in from the south, out of the Sudd, having paralleled the Bahr el Jebel for more than half the length of the swamp. Shortly thereafter, the first of the three tributaries from the Ethiopian highlands, the Sobat, flows in from the east, just before the river turns north again. At Khartoum, the White Nile meets the Blue Nile (Bahr el Azraq), the second tributary from Ethiopia. As a single stream they flow north another 300 kilometres before being joined by the last tributary (and the third from Ethiopia), the seasonal Atbara River, still 2,700 kilometres from the sea. From here the river flows in a great, S-shaped curve through the Nubian Massif, the area of the famous six cataracts, and then almost straight north from Aswan to the Mediterranean.

The river as we know it was formed very recently, as geological time goes — less than thirteen thousand years ago — and far more recently than Carrington had thought. However, he was aware that its future was threatened. The terraces and limestone cliffs flanking the lower channel of the Nile testified to the shrinking of the river as more of northern Africa became desert. As he noted: "The river was entering on the period of its battle with the desert, a struggle for survival against the combined forces of sun and sand. The battle still continues, for these two powerful allies may yet destroy the Nile as they have destroyed so many lesser African streams, by forcing it to expire in a desert morass before it can fight its way through to the sea."

* * *

In the forty years since Carrington's book was published, our understanding of the planet's geographical history has changed immensely. In the 1960s, the theory of plate tectonics was first seriously proposed, but, for a decade, it was not generally accepted. In the 1970s, proof was found that the Mediterranean Sea had been cut off from the rest of the world's oceans for half a million years and had completely dried up. In the 1980s, oil exploration in and near Egypt provided evidence concerning the Nile's early history. And in the last two decades, studies in geophysics and palaeo-climatology (the study of ancient weather) have painted a picture of the various stages of the evolution of the river to its present form.

Two hundred million years ago, there was a single giant continent, Pangaea. Under tectonic influences, primarily the creation and development of rifts like the one now in East Africa, Pangaea broke into the continental plates we know today. The European and northern African plates collided and slowly closed around the Tethys Sea which had separated them (like a pair of nutcrackers pivoted at the Straits of Gibraltar), creating the Alps and forming the Mediterranean Sea by welding their eastern ends together. This process began to subside about ten million years ago. After that the Straits of Gibraltar silted up, and finally closed about six million years ago.

Before this closure, a few shallow rivers drained the northern portion of Africa into the Mediterranean. Rivers in the area of Ethiopia and the Sudan, separated from Egypt by the Nubian Massif, drained into the Red Sea and the Indian Ocean. Rivers in what are now Uganda and western Tanzania flowed west over relatively flat land and fed into the Zaïre River, flowing to the Atlantic. For the preceding twenty million years, the Ethiopian highlands had been rising through volcanic activity and a general, but slight, lifting of the eastern third of the African continent. As the Mediterranean dried up, the evaporation was picked up by the prevailing westerly winds and forced to fall as rain on these relatively new highlands. This water flowed westward into the early Nile, letting the river carve its bed downward four thousand metres over the next half-million years as the surface of the sea fell. Even after the Atlantic Ocean broke through again at Gibraltar, the Nile was maintained by these rains. As the Mediterranean rose (at a rate, some have estimated, of 1,500 metres per century), the river slowed at the mouth of the Nile, and began depositing sediments to fill the deep gorge which now stretched inland as far as Aswan.

Beginning about two million years ago, rifting activity started again, this time along a series of fault lines stretching from the Sea of Galilee to the country of Mozambique, with a branch running west and north from Lake Malawi. The roughly parallel sides of these faults pulled apart and allowed the land between them to drop while forcing the outer edges upwards into escarpments. This stimulated volcanic activity nearby and created land-locked drainage basins. One result was that the Blue Nile was cut off from its original outlet, the Red Sea, and its lower courses were forced to flow successively south-east, then south, and then west, until it added its waters, along with those of the Atbara, to the giant Lake Sudd (covering the Sudd and Central Sudan basins). From its inception more than forty million years ago, Lake Sudd only intermittently had an outlet to the north and the Egyptian Nile, determined by a series of wet and dry periods, each lasting thousands of years.

To the south, the developing rift system shaped the Tanganyika craton, or mini-continent, between the two arms of the rift valley and a line of tectonic activity along what is now the Uganda–Sudan border. All the edges of the craton were forced upwards, creating an internally drained basin. The Katonga and Kagera Rivers, now cut off from the Zaïre River, reversed their flow as the land tilted, and began filling the central depression, thereby creating Lake Victoria. The rising escarpments changed the climate as well as the geography. The deep, narrow, rift-valley lakes (Tanganyika, Edward, and Albert) filled up. And the huge rifting pressures pushed up and tipped a large chunk of rock to make the non-volcanic, block-fault mountains we know as the Ruwenzoris.

During the extremely wet periods 40,000 and 26,000 years ago, water from the central lakes region may have briefly found its way to the Egyptian Nile. However, it was not until after the last glacial period that the Nile, as we know it, took shape. Fifteen thousand years ago, at the height of the glaciation, all the rift-valley lakes and Lakes Victoria and Sudd were at their lowest. In the wet phase immediately following the retreat of the ice, 12,500–12,000 years ago, all these lakes reached their highest water levels. Lake Victoria established its outlet to the western rift via Ripon Falls and Murchison Falls; Lake Albert got a permanent outlet to the north into the Sudd region; and Lake Sudd established a new route, the current one, through the Nubian Massif by means of the Shabluka reach (the so-called Sixth Cataract). Thus, today's Nile is a very young river indeed.

The future of the Nile is in doubt. About 10,000 years ago, the Intertropical Convergence Zone (ITCZ), the region of low pressure near the equator where the north-eastern and south-eastern trade winds meet (and the rains fall), started shifting northward, bringing rains to the Ethiopian highlands and large parts of the Sahel and southern Sahara. The Nile's catchment area grew. Lake Turkana in the eastern rift valley received so much rain that, about 9,500 years ago, its overflow went to the Nile via the Sobat River. This wet phase lasted about 2,500 years, with short, arid interruptions. The pattern now seems to have reversed.

✳ ✳ ✳

Any person — in any age — sets out on a remarkable adventure when he or she decides to follow all or part of the course of the Nile. The most logical and scientific way to discover the source of a river is to begin at the mouth and systematically explore each tributary. However, in the nineteenth century a number of formidable obstacles, such as the great swamp of the Sudd, several major cataracts, and the hostility of local populations, made this very difficult. Alternatively, the exploration might begin at a large reservoir, such as a lake, and follow outflowing streams. This was the course chosen by most of the Victorian explorers. But to reach the starting place — the lake or lakes that formed the reservoir — they had to set out from the east coast of Africa and cross the entire width of what is now Tanzania. Only then, laboriously, could they begin to trace the complex system of waterways that feeds the upper Nile.

Even before I became curious about the Nile and its mysterious beginnings, I had been fascinated by that enigmatic and elusive explorer Richard Francis Burton. He was a traveller and seeker of first-hand experience like no other. It is fair to say that what drove me to be in Africa in the very places in which the great explorers had been was the direct result of my compulsion to learn all I could about this man. He, in turn, led me to others, especially to John Hanning Speke, James Augustus Grant, Samuel and Florence Baker, David Livingstone, and Henry Morton Stanley. These great nineteenth-century figures were not the only Victorian explorers, but to me they were the ones whose work ultimately resulted in the mystery of the Nile's source being clearly articulated and eventually solved.

Richard Francis Burton was born on March 19, 1821, in Torquay, Devon, England. He died in Trieste (then in Austria-Hungary, now in Italy), on October 20, 1890, during the final posting of his long diplomatic career. The son of a relatively unsuccessful army careerist, Burton, with his brother, Edward, and his sister, Maria, was raised in France and Italy. From an early age, he manifested three characteristics that were to mark him for life: an exceptional skill at acquiring languages, an inability to submit to authority, and a restlessness bordering on nomadism, which caused him to observe, "England is the only country where I never feel at home."

Burton was expelled from Oxford for unruly behaviour in 1842, joined the Army of the Honourable East India Company, and served in India for seven years. While there, he often

Captain Richard F. Burton, 1863.

donned native garb, perfecting his ability to pass as a "local." It was this ability to shed his British persona that enabled him, in 1853, to travel to Mecca disguised as a Muslim Pathan (a native of north-west Pakistan or Afghanistan) and, the following year, to enter the forbidden city of Harar in Ethiopia. However, in his later African journeys, he played the role of British gentleman to the hilt. The year 1855 found him in Somaliland with John Hanning Speke, and it was then that the two first combined their ideas for a project to seek the source of the Nile in Central Africa.

In 1856–59, Burton and Speke made the difficult Nile journey which led to Speke's claim that, temporarily separated from Burton, he had himself found the true source of the river.

Captain John Hanning Speke, 1863.

The bitter controversy that followed terminated their association and permanently soured their relationship.

My personal fascination with Burton had involved me in exhaustive research on his years in India (1842–49), culminating in the journey I took and described in *Sindh Revisited*. Because I had studied Burton so thoroughly and followed his progress during the India years so closely, I found myself adopting his view of John Hanning Speke. The relationship between the two men was never without some spark of annoyance on the part of each. In Somaliland, when both were wounded, each blamed the other for less than perfect conduct. Burton chose Speke as his companion on the Nile journey, but heaped scorn on Speke's claim that Lake Victoria was the river's source. Steeped in Burton's point of view, as I was, I at first regarded Speke as an inferior figure. My experience of retracing the journey he made with Grant, however, changed my opinion of Speke completely.

John Hanning Speke was born on May 4, 1827, in Bideford, Devon, England, and died under mysterious circumstances while shooting in Somerset on September 15, 1864, on the afternoon before he was scheduled to debate Burton publicly on the Nile issues. He joined the Army of the East India Company in 1844, and his duties took him to the Punjab. He also travelled to Tibet and spent time in the Himalayas. Speke's untimely death meant that his only contributions to Nile exploration were the 1856–59 trip with Burton and the 1860–63 journey with Grant. But they were significant achievements, and in carrying them out Speke showed himself to be a man of single-minded determination. His writings also show him to be a man

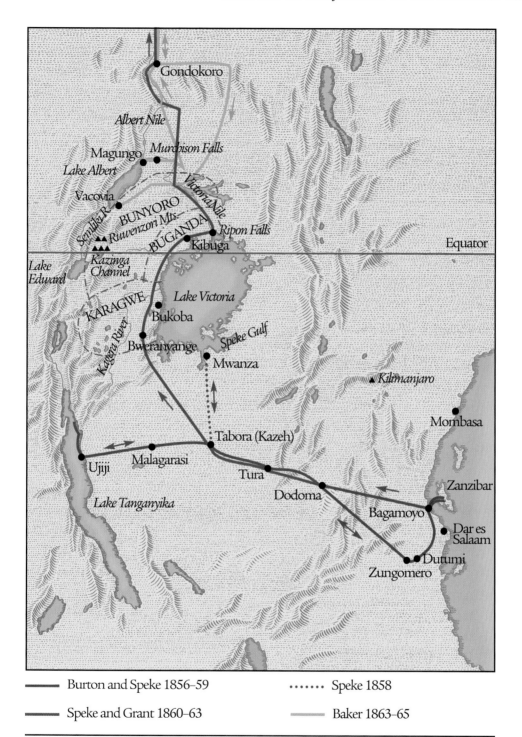

Burton and Speke 1856–59 · · · · · · Speke 1858

Speke and Grant 1860–63 ▬▬ Baker 1863–65

Map showing the journey of Burton and Speke to Lake Tanganyika (1856–59) and Speke's 1858 trip (without Burton) to Lake Victoria; the journey of Speke and Grant (1860–63); and the southern portion of Baker's journey (1863–65).

whose personality endeared him to Africans — both men and women. He was a man of curiosity, courage, good-will, and good humour. He was also a man whose greatest passion was the killing of game. And there were those who found him indiscreet (he had a hard time keeping his opinions to himself) — a trait far more negative in a Victorian than it would be in a person of our own era.

Captain James Augustus Grant, 1863.

Whatever Speke's shortcomings, they in no way marred the near adula-tion with which he was regarded by his partner on the 1860 expedition, James Augustus Grant. Grant was born on April 11, 1827, in Nairn, Scotland, and died there on February 11, 1892. Grant had been commissioned in the East India Company's Army in 1846, and served during the Sikh wars and the Indian Mutiny of 1857. Grant was loyal, obedient, and fully capable of carrying out his duties independently if necessary, but also willing to follow an order to the letter. His excellent service to Speke meant that, despite the usual difficulties of travel in Africa, there was no contention or animosity of any sort between the two men. Later in his career, Grant served in intelligence in Ethiopia under Lord Napier, eventually achieving the rank of lieutenant colonel.

One of the most exciting aspects of the nineteenth-century search for the source of the Nile was that it attracted not only those with military back-grounds, like Burton, Speke, and Grant, but also private individuals who, though sometimes sent on missions by organizations like the Royal Geographical Society, pursued exploration for purely personal adventure. Samuel White Baker epitomized this kind of man. He was born on June 8, 1821, in London, and died on December 30, 1893, in Devon. Baker came from a family wealthy enough to give him his independence. He lived on the island of Mauritius (1843–45) in the Indian Ocean, as well as in Ceylon (1846–55), and travelled in the Middle East (1856–60). In 1861, he went to Africa with a beautiful, brave Hungarian woman whom he had purchased out of slavery — Florence von Sass, who eventually became his second wife. His first wife had died in 1856, leaving four daughters, who remained with relatives in England while Samuel and Florence trekked south through Africa to find Lake Albert and Murchison Falls.

The Bakers initially carried with them food purchased at a fashionable London department store. They were larger-than-life figures who fought off adversity with bravura. When they returned to England, Baker was knighted (1866), an honour received only much later by Burton (1886). As an author, Baker was immensely popular. As an explorer, he later allied himself to the interests of the Ottoman Viceroy of Egypt, Ismail Pasha (1869), in whose service he helped quash the slave trade and was appointed a governor general of territories he had helped to annex.

Though I knew little of Baker before I began my own Nile journey, I came to admire him, even to emulate him, as I stood where he had stood and sailed where he had sailed. He was a true adventurer.

David Livingstone, the most famous Victorian explorer of all, was in many ways the opposite of Baker. He never appeared to think of himself at all. His was always the higher calling, the greater cause. There is no brief way to do justice to his many accomplishments. He was born, like Grant, in Scotland and he died in Africa. He lived from March 19, 1813, to May 1, 1873. He grew up in poverty, buoyed by devout faith. To prepare to be a medical missionary in China, he studied Greek, theology, and medicine, despite also having to work in a cotton mill, but the Opium War (1839–42) prevented him from going to China. Instead, after his ordination as a missionary in 1840, he set sail for Africa. Livingstone threw himself into African life and never looked back. He believed that the purpose of exploration was to spread the Christian gospel, to open Africa to trade, to "civilize" the African peoples, and to end the institution of slavery. His many journeys covered the decades between 1841 and 1873. Perhaps Livingstone's best-known journey, before his storied meeting with Stanley, was the 1858–64 expedition to the Zambezi, which added valuable knowledge about the interior of Africa, but caused the death of his wife. By time Livingstone was found by Stanley in 1871, the horrors of the slave trade had permanently darkened his views of Africa.

By contrast, Stanley was no crusader. In fact, he was notoriously high-handed and carelessly cruel to the Africans. He did, however, help to revive Livingstone's spirits in the last months of the great missionary's life.

Of all the explorers whose paths I trod, none was better organized, better equipped, more optimistic, or more confident than Henry Morton Stanley. And none had risen from so lowly a beginning. A foundling, he was born John Rowlands, on January 28, 1841, in Denbigh, Wales. When he was a boy he stowed away on a boat bound for New Orleans. He took the name of

Henry Morton Stanley, c. 1874.

the man who adopted him, and then began a life of adventure as a soldier, a sailor, and a journalist. He was covering the Spanish Carlist Civil War in 1869 for *The New York Herald* when he was summoned to Paris by his publisher, James Gordon Bennett, Jr., and given the assignment of the century — to find Livingstone. How he did this and with what result is an extraordinary story. When he died in London on May 10, 1904, his name was almost as well known as Livingstone's.

Dr. David Livingstone, c. 1864.

These, then, were the people in whose footsteps (to and along the Nile) I had chosen to walk. I felt that to a large extent they shared a set of attitudes aptly expressed by Anne Hugon in her book *The Exploration of Africa*: "Constricted by the conventions of 19th-century society, particularly those of Victorian England, they longed for a freer way of life. In leaving home to explore a world as different from their own as Africa, they escaped the rules and constraints that weighed on them so heavily.... In the European imagination it was the land of dark forces, of inaccessible places, of extraordinary peoples. Its fascination was charged with an element of fear which increased the prestige of the explorers even further. They themselves fostered this image by readily speaking of the 'dark' or the 'mysterious' continent. As a whole the explorers, like their contemporaries, entertained a vision of Africa that was coloured more by fantasy than by reality."

In order to experience astonishing adventure, the men and women of the Nile endured astonishing hardships. There were dangers from wild animals and disease-bearing insects. The climate could be harsh and debilitating. The terrain was often very difficult, they witnessed levels of poverty and ignorance that profoundly shocked them, and local chieftains and officials hindered or delayed them in various ways. It is no wonder that they sometimes felt like giving up. "I am thoroughly sick of this expedition," Baker revealed. "I shall plod along with dogged obstinacy, but God only knows the end. I shall be grateful if the day ever arrives once more to see Old England.... white ants and rats, robbers and smallpox, these are my companions and neighbours."

But the hardships the explorers endured were offset by moments of transcendent peace and unusual beauty far different from anything that could be experienced at home: "That night was the perfection of a bivouac," Burton said of one of his camp stops, "cool from the vicinity of the hills, genial from their shelter, and sweet as forest-air...." I, too, experienced time and again the sensation of the sweetness of the African night after a long

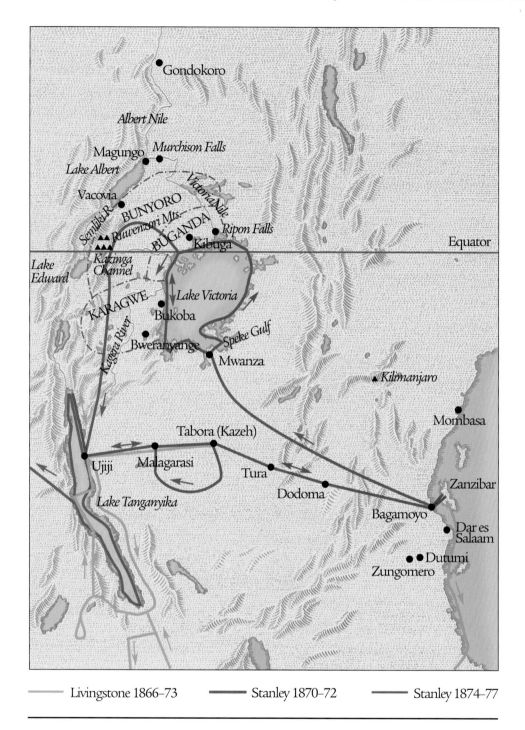

——— Livingstone 1866–73   ▬▬▬ Stanley 1870–72   ——— Stanley 1874–77

Map showing important part of Livingstone's last journey (1866–73);
Stanley's journey to find Livingstone (1870–72); and the eastern portion of
Stanley's exploration (1874–77).

day's travel in the unrelenting sun. At the end of each day's trek, like the Victorians, I looked forward to the quiet moments I could spend with my diary. Although I never hoped to match the skill of men trained as diarists by the army and by the Victorian age, nor to equal their experiences in novelty and freshness, I did aspire to avoid their prejudices. The nineteenth-century accounts embodied the biases of the culture the explorers came from. Nowhere is this more evident than in their depiction of the character and personality of the native Africans — people who could and would be discarded if they stood in the way of the Europeans' aims. Countless porters died under the threats — perhaps the whips — of explorers who thought only about their own goal and their own glory.

Armchair travel has its own built-in distortions, as I was to learn. As Speke once remarked, it is very easy to judge the decisions of a traveller when you are safe at home reading about what he was doing in the field. I often asked myself why this or that explorer had neglected to go somewhere, do something, or check something. Once I was in the field myself, I often saw difficulties I could not have understood from afar. Armchair travel is also a bargain. The real thing is an enormously costly undertaking; this was especially true in Victorian times, when an expedition could take years, require vast quantities of supplies, and involve hundreds of people. Expeditions to Africa were financed in a number of ways: personal wealth; the support of scientific societies, notably the Royal Geographical Society (formed in 1830 and merged with its predecessor, the African Association, in 1831); grants from newspapers such as *The New York Herald*, which sponsored Stanley; private patrons; the Foreign Office of England; or whatever combination of the above an explorer could wangle.

Frank McLynn, in his Burton biography, *Snow upon the Desert*, examines at length the complexities of the Royal Geographical Society's support of the 1857 Burton–Speke journey, approval for which was forthcoming from the Society in the second week of April 1856. When I studied letters that passed from Burton to Norton Shaw, then secretary of the RGS, I could not avoid noticing the tone of urgent request used by the explorer in trying to elicit the necessary funds from the Society: "I am prepared to start alone and if judged necessary disguised as an Arab merchant...." Considering how elaborate even a modest expedition had to be, it is not surprising that explorers often found themselves practically begging for money. Once the explorers reached Africa, the difficult task of recruiting able and loyal local workers had to be faced. Equipping the expedition leaders with the scientific tools they needed was probably less difficult than equipping everyone with the basic necessities of daily life. It was not unusual for an expedition to last for more than a year, and everything had to be brought along, from handkerchiefs to stoves, from soap to bullets.

In order to guarantee safe passage, explorers also had to have tempting items to barter in exchange for local goods and to pay for the unending series of tributes, tithes, taxes, bribes, fees, and reciprocal gifts expected by

Samuel White Baker and Florence Baker (née von Sass) c. 1866.

the tribal chieftains of the territories they passed through. All these supplies had to be carried, mostly on the backs of Africans. It must sometimes have seemed that the real mystery of the Nile was why anybody would go to so much trouble to find its source.

In most ways, of course, my own journey was simplicity itself compared with these elaborate and cumbersome outings. And I had started with a modest goal — to re-create the journey Burton and Speke had made, beginning in Zanzibar, then trekking across the width of what is now Tanzania. Fully prepared to do this, I threw myself into Burton research. Soon, however, it began to bother me that Richard Burton, like David Livingstone, never actually saw the source of the Nile. What he did see was Lake Tanganyika. And while his theories about the role of this lake in the Nile system were intriguing, I knew I could not be satisfied with them alone. So, I thought, why not add Speke and Grant's journey to the itinerary?

The thought pleased me immensely. The more I studied Burton, the more Speke seemed to emerge from his shadow. And Speke really had been the first European to see Lake Victoria, arguably the biggest piece of the Nile puzzle. He had also located the place where Ripon Falls emptied from the lake into a river that he assumed was the Nile. Of course, this would mean adding to my itinerary a trip to the opposite end and northernmost point of the second-largest lake in the world, and into Uganda. Nonetheless, I decided to follow in the footsteps of Speke and Grant.

In researching Speke and Grant, I read of their triumphant return to England, which meant I read of their meeting with Samuel Baker at Gondokoro on the way home. I learned that Speke, anxious to get home to report his findings, had been willing to forgo investigating the existence of another lake, Albert, which he told Baker about. Of course, I had long known about Lake Albert, but when I reflected that Speke had more or less handed its discovery to Baker on a silver platter, I realized that Baker was very much a part of Speke's story and therefore part of mine. I added Lake Albert to my itinerary, despite my concern about the growing unrest among refugees in the region.

Then I learned that Baker's efforts had been incomplete, that he had seen only a part of Lake Albert, that he had given up and gone home, satisfied with a modest discovery when a major one lay within his grasp. Rather than solving the mystery of the Nile, Baker had probably deepened it. It was, in fact, Stanley who eventually answered most of the questions that had thus far been asked about the source of the Nile. But he was drawn to Africa not to find a river, but to find a man, Dr. David Livingstone.

In a meeting on May 22, 1865, to celebrate the life and achievements of Speke, the Royal Geographical Society announced that it had chosen Livingstone, by then the best-known explorer in Great Britain, to resolve the controversy which had arisen from Burton and Speke's conflicting theories. By 1871, when Stanley found him, Livingstone had spent five fruitless years on this project, learning about the waters between the Zambezi River and the south end of Lake Tanganyika, but more and more consumed by the horrors of slavery and how to combat it. Livingstone and Stanley found something special in each other and formed something like a father-son relationship. Together they were able to eliminate Lake Tanganyika as a source of the Nile, but could do no more before Stanley had to leave. After Livingstone's death in 1873, and his funeral in Westminster Abbey, it was Stanley who organized the expedition which was to confirm Speke's opinions by circumnavigating Lake Victoria, and would add to the relevant information by exploring the region of the Ruwenzori Mountains. I decided I had to do that too.

That was how the plan for my journey to the source of the Nile evolved. I came to regard it as a double journey: a journey to experience what I had only read about, and a journey to seek answers to questions I could not yet frame — the questions that shape themselves in the traveller's mind only as the journey unfolds. Only the experience itself would tell me what else I needed to look for. Even as I set out, however, I felt instinctively that more than a river had been born in the geological cradle of the Nile. I vowed to explore this idea too.

And finally, I promised myself that I would try to see Africa today in the light of the long chain of European intervention and influence in Africa — the successive waves of non-African traders, missionaries, explorers, administrators, dictators, and democrats who had left their mark on the continent.

Between 1880 and 1902, Africa changed from a relatively uncharted continent, ruled by its own peoples, to a group of possessions held by rival European powers. Between 1902 and the present, it has evoked the highest hopes and the deepest despair of any continent in the world. In a way, perhaps I felt that understanding the difficult puzzle of the Nile's source might also give me some insight into a far more challenging riddle: the turbulent, complex, paradoxical enigma of Africa itself.

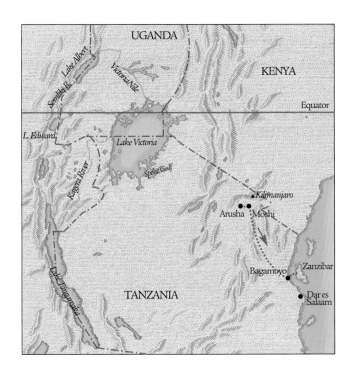

Fair Is This Isle:
Zanzibar

I find my journal brimful of enthusiasm. Of the
gladdest moments in human life, methinks, is the
departure upon a distant journey into unknown lands.
Shaking off with one mighty effort the fetters of Habit,
the leaden weight of Routine, the cloak of many Cares
and the slavery of Home, one feels once more happy.
The blood flows with the fast circulation of childhood....
A journey, in fact, appeals to Imagination, to Memory,
to Hope, — the three sister Graces of our moral being.

RICHARD F. BURTON
Zanzibar

2

FAIR IS THIS ISLE: ZANZIBAR

My first objective was Zanzibar, where Burton had gone to begin his expedition in 1856. To get there, he had sailed from Bombay. Speke, with Grant in 1860 and Livingstone in 1866, had sailed to Zanzibar from England via the Cape of Good Hope. I chose a different route: a long flight from London through Amsterdam to Kilimanjaro Airport. A balmy African night greeted me, the tropical heat expected, the muted croaking of tree frogs and the murmurs of the jostling airport crowd a soothing background accompaniment. Magic. It was marvellous to be back again. I went through the usual Customs and Immigration hassle, met Thad Peterson (he had not changed much in ten years), and then set out on the seventy-kilometre drive, west and a little north to the other side of Arusha, to the Peterson compound. I deliberately began my journey in Arusha not only because of its airport, but also because Thad Peterson's headquarters is there, and he had been the most flexible in adapting his operation to my extraordinary demands.

Thad is the son of a missionary who devoted his life to working in Tanzania. Thad was born in the country when it was still Tanganyika. His sensitive understanding of the ways and the people of Africa makes him an exceptional travelling companion. Despite the perils of the journeys on which he has been, his competence and relaxed manner instil complete confidence in fellow travellers and loyal workers alike. His encyclopedic knowledge of the outdoors is the product of his keen powers of observation, plus the fact that he would far rather be sitting on top of his Land Rover watching wildlife than doing practically anything else — except perhaps reading about what he has seen and hopes to see in the wild. He is secretly also a frustrated adventurer with a daredevil curiosity. Without Thad, I would have been as lost as Burton

[T]he fair sex has the laugh in its side ....

RICHARD F. BURTON
Personal Narrative of a Pilgrimage to Al-Madinah & Meccah

Previous page: A pale-blue sky covered the hazy land and sleeping sea as we steamed through the strait that separates Zanzibar from the continent. Every stranger, at first view of the shores, proclaims his pleasure. The gorgeous verdure,... the calm sea, the light gauzy atmosphere, the semi-mysterious silence which pervades all nature, evoke his admiration.

HENRY MORTON STANLEY
Through the Dark Continent

would have been without his substantial entourage of Britons, Arabs, and Africans.

I got to bed at 10:00 p.m. and, despite being quite keyed up, managed to stay asleep until I was rudely awakened at 4:00 a.m. by the sound of a high-pitched alarm. Still dazed by sleep, I was unnerved by the loud commotion. Sounds of gunfire and guards shouting followed — and then suddenly silence. I did not get up to investigate, and managed to get back to sleep for another hour before Thad sheepishly arrived at my door at 6:30 a.m. There had been a break-in, he explained. Thieves had stolen the large microwave oven out of the kitchen as well as some important bags and documents that Thad had accumulated for our journey.

Although we had planned the journey with two Land Rovers, because of the break-in we initially took only one, leaving Thad's assistant, Joshua Mbewe, to replace the stolen documents and get new entry forms, permits, insurance, and other papers we would need. We arranged to meet him later in the eastern seacoast city of Bagamoyo. Bagamoyo is the mainland port nearest to Zanzibar, the island and the city, thirty-five kilometres farther east, off the coast of Tanzania. Senyaeli Pollangyo and Ali Mbewe joined Thad and me as we started the long, hot, dusty drive about six hundred kilometres south-eastward through Tanzania.

An introductory word here about the rest of our company is in order. I already knew Joshua well from two previous African safaris and enjoyed renewing my friendship with him. A member of the Chagga tribe from Kilimanjaro, he lives in Moshi, some distance from the headquarters of Thad's company, Dorobo Safaris, at Arusha. He formerly worked for both the Tanzanian Game Division and the Tanzanian Wildlife Corporation, but he has worked in his current post in Thad's operation for many years. He is the father of seven children. His son Ali was born to a Muslim mother. Joshua is a Christian. They get on well together, and the difference in faith has never seemed to be a problem.

Ali, in his early twenties, is an excellent mechanic and getting to be a good cook. Always willing and enthusiastic, he seemed as glad to be working for Dorobo Safaris as Thad was to have him as an employee.

Pollangyo is around Joshua's age — somewhere in his fifties — and a member of the Meru tribe. He is something of an "elder" at Dorobo Safaris. Immensely strong and usually silent, he is also thoughtful and intelligent, and was invariably chosen to help us out of any difficult, or potentially difficult, situation, whether with police or overly conscientious officials. He knows when to talk and when to shut up. He has been with Dorobo Safaris for a long time and he and his wife are regarded almost as part of the family by the Petersons.

✳ ✳ ✳

Crossing the Ruvu (Kingani) River.

This initial stage of our journey took us first through Moshi, past the slopes of Kilimanjaro, through Same and the Pare Mountains, through Korogwe, and then sharp eastward along a shortcut north of Dar es Salaam to the coast. To do the final leg of the journey along the coast we had to cross the Ruvu River on a hand-pulled ferry. In all it took us about nine hours, not counting a very quick lunch break at the Pangani River. We arrived in Bagamoyo at about 6:00 p.m.

Bagamoyo, now a sleepy seaside town, is seventy-five kilometres north along the coast from Dar es Salaam. Its importance and power as a trading centre have changed over time. Initially a small trading post secondary to Kilwa and Mombasa, it was controlled by the Sultan of Oman. Then, in 1832, when the Sultan, Sayyid Said, decided to relocate his capital from Oman to Zanzibar, he used Bagamoyo's proximity to Zanzibar to increase its importance as a port. This arrangement continued until Bagamoyo was made the capital of German East Africa, becoming an administrative as well as a trading centre.

Livingstone, Burton, Speke, Stanley, and Grant all started journeys into the interior of Tanganyika from Bagamoyo. Livingstone's body returned to

Crewman cutting open a jak fruit.

Bagamoyo on February 15, 1874, carried the hundreds of kilometres from the interior to the coast by two African bearers, his devoted attendants during his last seven years in Africa.

* * *

I spent the night listening to a rat gnaw away at the foot of my bed, and greeted with relief the muezzin calling Muslim worshippers to prayer at a quarter to five in the morning. After a hurried breakfast of *ugali* (cornflour porridge) and spicy scrambled eggs, plus some extremely strong coffee, we set out for Zanzibar, boarding a fragile eight-metre-long dhow and heading eastward into the trade winds. The sun was up, and it was already hot by 8:30 a.m. Despite the extra power provided by a flimsy outboard motor, I was extremely doubtful about the dhow's ability to get us to the island, but the local sailors seemed quite confident of their craft. Indeed, the other lateen-rigged vessels around us seemed even more fragile than ours. So, relying on sail, engine, and some inborn nautical expertise, we chugged along for six hours, until at last, in the distance, the thin, uneven line that is the western coast of Zanzibar came into view. We approached slowly, steering our craft through sandy islands and coral reefs. The bright red buildings, white minarets, and lush green jungle seemed to me an exotic landscape filled with the promise of excitement and adventure. I breathed deeply to try to catch the scent of cloves. Instead, as we sailed closer into the main harbour, my nostrils captured the much more distinctive odour of dried fish.

Ignoring the smell, we ate on board our flimsy craft, feasting on *mchuzi* (fish stew), *dengu* (lentils), and rice, then sampling a whole array of local fruit: jak, Zanzibar apples, passion fruit, sweet lemons, papaya, and grapefruit.

Our craft nosed cautiously into the crowded harbour. Hundreds of Arab dhows, some elaborately decorated, others with huge bowsprits, were moored in the shallow, sheltered lagoon. Water lapped gently against the enormous wooden hulls, in peaceful contrast to the busy scene on shore. The waterfront was a pandemonium of hawkers, pedlars, fish vendors, children rushing to and fro on unknown missions, women in brightly coloured garb, and men in white robes, all shouting, arguing, questioning. I could not wait to throw myself into the crowd. But first the agony of official entry — again. Despite being very much a part of Tanzania, Zanzibar retains its independent attitude, and we had to endure intense questioning at Passport Control and again at Customs. The boat papers were studied even more carefully than our own documents.

The island of Zanzibar has enticed travellers and adventurers to its shores for hundreds of years. Burton recorded his first glimpse of it, saying he was awed by the sight of its distant hills and intrigued by its unique atmosphere: "Earth, sea, and sky, all seemed wrapped in a soft and sensuous repose, in the tranquil life of the Lotus Eaters, in the swoon-like slumbers of the Seven Sleepers, in the dreams of the Castle of Indolence.... all was voluptuous ... every feature was hazy and mellow, as if viewed through 'woven air'...."

The Bantu, the original inhabitants of the claw-shaped, 1,600-square-kilometre island, probably migrated from the mainland. A succession of Mediterranean, Middle Eastern, Asian, and European peoples have all had an impact on the island at one time or another. Many nations have stayed to settle and rule — notably the Shirazi Persians and the Omani Arabs. The latter came early in the nineteenth century and introduced the clove tree in 1818. Quite correctly, Zanzibar is also known as Spice Island. The island's importance grew after the Sultan of Oman decided to move his court from Muscat, near the entrance to the Persian Gulf, to Zanzibar. During his lifetime, Zanzibar became not only the world's largest producer of cloves, but also the most important slave-trading centre on the east coast of Africa. It is estimated that no fewer than fifty thousand slaves changed hands in the Zanzibar markets every year. The Zanzibar that Burton and Speke first knew was a very important centre.

Once we had satisfied the Immigration authorities as to our authenticity and intentions, we fought our way first through the busy dockside crowd, and then through the narrow, dirty alleys of Stone Town — the oldest part of Zanzibar — heading for Emerson's House, a very old building, now a small hotel. Despite the heat and humidity of the afternoon, small stores along musty alleyways did a brisk business, selling a whole array of local produce. I felt a familiar rush of excitement at once more being in an Eastern milieu. This was a completely different world. Clearly, hundreds of years of occupation by various cultures had left their mark. Overhanging balconies, tall, antique, carved and studded doors, narrow stone terrace houses — these gave the streets the air of a Muslim-inspired labyrinth. Surely there can be no map of this jumble of alleys. A map might prove meaningless, anyway. As Burton said in 1856, "It would be the work of weeks to learn the threading of this planless maze, and what white man would have had the heart to learn it?"

Above us the hot afternoon sky was nothing more than a narrow band of blue between the high stone walls — barely six metres apart — that lined the street. People stepped aside to let us pass, politely avoiding contact with the bags we carried. However, warned by the sound of oncoming bicycle bells, we nimbly got out of the way of errant cyclists — a real hazard. Pedestrians were very much second-class citizens.

The Zanzibar that Burton and Speke encountered in 1856 must have been very different from the Zanzibar that we visited 140 years later. The permanent population then was perhaps 50,000 (today it is close to 200,000), although their ranks would have been substantially increased by the transient population of slaves and slave traders.

Even after the Sultan of Zanzibar banned the export of slaves, slavery inside his dominion went on unabated, and Arab merchants continued their trade along the mainland coast. The slave trade of Zanzibar seems a remote fact of history. I was about to write that, of course, there are no slaves today. However, I have recently seen articles in Western newspapers about members of the Dinka tribe, slated for execution by the Sudanese government, being sold as slaves.

Slavery was very much in evidence in the mid-1850s when Burton and Speke arrived on the island, and Burton's many descriptions give us a grim reminder of the horrors of the lucrative slaving trade.

Fawn Brodie, in her excellent biography of Burton, *The Devil Drives*, takes a more sophisticated view of Burton's attitude towards slavery than biographers who simply assert that he was unsympathetic to the plight of Africans. Brodie says that Burton deplored the trade and understood that much of the moral and physical degradation that he witnessed was the direct result of the damage the Arab slave traders had wreaked on Africa. I agree that the ironies and complexities of the slave trade were not lost on Burton. He understood that neither a foreign traveller such as himself, nor those profoundly involved in the trade, could offer quick solutions to the economic realities of the awful business. Burton wrote that no matter how much the visitor might pity the slaves, he must restrain himself from interfering. "Were he to deal civilly and liberally with this people," Burton wrote, "he

The Arab never changes. He brought the custom of his forefathers with him when he came to live on this island. He is as much of an Arab here as at Muscat or Bagdad; wherever he goes to live he carries with him his harem, his religion, his long robe, his shirt, his slippers, and his dagger.

HENRY M. STANLEY
How I Found Livingstone

would starve; it is vain to offer a price for even the necessaries of life; it would certainly be refused because more is wanted, and so on beyond the bounds of possibility." Burton saw that the economics of slavery affected every commercial transaction. "Thus if the touter did not seize a house, he would never be allowed to take shelter in it from the storm; if he did not enforce a 'corvée,' he must labor beyond his strength with his own hands; and if he did not fire a village and sell the villagers, he might die of hunger in the midst of plenty. Such in this province are the action and reaction of the evil."

In Burton's description of the slave market at Zanzibar in 1856, he writes of lines of emaciated slaves, some in red nightcaps, standing like beasts or, if too sick to stand, squatting on the ground while the brokers called out the qualities of their wares. The ribs of the slaves, Burton says, protruded "like the circles of a cask." Always interested in rebellious and unusual human behaviour, Burton pointed out that the young boys who were for sale "grinned as if somewhat pleased by the degrading and hardly decent inspection to which both sexes and all ages were subjected."

* * *

That evening, as we waited for dinner on the rooftop of Emerson's, I enjoyed the extraordinary view over old Zanzibar. Sunset: a huge red ball of fire on the skyline, crossed by dhows sailing the Indian Ocean. Just beneath us the rooftops of old Stone Town began to disappear into the dusk as the sun slowly dropped below the horizon. The exotic clamour of the busy African town rose to meet our ears. As darkness descended, the city seemed to take on a completely different personality from that of only moments before. I had read somewhere of a modern travel writer who never went through the streets of Stone Town at night without a torch. A wise precaution. Torches can sometimes be handy weapons.

At dinner that first night, Pollangyo and Thad tried hard to explain the local Tanzanian political scene, and to give me an understanding of some of the basic facts about the country formed in 1964 by the union of Tanganyika and Zanzibar.

Tanzania, East Africa's largest country (945,000 square kilometres), is made up largely of high desert or semi-desert plateau and savanna. Much of the country is uninhabited. The offshore islands of Zanzibar, Pemba, and Mafia are part of the union, and the rift-valley lakes cover more than 53,000 square kilometres. The two highest mountains, Kilimanjaro (5,895 metres) and Meru (4,565 metres), lie in the north-east of the country, near the

Then commence negotiations about the Mahr or sum settled upon the bride; and after the smoothing of this difficulty follow feastings of friends and relatives, male and female.

RICHARD F. BURTON
Personal Narrative of a Pilgrimage to Al-Madinah & Meccah

Kenyan border. As with all climatic change, the rainy season depends on the prevailing winds, which here are the south-east trade winds that blow from the Indian Ocean from April to October, and the north-east monsoons that blow from November to March. The "long rains" fall from April to May, and the "short rains" in November and December — when the winds change.

The population of Tanzania exceeds twenty-five million, and there are more than one hundred different tribal groups, most of which are Bantu. Zanzibar, however, with its heavy Arab influence, has created a people who are a mixture of Shirazi, Arab, Comorian, and Bantu. Since the Arab traders' invasion of the country in the twelfth century, Islam has been by far the most influential religion, especially in the coastal regions and on the island of Zanzibar. Christianity, the second most influential religion, was first introduced by Europeans in the early nineteenth century, mainly in the interior. About 30 per cent of the population is Islamic, 25 per cent Christian, and 45 per cent followers of traditional native religions. For

Zanzibar's historic museum.

instance, the Maasai continue to worship Engai and his messiah Kindong'oi. Swahili is the official language of Tanzania, but English remains the main language of commerce.

Thad and Pollangyo explained that independence had come fairly quickly and easily to the old Tanganyika, mainly because of Julius Nyerere. In 1953, Nyerere was elected president of the Tanganyika African Association (TAA). Founded as a mutual-benefit society for urban Africans in the 1920s, it became a streamlined political organization under his leadership. On July 7, 1954, it changed its name to the Tanganyika African National Union (TANU) and adopted new aims: uniting all nationalists in the country and opposing tribalism with the eventual goals of self-government, independence, and African rule. The British planned a multiracial constitution to protect European and Asian minorities, but they eventually capitulated, and Tanganyika gained full independence on December 9, 1961, with Nyerere — the father of the new country and the "conscience of Black Africa" — as its first president.

Zanzibar had a much more turbulent transition. The British had ignored Tanganyika because of its limited agricultural potential, even after it became their protectorate after the First World War. However, they had been keenly interested in Zanzibar for almost a century when they made the Sultanate a protectorate in 1890. In the 1960s, local political parties arose with the prospect of joint independence with the island of Pemba. The Afro-Shirazi Party (ASP) was supported by the majority African population. The Zanzibar National Party (ZNP) and the Zanzibar and Pemba People's Party (ZPPP) had support from the Arab and Asian landowning and mercantile

Door lintel in Stone Town with a European coat of arms.

classes. The ZNP and ZPPP, like the British, wanted an Arab country with the Sultan continuing as head of state. In pre-independence elections, the ASP got the majority of votes but only a minority of seats in the new National Assembly. The ZNP and ZPPP formed a coalition under Sheikh Mohammed Shamte to become the first government of Zanzibar on December 10, 1963. A month later, the ASP, led by Abeid Aman Karume and with support from the mainland, started a bloody revolution. The Sultan was ousted and much of the Arab population killed or expelled. A Revolutionary Council, with Karume as leader, took over the new country and negotiated the creation of the Union of Zanzibar and Tanganyika on April 26, 1964 (renamed the United Republic of Tanzania). Thus was Tanzania born.

In 1965, Nyerere announced a "One-Party State" policy: TANU on the mainland and ASP on the islands until they could merge. This they did in 1977, taking the name Chamba cha Mapinduzi (CCM), the Party of the Revolution. Every five years, from 1965 on the mainland and 1980 in Zanzibar, elections are held for the president of Tanzania and the Tanzanian National Assembly. Karume, as the head of state of Zanzibar, said shortly after the revolution that there would be no need for elections in Zanzibar for at least sixty years, but after his assassination in 1972 (reputedly while playing poker) and constitutional reforms in 1977, that changed. Since 1980, the Zanzibaris have voted for a president of Zanzibar (who is *ex officio* a vice-president of the United Republic) and for their own House of Representatives.

Julius Nyerere, who still likes to be called *Mwalimu* (Teacher), stepped down as Tanzanian president in 1985 and was succeeded by Ali Hassan Mwinyi. Tanzania introduced a multi-party system in July 1992. President Mwinyi was succeeded by Benjamin Mkapa (of the CCM) in 1995, when all the new opposition parties ran candidates. Zanzibar's own president is currently Dr. Salim Amour.

Ten political parties, besides the CCM, are registered. These include the Civic United Front (CUF), seen as CCM's major rival; the Tanzanian People's Party (TPP); and Chamba cha Demokrasia na Maendelo (CHADEMA, Party for Democracy and Progress). The first test of the new system was the April 18, 1993, by-election in Kwahani, Zanzibar. Before this, each seat was contested by two CCM candidates chosen by the party's committees. The CCM and TPP had the only valid nominations; the other parties, especially CUF, campaigned for a boycott of the election, claiming it would not be fairly run. The TPP candidate lost even though that party is not tainted with pre-revolutionary politics. In Zanzibar there is still always the question of whether a candidate supported the revolution and hence is "one of us," or opposed the revolution and is "one of them," a supporter of the landowners and the Sultanate.

Financial sponsors are becoming disillusioned with the situation in Zanzibar and have threatened to withdraw funding. The next elections should take place in the year 2000, and if Nyerere, still a revered father figure, were to die before then, political unrest would almost certainly flare up, and a rival political party could promote Zanzibar's independence again.

✳ ✳ ✳

My bedroom at Emerson's House was an enormous old room — cluttered with antiques and tinged with the dusty, musty smell that is one of the perfumes of the tropics. Surrounding the huge four-poster bed was a mosquito net (with no gaping holes) draping to the floor. A silent fan wafted a breeze across the room. Though not luxurious, the accommodations were the best possible, given our location. There was an old-town atmosphere in the hotel in keeping with its position right in the centre of Stone Town.

To guide us around Stone Town, I hired Jean Baptiste da Silva, a well-known local artist who was born in Goa. He took us to several buildings that were in the old town when Burton, Speke, and the other British explorers were here in the mid-nineteenth century. The Customs House was particularly interesting. At one time an Arab fort, it was destroyed by Arabs and then rebuilt by Arabs. The old Customs House door (Arab) was definitely here in Burton's time. We also visited the old British consulate. Burton, Speke,

Jean Baptiste da Silva.

Livingstone, and other explorers stayed here. Captain Hamilton (the first British consul in Zanzibar) lived and died here.

We made it a point to visit the United Mission to Central Africa Anglican cathedral, completed in 1877, the first Anglican cathedral built in East Africa. Dr. Livingstone himself had begun raising funds for this church in the 1850s. The cathedral was built on the site of a slave market. An underground prison in which slaves were chained before being sold is still there and gave me the same gruesome feeling I had when learning of a nearby well into which weak and sick slaves were routinely tossed to die. Today, the baptismal font stands on the spot where the well had been, and the cathedral altar marks the location of a tree where slaves were chained and whipped. The church's cross was made from a tree under which Livingstone once preached.

United Mission to Central Africa Cathedral, first Anglican cathedral in East Africa.

Thoughts of Livingstone led us to Livingstone House, now the Department of Tourism, located off Malawi Road behind the fish market. At this house, between January and March 1866, Livingstone gathered all his essential supplies before setting off on his last journey. The house overlooks the dhow harbour, that bustling hub of sailing activity, from where I could still see sacks of Zanzibar cloves being loaded into waiting vessels that had arrived with the trade winds from India.

Stone Town is the only continuously inhabited historical city of East Africa, a city within a city. Captain J.F. Elton, vice-consul of Zanzibar, described Stone Town in his 1879 book *The Lakes and Mountains of Eastern and Central Africa* as having "an architectural background of Arabian arches, heavy carved wooden doors and lintel posts, circular towers, narrow latticed windows, recesses and raised terraces, combined with and worked into tortuous lanes and sharp turnings, wells in unexpected corners, squalor, whitewash, dirt, and evil smells as you penetrate further into the heart of the town." It is the Arab houses that give Stone Town its distinctive appeal. Every house has a magnificent door, often teak studded with brass. Elaborate carvings on the lintels and frames include quotations from the Koran which are believed to bestow a blessing on the home. There are hundreds of different doors, carved with symbols of lotus flowers for procreation, fish for fertility, dates and frankincense for abundance, and reinforced with chains for the safety and security of those within.

At the Department of Archives I caught Dr. Abdul Sheriff at his lunch break. He is not only the head of the Department of Archives, but also curator of the Peace Memorial, the Palace, and the House of Wonders. Before this job, Dr. Sheriff was a professor of history at the University of Dar es Salaam. I had a lot to talk about with Dr. Sheriff, and a great many questions to ask. Our conversation flowed freely. He felt that, despite all that has been written about the source of the Nile, a comprehensive discussion weaving together both the geographical and the historical dimensions is still needed. We also got onto the topic of explorers as "discoverers." "It certainly is a bit ridiculous to state that Speke discovered Lake Victoria," he commented sardonically. "People have been living there, walking around it, trading there, and have had kingdoms there for hundreds of years. It is a bit like the North American Indian who arrived in Italy in 1995 and on the Spanish Steps declared that he had discovered Rome!"

Dr. Abdul Sheriff.

Dr. Sheriff nevertheless has great respect for the information passed down from the explorers in their writing. "Burton was a very good observer and recorded everything," Dr. Sheriff commented. "He kept meticulous notes. For example, his two volumes on Zanzibar. And his 1860 book *The Lake Regions of Central Africa* is a lexicon of topographic and ethnographic information. Speke, on the other hand, was much more of a physical achiever. He came only to discover the source of the Nile, much as a warrior would go out, get his prize, and return home. Burton was more complicated. If you wiped Burton from the literature of the nineteenth century there would be an enormous gap."

He told me that the name Zanzibar comes from *zenj*, "black," from old Arabic or perhaps Persian, referring to black people; and *bar*, "coast," from Arabic. Burton, however, maintained that the origin was the Arabic phrase *zayn za'l barr*, which could loosely be translated as "Fair is this isle."

Later, at lunch with Thad and the others at an old Indian restaurant overlooking the harbour, we talked more about the European concept of "discovery." In 1848, Johann Rebmann, a German Lutheran missionary, claimed to have discovered Kilimanjaro. Pollangyo reported a discussion he had had some years ago with an illiterate game scout called Akwimbe. "That's absolutely ridiculous," Akwimbe had said. "The Chagga were living on the slopes of Mount Kilimanjaro then, and they live there now. How could Rebmann possibly have discovered Kilimanjaro?" For the Europeans, however, the experience of a European was apparently all that counted.

Thad then talked to me about the history of missionaries in East Africa. There were two phases. The first was from the early 1840s until about 1870. Then, after the death of Dr. Livingstone in 1873, there was a great wave of enthusiasm and support that led to the establishment of mission stations in the interior. The pioneer missionary in East Africa was a German, Dr. Ludwig Krapf, who started his work in southern Ethiopia in 1837. In 1844, Krapf came south to Zanzibar and later crossed to Mombasa, and established a mission station at Rabay. He was joined there in 1846 by Johann Rebmann and in 1849 by Jacob Erhardt. From this place, the missionaries travelled inland. Rebmann went to Teita in 1847 and Chagga the following year, when he first saw Kilimanjaro.

⋆ ⋆ ⋆

I am always on the lookout for knives and daggers to add to my personal collection. These fascinating weapons often tell more about a culture than you can learn from history books. I continued my search throughout Stone Town and eventually found two old silver Arab daggers at a small harbourfront boutique. This was lucky. I bought them both — although some ill-advised former owner had wrecked the blades with a rough grinding stone.

Plaque on house where Livingstone stayed and his body later rested.

Someone recommended Goan food for dinner, and so we went to the Chit Chat in the heart of Stone Town, at 500 Cathedral Street. This is a tiny restaurant owned by an Indian from Kerala. His wife, who is Goan, does the cooking. We were served traditional Goan cuisine: pork *sorpatel*, prawns *rechad*, chicken *xachut*, crab in coconut, *puri bhaji*, squid in coconut — a fabulous treat! However, walking back to Emerson's through the dark, shadowy streets of Stone Town was far from pleasant. As the evening darkened, the lanes of Stone Town became really claustrophobic. Figures lurked in every archway, and we were studied very closely as we walked quickly back to the safety of our small hotel. I would certainly not have liked to make the journey across town on my own.

The next day, getting ready to leave Zanzibar for our trek on the mainland, we encountered another serious tangle of red tape, mainly because we insisted on sailing to Bagamoyo by dhow — in the same boat on which we had sailed to Zanzibar. I had wanted to sail, rather than fly or take the motor launch, feeling that this way my experience would parallel Burton and Speke's more closely. As a result, we had to wait for three hours until the dhow was brought around to the Immigration official for his inspection and approval. We killed time by visiting some more of Zanzibar's historic sites. First, the old, run-down palace of Tippoo Tip, certainly the most notorious slave trader in Zanzibar. Then, along the coast from the old town, we saw the palace of Sultan Bargash (1870–88). He had ninety-nine wives — and three swimming pools. He also had a balcony (now destroyed) from which he picked his three beauties for that day's pleasure. Farther inland we visited the old Persian ruins built by the Sultan Said in 1850. They are called the Persian ruins because the Sultan had a Persian wife, and he commissioned this small palace's ornate decorations to please her. Eventually, back again at the Immigration Office, we waited a further exasperating hour before we were allowed to leave in our dhow.

We had been in Zanzibar for two days. Burton and Speke stayed for six months — from December 17, 1856, until June 1857 — before sailing in the Sultan's corvette, *Artémise*, for the mainland and the start of their historic journey.

As the *Artémise*, which Burton called a "jackass-frigate" full of "a legion of rats and an army of cockroaches," pulled away, he and Speke were on their way to fulfil their mandate from the Royal Geographical Society: "to penetrate inland from some place on the East Coast and make the best of your way to the reputed great lake in the interior."

"Africa lay before them," says Edward Rice grandly in his Burton biography, "a giant, cruel, fetid, miasmic, challenging continent whose mysteries lay wrapped in enigmatic myths and legends." Burton was less magniloquent, though his spirits were buoyant as the corvette set sail. "After the usual expenditure of gunpowder which must in eastern lands announce every momen-

Arab fort in Zanzibar.

tous event, from the birth of a prince to the departure of a bishop," they glided out of Zanzibar harbour with a farewell glance at the white buildings.

With relief we, too, eventually sailed out of Zanzibar harbour — past the Customs House, past the House of Wonders, past the old Arab fort, westward towards the mainland and Bagamoyo. A dhow sailed lazily downwind between us and the old British Club — now Africa House. We passed the president's office, its flag whipping in the breeze, then the Zanzibar Hospital with its bright red roof. It was good to sail away and escape the island's bureaucracy. Several officials had tried very hard to extract money from us, but the dhow's stubborn owner had preferred to tack back and forth from one official to the other until finally, finally, we were allowed to leave. The three brightly clad sailors who navigated our boat across to the mainland were obviously glad, too, to be setting out at last.

It was a brilliant day, the sky almost cloudless, the sea a vivid blue. The sun beat down on us, and we cut open three *madafu* (young coconuts) to moisten our parched throats. As we drank, Zanzibar disappeared into the distance behind us, the white bleached faces of the buildings with their occasional red crowns stark against a dark green background of low-lying hills.

[A] large house ... possesses an ambitious doorway raised 3 feet above the street, and reached by four or five broad and circular steps.... [A]t the tall doorway of each sits the porter — as comfortable as his circumstances will permit....

HENRY M. STANLEY
Through the Dark Continent

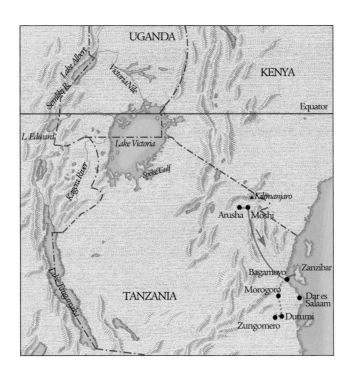

Lay Down the Burden of Your Heart:
Bagamoyo to Zungomero

*The first, or maritime region, extends from the shores
of the Indian Ocean ... to the mountain chain forming
the land of Usagara ... its breadth is therefore 92
geographical miles .... The average rise is under four
feet per mile.... The natives of the country divide it into
the three lowlands of Tunda, Dut'humi, and
Zungomero. Its undulations present no eminences
worthy of notice; near the sea they are short and steep,
farther inland they roll in longer waves, and every
where they are covered with abundant and luxiant
vegetation, the result of decomposition upon the
richest soil.*

RICHARD F. BURTON
The Lake Regions of Central Africa

3

LAY DOWN THE BURDEN OF YOUR HEART: BAGAMOYO TO ZUNGOMERO

In a few hours we arrived on the mainland at Bagamoyo after a spectacular sunset, our dhow sailing into the golden orb that descended slowly into the sea. With the wind behind us, we coasted smoothly along, enjoying absolute quiet, absolute peace. A wonderful way to travel, worth the waiting and the bureaucratic snarl it had caused. No one said anything. The only sounds were the wind and the rushing of the waves being cut by our bow.

It was low tide when we arrived, and so we rammed the dhow onto the tidal flats, then walked a good fifty metres to shore, wading up to our waists, carrying our bags and other equipment above our heads. Thad Peterson and I set foot on the sand. Unlike our nineteenth-century predecessors, we had only our curiosity to impel us. When Burton and Speke reached Bagamoyo, they had on their shoulders the weighty expectations of the Royal Geographical Society and the keen interest of Victoria, their sovereign queen.

I was aware of my good fortune in being able to travel light and with only a handful of fellow adventurers. By the time we got to Bagamoyo, Joshua had arrived with the second Land Rover and our papers. Being able to travel with such vehicles was perhaps the most obvious and constant reminder that our trip would be different from that of the Victorian explorers — for they either walked or were carried by man or beast for thousands of kilometres. The Land Rovers and our compact, up-to-date equipment allowed us to set up an efficient routine of daily travel and nightly camping. The explorers, too, had set up their routines, but ours were much lighter and faster.

Despite his usual devil-may-care attitude, Burton was well aware of the seriousness of his undertaking. "In writing our adventures," he said, "I was

[T]he next day saw us rolling down the coast, with a fair fresh breeze ....
RICHARD F. BURTON
The Lake Regions of Central Africa

Previous page: Zungomero is the greatest Bandárí or centre of traffic in the eastern ... regions. Lying upon the main trunk-road, it must be traversed by the up and down-caravans, and , during the travelling season, ... large bodies of some thousand men pass through it every week.
RICHARD F. BURTON
The Lake Regions of Central Africa

Coming ashore at Bagamoyo.

careful not to make a sensation of danger ... but future travellers will do well not to think that when about to explore Central Africa, they are setting out on a mere promenade."

Fawn Brodie, in *The Devil Drives*, points out that when Burton and Speke set sail from Zanzibar, at noon on June 16, 1857, they began a twenty-one-month expedition into unimaginable hardships. Neither was used to organizing large groups of men. They had both been army officers — travelling in a world of established discipline. Now there was no discipline except what they themselves imposed. They had to organize a caravan of up to two hundred men, including porters, guards, "ass-men," and guides. By the end of their two-year journey, all but a few had tried to desert.

Near sunset, on Wednesday, June 17, 1857, the *Artémise* anchored off Wale Point, which Burton describes as "a long, low, bush-grown sand spit, about eighty-four miles [135 kilometres] distant from the little town of Bagamoyo." The ship remained at anchor for ten days while the Arab Said bin Salim, who would accompany Burton and Speke, attempted to hire the porters to carry their tons of equipment and supplies. Said bin Salim had gone to the mainland for this purpose, and with him had gone a Customs clerk from Zanzibar named Ramji, hired to accompany the expedition, who eventually supplied slaves to serve as porters. There was a great deal of reluctance on the part of the Africans to travel with the *mzungu*, the white man, and some porters fled at the news without having taken a single step — but after taking their pay. These early efforts at procuring porters for Burton's trek netted 36 out of the required 170 men.

The most favoured items to barter for grain and goats along the way were

The beach at Bagamoyo.

> *During the day the beach throughout its length is alive with the moving figures of hamals, ... with sailors from the shipping, and black boatmen discharging the various imports on the sand. In the evening the beach is crowded with the naked forms of workmen and boys from the "go-downs," preparing to bathe....*
>
> HENRY MORTON STANLEY
> ***Through the Dark Continent***

cotton cloth, brass wire, and porcelain beads. All were used for personal adornment, and Burton said that he went through seventy loads in a year and nine months. This meant that, at the start of the journey, he would have needed seventy men alone to carry what he called "African specie." He also carried enough firearms ammunition for two years. Much of this was made of metals such as brass and lead, a crushingly weighty addition. He made sure, too, that there was enough ammunition for "each individual of the party," which meant that the weight of the guns had to be carried as well.

The goods for barter and the ammunition were only the beginning. They needed complete equipment for more than six hundred nights' worth of camping, including tents, which were made of sail canvas, not light nylon in those days, seats, beds, tables, cooking equipment, washing equipment, and every item necessary for the comfort of a British gentleman. They also carried staple food items that could not be traded for *en route*: coffee, tea, sugar, brandy. They had to take a wide variety of tools to maintain and repair equipment and to meet various needs along the way (axes to cut firewood, for example). Then there were the tools of the explorer's trade: books, charts, maps, and instruments, such as a chronometer, a sextant, and a compass to help them determine latitude and longitude; along with a sundial, rain gauge, barometer, pedometer, and Boiling Point thermometer.

✷ ✷ ✷

The objective of all these journeys was not simply to reach parts of the Nile River system, but to bring back proof of what had been found. The proof, of course, would be in the form of maps constructed from data collected on the ground. The data were accurate recordings of the latitude, the longitude, and, because the whole exercise had to do with the flow of water, the altitude of as many points as possible.

Geography of this kind is the daughter of astronomy and trigonometry. Enough was known by the second century A.D. for Ptolemy to be able to argue that geography needed to be based on latitude and longitude, and describe methods for determining them. And as long as one knew the mathematics, this was possible anywhere on land on the planet, even then. However, as soon as sea voyaging began in earnest, things became more difficult. The Age of Exploration stimulated the development of tools (the sextant, the compass, the chronometer), methods, and textbooks (Norie's *Complete Epitome of Practical Navigation*, Bowditch's *American Practical Navigator*, Thompson's *Lunar Tables*, Gordon's *Time Tables*, Buist's *Manual of Observation*, Jackson's *Military Surveying*, the British Admiralty manual, Keith's *Trigonometry*, Belcher's *Mast Head Angles*, and up-to-date nautical almanacs, all of which Burton and Speke had with them) which would allow the same degree of accurate measurement anywhere on Earth, on land or sea.

For latitude, all one needs to do is accurately determine the angle (the "elevation") between lines of sight to some celestial object and to the horizon. On a clear night, in the northern hemisphere, this was simplicity itself because, if Polaris is used as the celestial object, the observed angle is equal to the latitude. With an ephemeris (a table listing the position of celestial bodies for each day of the year) and more complex mathematics, one could use almost any object observable in the sky: the sun, the moon, most stars — even in the southern hemisphere. Longitude could be determined from celestial observation and knowledge of the correct time at some point whose longitude was already known (like Greenwich in England). Therefore, the explorers took along lever watches (that is, with a lever escapement) and chronometers (which were more accurate than the lever watches, but also more delicate). Altitude, or elevation above sea level, could be accurately determined by time-consuming surveying methods. But the facts that atmospheric pressure is proportional to height above sea level, and that the temperature at which a fluid will boil is proportional to the ambient air pressure (all other things being equal) allowed for a simple, portable, and reasonably accurate method for determining altitude. The explorers took along Boiling Point (B.P. or "bath") thermometers and a small, easily heated pot, or "bath," in which water could be boiled.

Nothing could be done about the weather, but as well as cloud cover, there were other difficulties. Determining a natural horizon was difficult in forests or mountains; a device to provide an artificial horizon (basically a small dish to hold a pool of mercury) addressed this problem. Clocks and watches had to keep time reliably for long periods but also be rugged enough to withstand the rigours of caravan travel in the tropics; Burton and Speke's chronometers and lever watch succumbed. Local variations in air pressure (for example, a passing low-pressure cell) and the purity of the water used (since impurities affect the boiling point) would throw off the measurements for altitude. The adventurers never solved these problems.

One check on the longitude and latitude, in the face of such observational difficulties, was the use of compasses and pedometers to determine the distance and direction travelled from point to point by "dead reckoning." But thick vegetation, swamps, and hilly ground often thwarted the attempt.

✳ ✳ ✳

It was no easy task to find men willing to carry the enormous burdens from the African coast to the interior. But even with enough porters, theft, loss, and abandonment caused considerable "shrinkage." Much of what was carried never made it anywhere near the intended destination.

It was not only items that got lost; people, too, fell by the wayside. The bearers were never clear as to what Burton and Speke intended. In the minds of the local population, both those accompanying the explorers and those encountered in the course of the journey, sorcery and evil were much more likely explanations of Burton and Speke's motives than exploration — a notion not at all familiar to the Africans.

Burton's expedition was organized according to a fairly typical hierarchy of command. He, of course, was in charge, and Speke was his co-explorer or partner. Serving as second in command was Said bin Salim, an Arab lent to the expedition by the Sultan of Zanzibar. Burton had two African gun bearers, Sidi Mubarak Mombai (called Bombay) and Mwinyi Mabruki. These two also served in the capacity of officers with considerable authority. "Sidi," a title of respect like "Sir" or "Lord," is related to the Arabic *sayyid* (sultan), and was originally used to address someone holding high office under a king. "Mwinyi," according to Burton, is "the title for an African freeman," and when used by Ramji's slaves was supposed to indicate noble descent. Burton's cooks were two Goans, and as armed escorts, he had, in addition to slaves, several Baluchis — men from Baluchistan, who had also been lent by the Sultan. It was not uncommon for Arabs to occupy a position of high authority in a European expedition. Beneath them would come the African leaders of the porters. Each porter was supposed to have a specific place in the line of march and a specific pack to carry. The Africans would form most of the labour force of an expedition, and the personality and competence of their African leader could make or break the journey. In Sidi Bombay, Burton had a man who was to become absolutely indispensable.

Sidi Bombay was born a slave, but, through his service to the African explorers, by the end of his life he was nearly as famous as the men he had served. He travelled with Burton in 1857, Speke in 1860, Stanley in 1871, and Verney Lovett Cameron in 1873. Bombay was strong, wise, fearless, smart, and skilled. Burton called him "an active servant and an honest man."

Like the men he served, Bombay must have been something of a visionary. He surely had an inkling that his involvement with Burton was a unique opportunity. Though he claimed that he was not excited by Speke's discovery of Lake Victoria, saying that as a Muslim he was more content with ordinary things, he was clearly excited by the prospect of working with these outstanding men. He was an exceptional man himself, a free spirit in the service of other free spirits.

As Burton and Speke waited off Wale Point, asses were collected to help carry personal baggage and equipment. They managed to collect thirty of them, some already in bad shape, and all destined, it turned out, for a horrible fate. Burton's descriptions of the hard time he had with these animals form an unforgettable part of his writing about the trek, and it is to be assumed that the asses had as much trouble with him as he had with them.

At Kaole, attempts were made to intimidate Burton and his workers by spreading alarming reports of the hostility of the tribes through whose territory they would have to pass. When the members of the armed escort left the *Artémise*, fellow soldiers had told them horror stories about what they would have to face if they went with Burton. One of the Baluchi told them that they would need a hundred guards to fight their way into the interior. Burton had twenty. There was also a rumour that they would be passing through the territory of "savages" whose practice it was to sit in the trees and rain poisoned arrows down on travellers. These marksmen were rumoured to be so accurate they never missed wounding the traveller in the head. The only way to avoid them, it was said, was to avoid trees altogether. "No easy matter," Burton wryly remarked, "in a land of all forest." It was also reported that certain chiefs had expressly forbidden any white men to enter their territory.

Throughout their journey, Burton and Speke encountered attempts by the Africans to scare them away. Because the history of exploration has so often been told from the point of view of the explorers, rather than the natives, it is easy to forget that the Europeans were as terrifyingly exotic to the Africans as the Africans were to the Europeans. Burton, sensitive to the viewpoints of other cultures, recorded some of the Africans' mistaken notions:

> *I was questioned by the chiefs concerning Uzungu, "White Land," the mysterious end of the world in which beads are found under ground, and where the women weave such cottons. From the day of our entering to that of our leaving the country, every settlement turned out its swarm of gazers.... I afterward learned ... malevolent reports concerning the*

Wazungu [white people]. They had one eye each and four arms; they were full of "knowledge," which in these lands means magic; they caused rain to fall in advance and left droughts in their rear; they cooked water-melons and threw away the seeds, thereby generating small-pox; they heated and hardened milk, thus breeding a murrain among cattle; and their wire, cloth, and beads caused a variety of misfortunes; they were kings of the sea, and therefore white-skinned and straight-haired ... as are all men who live in salt water....

RICHARD F. BURTON
The Lake Regions of Central Africa

One morning Burton overheard a conversation between Ramji, the Customs clerk, and his boss, the Customs collector Ladha Damha. Burton had asked them how much it would cost to purchase a boat on the "Sea of Ujiji" — one of the names for Lake Tanganyika. "Will he ever reach it?" the collector asked. "Of course not," answered Ramji, "he won't even make it half way...." The collector was later startled when Burton revealed that he not only could understand the Cutchee dialect in which they had spoken, but also was sure he *would* reach Ujiji. As a final demonstration that they should not try to put anything over on him, he insisted that he could decipher their financial balance sheets as readily as their language.

✷ ✷ ✷

Burton's anthropological and linguistic abilities were considerable:

> *It must be borne in mind that, in the Kisawahili and its cognates, the vowel u prefixed to a root, which, however, is never used without some prefix, denotes, through a primary idea of causality, a country or region, as Uzaramo, the region of Zaramo. Many names, however, exceptionally omit this letter, as the Mrima, K'hutu, Fuga, and Karagwah. The liquid m, or, before a vowel and an aspirated h, mu, to prevent hiatus, being probably a synaeresis of mtu, a man, denotes the individual, as Mzaramo, a man or woman of Zaramo. When prefixed to the names of trees, as has been instanced, it is evidently an abbreviation of mti, a tree. The plural form of m and mu is Wa, a contraction of Watu, men, people; it is used to signify the population, as Wamrima, the "coast-clans, " Wazaramo, the people or tribe of Zaramo, and Wasawahili (with a long accent upon the penultimate, consonant with the spirit of the African language, and contrary to that of the Arabic), the population of the Sawahil. Finally, the syllable ki — prefixed to the theoretical root — denotes any thing appertaining to a country, as the terminating ish in the word English. It especially refers in popular usage to language, as Kizaramo, the language of Zaramo; Kisawahili, the language of the Sawahil, originally called*

Kingozi, from the district of Ngozi, on the Ozi River. It has been deemed advisable to retain these terse and concise distinctions, which, if abandoned, would necessitate a weary redundance of words.

RICHARD F. BURTON
The Lake Regions of Central Africa

The "Kisawahili cognates" are, of course, the huge family of Bantu languages. His summary is still valid today, and helped me make connections between his journey and mine. When I encountered a Wagogo tribesman, for instance, I could be fairly sure I was in the country that Burton called Ugogo. These rules are not, however, universal: some Bantu languages use different prefixes, for example, Ba instead of Wa, for the people, and Burton sometimes applied these rules to non–Bantu-speaking peoples.

✳ ✳ ✳

Early one morning, we went to Kaole to find Professor Samahani M. Kajeri. In reading Burton, I had encountered dozens of tribal names. In Burton's time, there may have been seven hundred tribes and seven hundred tribal languages whose existence he was aware of. While waiting to set out on the expedition, he made some notes on the way of life of the coastal people, the Wamrima, taking careful notice of their drinking, dancing, squabbling, and eating habits. In a casual conversation with Professor Kajeri's wife before we met the professor, I asked her who the Wamrima tribe were. According to her, "the word Wamrima probably comes from *milima*, or 'hills.' Therefore, this means the Wamrima were probably the people who came from the hills or the interior."

Professor Samahani M. Kajeri and his wife.

Professor Kajeri is a local expert and the author of *Bagamoyo — The Beauty at the Beach*. We were lucky to get him. He was out hunting wild pigs in his fields, but his wife coaxed him into giving us a full day of his time. The professor's own tribe, the Ndoe, migrated eastward to the coastal area from the Tabora region five hundred years ago. The verb *doezi* means "to better yourself, to be an opportunist or a freeloader." According to the professor, people of whom such behaviour was characteristic were automatically called "Ndoe."

When the fun threatens to become too fast and furious, the song dies, and the performers, with loud shouts of laughter, throw themselves on the ground, to recover strength and breath.

RICHARD F. BURTON
The Lake Regions of Central Africa

Professor Kajeri gave us an extensive tour of Kaole and Bagamoyo, including the fourteenth-century Kaole ruins left by the Arabs and Shirazis from the Persian Gulf. The ruins are very like those in Gedi and around the Lamu Archipelago, farther north, in Kenya. I was fascinated both by these ruins and by a tumble-down house where Burton and Speke might have stayed 140 years ago.

At Bagamoyo we visited the first Arab house, built in the eighteenth century and now a museum housing African antiquities. We saw the Bagamoyo market, the first mosque (also from the eighteenth century), slave quarters, and a small church in which Dr. Livingstone's body rested after its long journey from the interior in 1874, *en route* to England. A sign above the door states simply: "Dr. Livingstone entered here." There is also a plaque commemorating Burton and Speke's 1857 departure from Bagamoyo.

The town has long been a place of endings and beginnings, of tragedy and beauty. Bagamoyo is derived from the phrase *bwaga moyo*, which has the meanings "throw off your cares," "rest," and "lay down (the burden of) your heart." The name reflects the relief of the slave in finally being able to put down the heavy pack he had carried across East Africa, and also resignation, for he knew he would now be shipped off to some other land to be a slave there. As the beginning and end of the slave route, as well as the jumping-off point for exploration, Bagamoyo had a chequered past that in some respects lives on. It is currently known for housing an uncommon number of muggers and thieves. In fact the *Lonely Planet* guidebook to East Africa warns travellers to the town that they can be robbed day or night by brigands wielding machetes and suggests they should "make a determined effort to look poor" when visiting the beach at Kaole.

Bagamoyo was the administrative headquarters of German East Africa from 1886 to 1891, when the capital was moved to Dar es Salaam. The Society for German Colonization was formed in 1884, mainly because of the persuasive arguments of Karl Peters. Peters was a German nationalist who felt that African colonization should be vigorously pursued. When he could not get his government's support, he and two friends went to Zanzibar in November 1884, posing as mechanics to escape British scrutiny. They slipped away to the mainland, where for several weeks they met with as many tribes as they could, signing a "treaty" with each. When Peters returned to Germany, he signed over his rights in these treaties to the Society, later incorporated as the German East Africa Company. This put the German government in the awkward position of having treaties between African tribes and a non-governmental German entity. The territories in the German East Africa Company's jurisdiction were declared a protectorate of the German state. In fact, the Anglo-German Agreement of 1886 gave Tanganyika, Rwanda, and Burundi to Germany, while Britain took the more fertile Kenya and Uganda. Colonization had begun, and railways, roads, hospitals, and schools were built. The agreement also encouraged the entry of a great number of Christian missionaries, and the first German governor, von Soden, tried to use them as agents for colonization in his plan for peaceful economic expansion.

Two mainland uprisings against German rule, in 1889 and 1905, caused major bloodshed and bitterness, but German occupation of the area continued until the end of the First World War, when Tanganyika was mandated to the British, and Rwanda and Burundi to the Belgians. Buildings from the German period can still be seen in Bagamoyo.

People have described Bagamoyo as being like Zanzibar or Mombasa on a smaller scale, having a historic centre with winding alleys, tiny mosques, cafés, and whitewashed German colonial buildings. Near the waterfront there is an area like this, but it is now close to irredeemable decay. The Customs House at the beach is being restored, but most buildings from the colonial period have a neglected appearance.

The small museum at the Catholic Mission north of town has relics of the slave trade and displays about the early European explorers, including Burton, Speke, and Stanley. Some of the photographs of the slave trade are extraordinarily dramatic and quite gruesome. At Kaole we also saw what Moorehead describes as "the ruins of a coral mosque, and of graves and houses dating back to the thirteenth century, an incredible antiquity in this climate where every man-made thing seems destined to be overwhelmed by nature and forgotten."

Burton writes that Kaole was an abbreviation of "Kaole Urembo," which in ancient coastal dialect meant "to show beauty." It never ceased to amaze Burton, as he made his way through Africa, that architecture was not an art with which the Africans appeared to be familiar — at least not the European notion of architecture — and, even at Kaole, he was struck by this characteristic. "The only attempt at masonry in the settlement," he said, "is the 'gurayza' or fort...."

✳ ✳ ✳

On June 27, 1857, with Burton mounted on an ass, the travellers finally left Bagamoyo and headed towards the Kingani River, now called the Ruvu. Their first major goal was to reach Zungomero. That was our goal, too, but we had a problem: Zungomero has completely disappeared from all modern maps. Undaunted, I noted the reading on the Land Rover's odometer, intending to use it as a gauge of our progress, and we prepared to set out.

My research for the Burton portion of our journey was extremely precise. I had combed Burton's account in *The Lake Regions of Central Africa* and prepared a sort of handbook with a page for every stop he had made, listing the date he had been at that location; the name of the place; its translation (by Burton) into English; and any significant geographical, historical, anthropological, botanical, or geological observation Burton had made there. I had also painstakingly studied a detailed map Burton had made of his journey and meticulously grafted onto that map Burton's division of his journey

into five "regions," each region made up of a number of "stations," an Arab method of measuring distance based on a day's travel.

I then tried to match this map with a map of modern Africa, because my simple plan was to follow Burton's journey. Initially, I was reassured to see that the old caravan route that Burton followed now fairly closely corresponded to the railway across Tanzania built by the Germans before 1910. However, except for a very few places, I could not find any similarity between the place names on Burton's map and the place names on the modern map. I thought this a minor problem when I did my research amid the comforts of England and Canada. But it became a major problem in my trek across Burton's first region — from Bagamoyo, which had been easy to find, to Zungomero, which was a different story altogether.

Kaole, the starting point of the Burton–Speke expedition, 1856.

After a mosquito-infested night of breezeless heat and humidity, Thad Peterson, Pollangyo, Joshua, Ali, and I said our farewells to our Bagamoyo hotelier and host, jumped into our long-wheel-base Land Rovers, and struck out into the interior for the first phase of our journey along the old slave-caravan route.

We passed a string of villages, not one of which I recognized from the research: Sanzare, Kigongoni (which literally means "ridge"), an area that houses the local prison and includes the villages of Matimbwa, Kitgongoni, Yombo, Miswe, and the district of Kibaha. An elder who seemed to know the area well confirmed that these places were indeed along the caravan route. We needed this confirmation, as it soon became apparent that we had absolutely no idea where we were. After travelling for a time along the old Dar es Salaam road to Morogoro, we left the Ruvu River valley and hit the new Dar es Salaam–Morogoro road, which was much wider, paved, and crowded. Boutiques lined the sides of the road in a benign display of commerce. As I watched them go by from the safety of the Land Rover, I recalled a story told by Burton, which would no doubt terrify and titillate the readers back home, about M. Maizan, who in 1845 was "the first European known to have penetrated beyond the sea-board." Foolishly leaving behind his armed escort and accompanied by only a few locals, Maizan had visited the village of the chief of a subtribe of the Wazaramo. Maizan was received

Men never appear in public without an ostentatious display of arms. The usual weapons, when they cannot produce muskets, are ... long knives ... made by themselves with imported iron.

RICHARD F. BURTON
The Lake Regions of Central Africa

Termite mound and impala.

politely at first, but after several days of cordial treatment, the chief suddenly accused his visitor of having given goods to other chiefs, and declared, "Thou shalt die at this moment!" Burton carefully described the torture inflicted on his predecessor: "The unfortunate man's arms were then tightly bound to a pole lashed crosswise upon another, to which his legs and head were secured by a rope tied across the brow. In this state he was carried out of the village to a calabash-tree.... The inhuman Mazungera first severed all his articulations, while the war-song and the drum sounded notes of triumph. Finding the *simé*, or double-edged knife, somewhat blunt, he stopped, when in the act of cutting his victim's throat, to whet the edge, and having finished the bloody deed, he concluded with wrenching the head from the body."

At Mlandizi the new highway departs from the old caravan route. Modern engineering has straightened the road, which now crosses and recrosses the Ruvu River, rather than paralleling its windings. We planned to cut south to Kisaki, which we hoped was at or near Burton's Zungomero. On the way we noticed a friendly highway sign: *Safari Njema*. I asked what it meant. "Safe Journey."

The later explorers, such as Stanley, may have taken a much more direct route into the interior, staying closer to the current Dar es Salaam–Morogoro road. Obviously following the Ruvu (or Kingani) River, as Burton and Speke did on their 1857 journey, was a somewhat indirect route, but the difficulties were known. On the other hand, the traders and the locals were familiar with the power of the Sultan of Zanzibar under whose protection they travelled. And the frequent caravans allowed mail to pass to and from the coast. As we motored along, we could see the Dar es Salaam–Ujiji Railway running about ten kilometres south of the main road and almost parallel to it.

Ninety-three kilometres from Bagamoyo, we stopped for petrol, and soon after headed south. Long, thin, red-and-black termite mounds dotted the highway, looking like mileposts or odd single fingers pointed at the sky. In East Africa, the terrain can change suddenly and dramatically. As we followed the winding red road we suddenly found ourselves in the *miombo* (woodland), which covers most of southern Tanzania. The *miombo* is characterized by trees that have adapted to a long dry season, the three dominant species being *Brachystegia*, *Isoberlinia*, and *Julbenardia*. Although the area receives a lot of rain — 80 to 120 centimetres a year — it all falls from November to May, during and right after the monsoon season. The *miombo* has grass underbrush, unlike the lush, complex underbrush that is typical of swamp forest and lowland rainforest. The *miombo* is home to insects and animals suited to the two extreme seasons. We travelled through a lot of *miombo* in the course of our journey, and we encountered quite a number of these insects and animals, which include the tsetse fly, termites and their predators, bees, and the honey badger, hartebeest, sable, bush rat, gerbil, mole rat, and Burchell's zebra. During the dry season, which was just ending, the *Brachystegia* and *Isoberlinia* bark provides fodder for elephants, and fuel for the fires of hunters and honey gatherers. The sparseness of the underbrush in some places was a sign of heavy use.

After a place called Kizuka, we passed through a military zone, finally reaching Ngerengere, 133 kilometres from Bagamoyo. It had taken us only a few hours, whereas only on the very best days would Burton and Speke have even achieved 17 kilometres. Ten kilometres a day would have been considered much more usual.

Suddenly, our road came to a dead end. What had been a serviceable road ten years before had not been kept up and was now impassable. Even if we had reached the Ruvu River, we would have been stranded and would not have been able to get across. In the dry season, when the water is very low, a vehicle might be able to cross the river, but certainly not now, when the heavy rains had already started to fall. It began to rain again. We had to turn back to the main road. This was a thirty-six-kilometre mistake — but at least it was not a several-days mistake, as it would have been in Burton's time.

Back on the main road the way was clearly

Black-and-white colobus monkey.

Trying to match Burton's place names to those remembered by an elder.

defined but not nearly so exciting. We turned off it at Mikese (189 kilometres from Bagamoyo) and found ourselves on another dirt road, rutted and in very bad condition. That took us to the railway through woodlands and past an old German settlement with a kapok-processing plant. The kapok, or silk-cotton tree, was introduced from its native America. The fibre, removed by hand from the ripened pod, is a lustrous, yellowish floss after cleaning. Its resistance to water and decay led to its use as stuffing for life-preservers, bedding, and upholstery. The fatty oil from the seed kernels is used for soap or refined into an edible oil, with the residue used as fertilizer or fodder.

The rain had produced a wet, slippery road as we drove through stands of

[A] final march of four hours placed us in the plains of Ugogo .... [T]he scenery became curious. The Dungomaro appeared a large crevasse in lofty rocks of pink and gray granite, streaked with white quartz, and pudding'd with greenstone and black horneblend .... Farther down the bed huge boulders ... rose, perpendicularly as walls, to the height of ... one hundred and twenty feet, and there the flooring was a sheet of shiny and shelving rock ....

RICHARD F. BURTON
The Lake Regions of Central Africa

93

tall elephant grass, kapok trees, and mango trees (which are native to East Africa and may well have been cultivated here for six thousand years). Banana trees lined the roadside. On the outskirts of scattered villages, pedestrians in colourful tribal dress carried sticks, bundles, earthenware pots, and baskets of fruit. We spotted the occasional cyclist, hanging onto upright handlebars, bare body glistening. We ran over a chicken and debated whether to stop, but decided to let Joshua and Ali in the following vehicle sort out the problem. At Kikundi (which means "gathering"), 207 kilometres from Bagamoyo, *togwa*, a non-alcoholic beverage made from millet, was being sold by the side of the road, and many of the locals sat around drinking it. We were still not having much luck matching any names we had from Burton. Later on we stopped to investigate some extraordinary rock caves near the village of Bagalala. The caves were once used as dwellings, but not any longer.

The road now took us into an equatorial rainforest, where we saw the black-and-white and the red colobus monkeys, a first for me. The colobus is a forest monkey found all over East Africa. There are two major types: the black-and-white and the red. They have long limbs and a long, bushy, white tail. They differ from other monkeys in lacking a thumb.

Next we passed teak plantations, and then, quite suddenly, found ourselves down at the Ruvu River again, its fast-flowing brown water rushing between banks heavily forested with breadfruit trees and a dense, soaking undergrowth of bamboo, thick vines, and ferns. Then Matombo, at 245 kilometres.

Of course, the many changes in terrain that we encountered in one day Burton and Speke would have experienced much more gradually and therefore would have seen very differently. This was one way in which my journey could not parallel Burton's — nor would I really have wanted it to. On a more leisurely journey, I would not have been so struck by the tremendous range of features in the landscape. I think Burton probably — and Speke definitely — would have preferred the drama of travelling at my pace, if they had had the choice.

✳ ✳ ✳

To judge from their dialect they are, like the Wakwafi, a tribe or a subtribe of the great Masai race, who speak a language partly South-African and partly Semitico-African, like that of the Somal. The habitat ... extends from the north of Usagara to the eastern shores of the Nyanza or Ukerewe Lake; it has been remarked that a branch of the Mukondokwa River rises in their mountains. The blue highlands occupied by this pastoral race, clearly visible, on the right hand, to the traveller passing from Ugogo westwards, show where the ancient route from Panganitown used to fall into the main trunk-road of Unyamwezi.

RICHARD F. BURTON
The Lake Regions of Central Africa

An African graffito near Zungomero.

On and on we went, taking a twisting road through hills of yellow limestone laid down eons ago, when this part of Africa was covered by ocean. We marvelled at the precipitous drop to the valley below, proof of the river's vigorous erosive power. In the distance we could just make out the plains that border the northern edge of the huge Selous Game Reserve.

Near Mvuha we crossed a tributary of the Ruvu River and got directions to Kisaki, where, the elder said, there definitely was a region called "Zungomero." We were now 266 kilometres from Bagamoyo.

At 5:15 p.m., exhausted by the travels of the day, we nonetheless resisted the temptation to camp in an open field. It was still raining. We sped onwards to Dutumi (which Burton called Dut'humi), which we reached at 6:00 p.m. It was dusk and heavily overcast during the last hour as we drove through savanna — grassy plains marked with clumps of trees. The rain descended monotonously. Several troops of colobus monkeys swung from overhanging trees. We also passed some settlements of the blue-cloaked Parakuyu (or Baraguyu) Maasai. The men wore blue and red, the women only blue. This branch of the Maasai inhabit the northern Selous Plains from near Morogoro all the way to Dar es Salaam. Near Arusha and in South Maasailand, the Maasai wear much more distinctive red cloaks.

Burton reached Dutumi around July 18 — about a month after setting sail from Zanzibar — and stayed there until July 24. By this time, after several false starts, his caravan was becoming more organized. Burton felt obliged to apologize in his writings that his complement of porters included slaves. His attitude towards slavery was never blasé, though he was often ironic. I sometimes suspect that Burton's negative attitude towards the African was a socially acceptable way to hide deeper, more sympathetic feelings:

I must explain to the reader why we were accompanied by [slaves], and how the guide and escort contrived to purchase them. All the serving men in Zanzibar Island and on the coast of East Africa are serviles; the Kisawahili does not contain even a word to express a hired domestic. For the evil of slaver-service there was no remedy: I therefore paid them their wages and treated them as if they were freemen. I had no power to prevent Said bin Salim, the Baloch escort, and the "sons of Ramji," purchasing whomever they pleased; all objections on my part were overruled by "We are allowed by our law to do so."... I was fain to content myself with seeing that their slaves were well fed and not injured, and indeed I had little trouble in so doing, as no man was foolish enough to spoil his own property. I never neglected to inform the wild people that Englishmen were pledged to the suppression of slavery, and I invariably refused all slaves offered as return presents.

RICHARD F. BURTON
The Lake Regions of Central Africa

At Dutumi that night we camped in the district commissioner's bungalow, a dilapidated structure high on a bluff overlooking the plains. The bluff was actually the edge of an offshoot of the Great Rift Valley, continuing the line of the escarpment running from the northern tip of Lake Malawi through Mikumi. From Mikumi the main rift valley stretches north and west, while this side branch runs east–north–east, petering out near Ngerengere on a line leading straight to Bagamoyo. The rain stopped, and wonderful African smells filled the cool, clear air. Rain seems to bring out the best in Africa — a fresh earthy quality. We heard doves cooing and in the distance the unique sound of a hornbill drumming. Joshua and Ali cooked up a strange mixture of rice and vegetables, which we washed down with a Serengeti beer. Then a slice of pineapple.

I was tired, but before I crawled into my sleeping bag for the night, I reviewed my research on the First, or maritime, Region. We were at the second-last stage of Burton's trip in the region: Dutumi to Bakera. The last was Bakera to Zungomero. Tomorrow we would have to start hunting again for Burton's elusive places. For the time being, however, I decided just to relax and reread Burton's diary account of some of his adventures in the region.

Near the first station, Mgude, "the cocoa-plantation near the sea," Burton came across a medicine man. This reminded me of a similar person I had "consulted" when I had followed Burton's travels in Sindh. "I sent for a mganga or medicine-man," Burton wrote, "a dark old man, of superior rank, as the cloth round his head and his many bead necklaces showed." The old man arrived with his doctor's bag full of implements and demanded to be paid before he began. When he was satisfied with the amount Burton offered, he began his "treatment," producing a gourd full of medicine that to Burton sounded like pebbles and bits of metal when the gourd was

Off the main road, in savanna, searching for Zungomero.

shaken. I have always admired the way in which Burton — and Speke and Livingstone, too — threw themselves into African life without fear. Burton did not even flinch when the next step in the "doctor's" procedure proved to require "two thick goat's horns connected by a snake-skin." This odd instrument was decorated with "curiously-shaped iron bells," which the medicine man jangled as he gyrated the object, whispered, swayed, and finally pronounced that Burton's trip was destined to be prosperous. There did not, mercifully, appear to be a physical component to this encounter, unlike my own appointment, at which curious ointments and oral medications were prescribed.

At Nzasa, the fourth station, Burton learned from his Arab assistant that to impress the natives it was essential to appear extremely proud and disdainful. "At 4 p.m. a loud drumming collected the women, who began to perform a dance of ceremony with peculiar vigor. A line of small, plump, chestnut-colored beings ... advanced and retired in a convulsion of wiggle and contortion.... I threw them a few strings of green beads, which for a moment interrupted the dance. One of these falling to the ground, I was stooping to pick it up when Said whispered hurriedly in my ear, 'Bend not; they will say, "He will not bend even to take up beads"!'"

At Sagesera, the eighth station, Burton had a run-in with warrior tribes determined to extract tribute:

My companion, who was leisurely proceeding with the advance-guard, found his passage barred by about fifty Wazaramo standing across the path in a single line that extended to the travelers' right, while a reserve party squatted on the left of the road. Their chief stepping to the front and quietly removing the load from the foremost porter's head, signaled the strangers to halt. Prodigious excitement of the Baloch, whose loud, "Hai, hui!" and nervous anxiety contrasted badly with perfect sang froid of the barbarians. Presently, Muinyi Wazira, coming up, addressed to the headman a few words, promising cloth and beads, when this African modification of the "pike" was opened, and the guard moved forward as before. As I passed ... I could not but admire the athletic and statuesque figures of the young warriors and their martial attitude, grasping in one hand their full-sized bows, and in the other sheaths of grinded arrows, whose black barbs and necks showed a fresh layer of poison.

RICHARD F. BURTON
The Lake Regions of Central Africa

It was near Dutumi, too, that Burton and Speke began to experience the debilitating bouts of strange infirmities that would severely plague them for the remainder of their journey: "At Dut'humi we were detained nearly a week; the malaria had brought on attacks of marsh fever, which in my case lasted about 20 days.... My companion suffered even more severely; he had a fainting-fit which strongly resembled a sun-stroke, and which seemed permanently to affect his brain."

✳ ✳ ✳

It was a very peaceful night, but I slept fitfully in my sleeping bag on the hard, hard bed until 5:30 a.m. The four of us got up to a whole morning chorus of insects and birds — but no mosquitoes. Though I never discovered the reason for their absence, it made a welcome change. I washed, dressed, and had a cup of Tanzanian coffee: gritty, cloudy, and strong. Just the thing to start the day. A slice of papaya and of pineapple, and we were ready to pack up and move on. The sounds of Africa surrounded us. The mist still on the plains in the distance enshrouded hill and mountain, lending more magic to the African morning.

Determined to locate Zungomero, I wanted to leave camp the minute breakfast was over, but we left at about 8:00 a.m. — a late start. Later on we would get much better at stowing our considerable gear onto and into the Land Rovers, but at this stage we spent far too much time packing and unpacking and rearranging. We missed a good chunk of the early morning. Burton's account of his journey is full of complaints about how chaotic his march was, primarily because he and Speke were inexperienced at organizing the workers — and the animals. But for him, too, the daily routine eventually acquired its own brand of order. In Burton's time, the caravan route consisted of paths from village to village, and it would not have been unusual to pass other caravans — often of slaves carrying ivory — travelling in the opposite direction. Each day began before dawn, when it was still cold. Burton and Speke breakfasted, perhaps while the Arabs prayed, facing northward here, towards Mecca. (The Islamic injunctions about these five-times-daily prayers required a knowledge of where one was with respect to the Holy City, and in the context of continuous Arab travel it provided a powerful stimulus for the acquisition, retention, and refinement of geographical knowledge in the Arab world.) As the sky began to lighten, everyone — man and beast alike — was roused and rounded up, and all the many burdens were assigned. Of course, the entire camp had to be dismantled in order to be packed and loaded on the asses. Before leaving camp, it was the practice to burn any rough shelters that had been erected to discourage followers and avoid giving an advantage to potential marauders.

Red-billed hornbill. Was Burton the first European to see this bird?

Their march would have had a military flavour, being led by a sort of honour guard consisting of a bearer carrying the Sultan of Zanzibar's red flag, immediately followed by a drummer. Next came those who carried the "specie," or items for barter. The porters and the asses carrying camp supplies followed. Caravans included the wives, children, and domestic cattle of the bearers, and the personal slaves of the armed guards. These guards usually carried a musket, a sabre, a leather box, and a cow-horn for ammunition. Weapons were always at the ready, not only in case of an attack by hostile tribes, but also because they might be needed for hunting game.

The march was thus an extremely noisy procession designed both to intimidate local populations and to entertain the marchers. Burton wrote: "The normal recreations of a march are, whistling, singing, shouting, hooting, horning, drumming, imitating the cries of birds and beasts, repeating words which are never used except on journeys...."

Because of the heat, it was unlikely that the march could proceed after 11:00 a.m. each day, and might even have to halt as early as 8:00 a.m. Burton and Speke, who travelled at the rear of the march, walking, riding asses, or carried in hammocks when ill, would cover about sixteen kilometres if the march lasted until 11:00 a.m. Between the halt and dinner at about 4:00 p.m., the explorers were busy with their writing, sketching, observations, and the continuing business of the caravan. Barter was conducted with villagers if a village was nearby, the porters being assigned goods for trade by their leaders.

At night there was dancing, and no doubt a good deal of drinking, too. Burton always seemed to take delight in watching the dance. He recorded his observations of African dancers with as much detail as he lavished on the dancers of Sindh and as much knowledge as he later showed for the ballet at home.

As our own "march" for the day began, I was not sorry to leave the filthy guest house that had served as our camp. When Joshua and Ali cooked dinner, a rat had skulked around the veranda, watching us, then darted into our rooms to see if we had left any food. Most of the night a bat had flown around the rafters of my flimsy room. But it could not have been quite as bad as what Burton and Speke experienced in Zungomero. Burton called it "that hot-bed of pestilence" and went on to report: "The roof was a sieve, the walls were systems of chinks, and the floor was a sheet of mud."

When we drove down from the guest house, we noticed the remains of an old cotton mill. Most of the inhabitants of Dutumi at one time used to work in the cotton fields around the mill. They would have come from the Waluguru and Warutu tribes and would have known how to make for themselves the cloth "piece-goods" like those that Burton had brought from India to give to their forbears. Cotton has had a long history in Africa. There may have been cotton plants native to Africa cultivated as early as 3000 B.C., and there was certainly an established cotton industry in Africa in the Middle Ages, though its use would have been reserved for the wealthy, as cotton cloth was a luxury. We would pass cotton fields later in our journey.

*Palmyra palm tree
(Borassus flabelliformis).*

We drove through the actual Dutumi village to Vwakira, a sparsely populated settlement, probably Burton's Bakera, which sits within view of the Uluguru Mountains, a view framed by tall elephant grass. Bakera was the last station before Zungomero. Passing through Dakawa and then Sesenga, we reached and forded a tributary of the Mgeta River called the Mgeta Kafa. In this part of Africa, most such small rivers disappear in the dry season.

We were then told that Sesenga had in fact been Zungomero. So we backtracked for three kilometres and travelled up the road another five kilometres, only to discover that the information was hopelessly wrong. We did come to another village, and it was still "Sesenga." And so we backtracked again, returning to the river and passing through Kisaki, another nine kilometres. The road took us across an iron bridge, then through tall grass. Pollangyo told me that this tall grass harbours *upupu* (buffalo vine), a type of creeper that is completely covered with tiny hairs that sting. Being stung by this vine is one of the worst African experiences, I was told. Farther on, coconut trees, now more than a hundred years old, grew along the road. We also passed through an area of mango trees and old kapok trees which had certainly been some sort of settlement — a meeting place for the caravans in the old days.

As we struggled along, we found people eager to help us, sometimes surrounding the car and offering numerous pieces of advice simultaneously. When we asked village elders where Zungomero was, they simply told us that the entire area was called Zungomero and that the name had been passed down from their grandfathers to their fathers.

About four kilometres farther on, several small roads and trails converged on a school, now called Nyaratanga, set in a grove of mature trees—old, gnarled kapoks, twisted by nature into interesting shapes. It gave me a strong feeling of the past, of history. One elder, Juma Abdullagh Nzgula, explained that in the old days the place was called Zungomero Mahinda (*mahinda* means "ancestral spirits"). These spirits were consulted in cases of sickness, famine, and other difficulties. The elder's father had been born in Zungomero, as had his grandfather. Many years ago, he told us, the population of Zungomero had been decimated by the Wakutu, and the Arabs had bought, bartered for, and simply taken slaves from the area. In those days, he said, "if you needed money, you could go to your sister and take her son and then negotiate a price for the son. This was possible. The proceeds were divided."

So we *had* finally reached Zungomero. It was still a place; and it did have a definite if somewhat gruesome history.

✳ ✳ ✳

Leaving Zungomero, we drove westward for many kilometres on a rough game track — just above the railway, sometimes through the Selous Game Reserve, sometimes through a buffer zone to the park. Game was abundant — impala, wildebeest, warthogs, hornbills, a Marshall eagle. We stopped for lunch in dry, wooded scrubland, but thousands of African ants ruined our picnic and we had to move on. A little later we stopped again on a woodland road, where it was well treed and shady and where there were not so many ants or tsetse flies. Selous is famous for tsetse flies.

After lunch we arrived at a game-scout outpost, Bwaga, inside Mikumi National Park. The scout estimated that in another forty-six kilometres we would be out of the park at Mikumi (the main town), from where we could hit the direct road north to Kilosa — our next main destination. This sounded promising.

Just after 3:00 p.m., having travelled 220 kilometres as the crow flies in less than two days, we crossed a dry tributary of the Ruaha River. Away in the distance shone the Ruaha itself, glistening in the afternoon sun. An hour later we reached the Mahondo Ranger post on the outer edge of the Mikumi Game Reserve. There were more villages now along the hot, dry, dusty road that ran through sugar-cane fields, banana plantations, and groves of dark green mango trees. Tall, spreading kapok trees arched over the roads, their opened pods like white blossoms. There were mud huts roofed with thatch. In the distance ahead, south of the Great Ruaha River, the Udzungwa

Mountains marked the edge of the Great Rift Valley. Finally, we reached Mikumi and drove to the wildlife lodge a few kilometres beyond the town — probably the best place to spend the night.

In *Burton and Lake Tanganyika, 1857*, Charles Richards says: "The first stage of the journey was completed when after marching for over three weeks during which time Burton and Speke had suffered much from fever, and other illnesses, the expedition reached Zungomero on July 25, 1857."

They stayed until August 7, Burton reporting:

> *We were martyred by a miasma; my companion and I were so feeble that we could scarcely sit our asses, and weakness had almost deprived us of the sense of hearing. It was a day of severe toil. We loaded with difficulty; for the slaves and porters did not assemble till past 8 A.M., and, instead of applying for their loads to Said bin Salim, every man ran off with the lightest burden or the easiest ass.*
>
> RICHARD F. BURTON
> **The Lake Regions of Central Africa**

As I rested, relatively secure in the lodge, I read what Edward Rice had said about Burton and Speke at this stage of their journey:

> *Struggling under appalling conditions, two sick men, handicapped by insufficient resources, a shortage of porters and animal transport, lack of equipment, and a rebellious caravan, pushed ahead into an Africa that no European had ever seen and which even the long-experienced Arab slavers and traders approached with caution and fear.*
>
> EDWARD RICE
> **Captain Sir Richard Francis Burton**

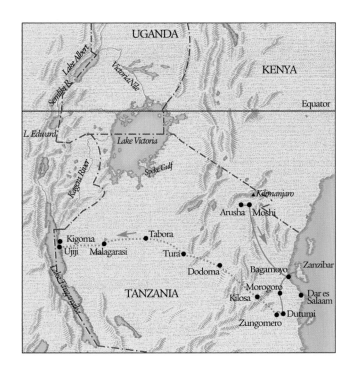

The Rough Nurse of Rugged Men:
Zungomero to Ujiji and Kigoma

There was nothing of effeminate or luxuriant beauty, nothing of the flush and fullness characterizing tropical nature, in this first aspect of Ugogo. It appeared what it is, stern and wild — the rough nurse of rugged men....

RICHARD F. BURTON
The Lake Regions of Central Africa

4

THE ROUGH NURSE OF RUGGED MEN: ZUNGOMERO TO UJIJI AND KIGOMA

When we left Zungomero, we left what Burton called the First Region of his trip and entered the Second, or mountain, Region. Ahead of us, between Zungomero and Lake Tanganyika, lay four more of his regions. Traversing the Second Region would take us from Zungomero over the Rubeho Mountains to the edge of a country Burton called Ugogo, which is near present-day Dodoma. The trek through the Rubeho Mountains was a difficult one for Burton because of the rugged terrain. For us it was also difficult, but mainly because we could not be sure what route Burton's expedition had taken to reach the mountain pass.

Beyond Dodoma, the explorers passed through the Third Region and part of the Fourth Region to reach Kazeh (present-day Tabora), where they rested for five weeks. From Tabora they proceeded to the Malagarasi River, which marked the beginning of Burton's Fifth Region; and from there they plodded laboriously on, reaching Lake Tanganyika at Ujiji on February 14, 1858, seven and a half months after leaving Bagamoyo. When I glanced at Burton's careful list, I counted ninety stations between Zungomero and Lake Tanganyika.

Our own expedition telescoped Burton and Speke's seven and a half months of travel into eight days. We left Bagamoyo on October 25, and arrived at Lake Tanganyika on November 1. Swift though our progress was, however, when we set out from Zungomero I had hoped to cover the distance much more quickly than we actually did. The trip to Lake Tanganyika turned out to be a difficult slog as we detoured and backtracked ceaselessly, trying to identify some of the more elusive portions of Burton's trail.

The women are well dressed as the men — a circumstance rare in East Africa....
[T]hey never veil their faces, and they show no shame in the presence of strangers.
The child is carried in a cloth at the back.

RICHARD F. BURTON
The Lake Regions of Central Africa

Previous page: Black cattle are seldom driven down from the interior, on account
of the length and risk of the journey.... The price of full-grown bullocks varies,
according to the distance from the coast, between 3 and 5 doti; whilst that for cows
is about double.

RICHARD F. BURTON
The Lake Regions of Central Africa

On leaving Zungomero, our winding, although generally westerly, route took us south, to the Mikumi National Park. For this part of the trip we did not follow Burton's more northerly route. He skirted the south slopes of the Uluguru Mountains; we detoured much farther south, eventually rejoining his route at the town of Kilosa.

The red road away from Zungomero.

By the time he entered the Second Region, Burton had been travelling much longer than we had and the daily routine of his march was well established, although he had a great deal of trouble with careless, rebellious, and larcenous porters. Our routine, on the other hand, was very quick and efficient. We worked hard, got on well together, and had fun.

I had made it clear at the start of the trip that I did not want too many modern conveniences to distance me from the experiences a nineteenth-century traveller would have had. I felt instinctively that, if I spent the nights surrounded by four solid walls, with proper beds and hot and cold running water, and ate meals prepared in restaurant kitchens, I would miss the essence of what I was seeking to understand: the sights, scents, sounds — even the tastes — of the explorers' life on the trail. So, except in urban places, such as Zanzibar, Bagamoyo, and Kigoma, we slept in tents, making our camp every night, eating our improvised meals around the campfire, and packing it all up again every morning.

I had a small tent to myself. Joshua had one that he usually shared with his son Ali, although Ali had a small tent of his own which he sometimes used. Thad Peterson shared his tent with Pollangyo. So almost always there were five of us in three tents, arranged around a campfire. The first time I saw the three set up, I remembered the descriptions I had read of Burton and Speke's three tents in Somaliland in 1855 and of the dangerous attack they underwent there. Wherever we had come to at the end of the day, usually just before sunset, we pitched our tents before it got dark and before the mosquitoes came out.

Especially while we were following Burton's map on the first part of our journey, we were so exhausted with our travelling and looking for places and arguing and trying to decide where we were that we needed a good strong drink of *pombe*, locally brewed beer, as soon as a campsite was decided. We would pitch the tents and have a shower outside. Our portable shower was a plastic bag full of water hung over the bough of a tree. It could be either cool or hot, depending on whether the bag was left in the sun for about half an hour. From the bottom of the bag protruded a long, thin, plastic tube ending in a nozzle that could be extracted or inserted. The extraction released the water through a shower head. Very simple. I wondered why I had not seen this anywhere else.

After we had worked together to pitch the tents, we all got wood for the fire. Ali usually did the cooking as we sat around and talked about what we had done that day and what we planned on doing the next day. I would quiz the others about their observations and write for at least an hour, recording the day's events. I also used this time to get myself ready for the next day's travels, reading about Burton's journey, what he had written, and what others had written about the towns that he travelled through. Beyond Mikumi, the first place name that seemed similar to any on Burton's itinerary was Miyombo, just south of Kilosa. After Kilosa, Burton's route took him south of Dodoma, a name not found on his itinerary. Between Kilosa and Dodoma are the Rubeho Mountains — which I found both on Burton's maps and on my modern maps. In a sense, what we were trying to do was to hack our way through the wilderness mentally before we did it physically, trying to imagine what Burton would have done as an explorer in the same place, dealing with his own camp and his band of bearers.

Each day we went as far as we could, then looked for a place to camp, usually off the road, in some kind of clearing. Each of these places turned out to be extraordinary in its own way. Occasionally we camped in some filthy little dwelling we found along the way, but usually we were in our tents at the edge of the jungle or by a river. It was pleasant and relaxing. We were always exhausted, and so we tended to go to sleep by about nine, and got up early in the morning to get going as soon as possible.

We did not carry much food, but bought it along the way. Burton and Speke did something similar, only they shot animals for food when they could.

When we were at sea level, it was as hot as hell at night. During the day we were tormented by mosquitoes and pestered by bees. And then there were ticks. I got a tick bite on my stomach. I tried to pull the tick off while I was having a shower. You have to get the head out by twisting counter-clockwise or else you are supposed to burn it off. I did neither, and the thing festered. I had to put up with it for the remainder of the journey.

There were other minor irritations — rashes and things — but mercifully nothing like the ravages of smallpox, which Burton witnessed at first hand near Mzizi Mdogo, "Little Tamarind," shortly after leaving Zungomero:

> On the way we were saddened by the sight of the clean-picked
> skeletons, and here and there the swollen corpses, of porters who had
> perished in this place of starvation. A single large body, which had lost
> fifty of its number by small-pox, had passed us but yesterday on the
> road, and the sight of their deceased comrades recalled to our minds
> terrible spectacles; men staggering on blinded by disease, and mothers
> carrying on their backs infants as loathsome objects as themselves.
> The wretches would not leave the path, every step in their state of
> failing strength was precious; he who once fell would never rise again;
> no village would admit death into its precincts, no relation nor friend
> would return for them, and they would lie till their agony was ended
> by the raven and vulture, the fisi [hyena] and the fox.... Under these

Grant's gazelles (Gazella granti).

circumstances, as might be expected, several of our party caught the
infection; they lagged behind, and probably threw themselves into
some jungle, for the path when revisited showed no signs of them.

RICHARD F. BURTON
The Lake Regions of Central Africa

Burton was a keen observer of flora and fauna. For instance, "We left Mzizi Mdogo on the 9th August, much cheered by the well-omened appearance of a bird with a red bill, white breast, and long tail-feathers." This description fits the red-billed hornbill: Burton may have been the first European to see this bird, and, if so, perhaps it should be called Burton's red-billed hornbill. Speke has a weaver-bird named after him; and Grant a gazelle. We saw red-billed hornbills all along the route that Burton and Speke travelled on their way from Bagamoyo to Lake Tanganyika.

Burton also made some interesting observations about the tsetse fly. His love for it was no greater than ours:

In this foul jungle our men also suffered severely from the tzetze
[fly].... On the line followed by the expedition, the tzetze was found
extending from Usagara westwards as far as the central lakes; its
usual habitat is the jungle-strip which incloses each patch of cultivated
ground, and in the latter it is rarely seen. It has more persistency of

purpose even than the Egyptian fly, and when beaten off it will return half a dozen times to the charge; it can not be killed except by a smart blow, and its long, sharp proboscis draws blood even through a canvas hammock.... In the vicinity of Kilwa it was heard of under the name of "kipanga," the "little sword." It is difficult to conceive the purpose for which this plague was placed in a land so eminently fitted for breeding cattle and for agriculture.... Possibly at some future day, when the country becomes valuable, the tzetze may be exterminated by the introduction of some insectivorous bird, which will be the greatest benefactor that Central Africa ever knew.

RICHARD F. BURTON
The Lake Regions of Central Africa

Needless to say, Burton's hope has not yet been realized. Nor were tsetse flies the only insects to menace him and Speke in the Second Region:

Late in the morning of the 24th of August,... we followed the path that leads from Mbumi along the right bank of the Mukondokwa River to its ford.... The path was slippery with mud, and man and beast were rendered wild by the cruel stings of a small red ant and a huge black pismire. The former crossed the road in dense masses like the close columns of any army. They are large-headed, showing probably that they are defenders of the republic, and that they perform the duties of soldiers in their excursions. Though they can not spring, they show great quickness in fastening themselves to the foot or ankle as it brushes over them. The pismire, known to the people as the "chungu-fundo," or "siyafu" from the Arabic "siyaf," is a horse-ant, about an inch [2.5 centimetres] in length, whose bulldog-like head and powerful mandibles enables it to destroy rats and mice, lizards and snakes. It loves damp places upon the banks of rivers and stagnant waters; it burrows but never raises hills, and it appears scattered for miles over the paths.

RICHARD F. BURTON
The Lake Regions of Central Africa

Given the hardships they had to endure, it is not surprising that during the next few weeks Burton's Baluchi escorts mutinied for more food and threatened to desert with their slaves. Burton and Speke had to consider the possibility of burying most of their baggage and carrying on with the expedition, trusting only to their Wanyamwezi porters to bring them to the lake. However, the storm blew over, Burton says, and they were able to continue. On the way, they caught sight of something that also caught my eye — strange beehives that looked like cannons sticking out of the trees, but were actually constructed of logs or rounds of bark from other trees.

★ ★ ★

Cannon-shaped beehives, or mazinga.

We left the Mikumi Lodge at 8:00 a.m. Our route cut through a valley, past an enormous herd of elephants. Near the lodge entrance, a herd of buffalo grazed on a parched brown hill.

I was still trying very hard to follow the exact route of the explorers. From the coast to Dodoma was about one-third of the distance to Lake Tanganyika, and for this first third of our trip it was a struggle to follow Burton's route and to match modern settlements to his place names. What happened, I think, was that the villages grew, or moved, or a town name came to be applied to an area. Also, before the influx of Europeans, the

When I returned in the evening, small boys brought me sparrows for sale.
JOHN HANNING SPEKE
Journal of the Discovery of the Source of the Nile

Overleaf: The Wanyamwezi tribe, the proprietors of the soil, is the typical race in this portion of Central Africa.... The aspect of the Wanyamwezi is alone sufficient to disprove the existence of very elevated lands in this part of the African interior. They are usually of a dark sepia-brown, rarely coloured like diluted Indian ink, as are the Wahiao and slave races to the south, with negroid features markedly less Semitic than the people of the eastern coast. The effluvium from their skins, especially after exercise or excitement, marks their connection with the negro.... The normal figure of the race is tall and stout, and the women are remarkable for the elongation of the mammary organs.
RICHARD F. BURTON
The Lake Regions of Central Africa

language of this area had no written form and Burton could have misheard names. There were times when I wished I had not decided to try to trace Burton's exact route. But then I would not have made the journey I wanted to make. Burton was a careful and complete diarist. He was exact about where he had gone and why. We found that, west of Dodoma, we could match our route to Burton's much more precisely.

Along the road from Mikumi to Kilosa we saw *Sterculia* trees. Tall and straight, with pale yellow bark, it is a dramatic deciduous tree with a dense rounded crown. We noticed it all over the countryside. As well, enormously tall, deciduous kapok trees lined the road. They had light-coloured bark and pods hanging from their branches, dark brown outside, like cocoa pods, that split open to reveal the fluffy white substance inside.

The road was bad, not paved, but we kept on, heading directly north. One town we passed through was called Ulaya, meaning "Europe," so called because the first person to camp in this place was a European. We also crossed a road leading to the town of Rumuma, another Burton place name. This region is home to the Sagara tribe.

At Kilosa — quite a big town — there was a definite Arab influence. In this area, Burton reports seeing a ruined village — possibly Kilosa — from which Arab slavers had kidnapped most of the inhabitants and laid waste to their homes. The experience deeply disturbed Burton: "A pitiable scene here presented itself. The huts were torn and half-burnt, and the ground was strewed with nets and drums, pestels, mortars, cots and fragments of rude furniture.... Two of the wretched villagers were seen lurking in the jungle, not daring to revisit the wreck of their homes."

When we realized that there was no road from Kilosa through the Rubeho Mountains to Dodoma, we backtracked to Miyombo to pick up the Miyombo-Dodoma road. I was now convinced that Burton and Speke had to have taken this route. A twisting, red-earth track took us westward into the Rubeho foothills, through occasional banana plantations in the valleys, sisal, tall elephant grass, and dry scrub. It was a hot trip on a rough road, undulating and full of potholes. Occasional villages with thatch-roofed mud houses broke the monotony of the journey.

At noon, after a quick lunch of rice pancakes, and local "cheddar" cheese, tomatoes, and samosa (a triangular patty with a meat or vegetable filling), we continued through torturous, rock-strewn terrain. I was deeply thankful we had four-wheel drive. The going was very slow. We made sure we were always within sight of a river tributary — something all the early explorers seemed to do. As the afternoon wore on, we made our way over the foothills and down to Rumuma, grateful to guzzle some *pomoni*, locally brewed from cornflour. After some questioning we learned that the river running

Carpentering amongst the East Africans is still in its rudest stage....
RICHARD F. BURTON
The Lake Regions of Central Africa

through Rumuma is a tributary of the Mkondoa.

We moved on, through an avenue of cassia trees (whose bark is harvested for a rough kind of cinnamon), next to a Catholic mission, then headed north. Here on the leeward side of the foothills and mountains the climate is dry and perfect for the baobab trees we saw everywhere. By 5:00 p.m., still some distance from the Dodoma road, we decided to give up for the day and camp on a bluff overlooking the plains.

We set up camp under a baobab tree, first unloading the Land Rovers, unpacking the cooking utensils, making the fire, and constructing a lean-to under which we put the provisions and a rudimentary table in case of rain. So we had the three tents around a sort of bivouac in the middle.

Baobab tree and beehive.

We tried to lay the supper out with a little bit of style. We got our plates from Ali, and squatted down on a stone or a log to eat. Ali always worked his magic. We only got sick once, when he bought some ghastly-looking meat from the side of the road. That experience reminded me of a complaint Burton had about the kind of food he bought at the side of the road: "the milk falls like water off the finger, the honey is in the red stage of fermentation, of the eggs there are few without the rude beginnings of a chicken, and the ghee [clarified butter], from long keeping, is sweet above and bitter below."

By the time we sat down to supper each night, we were usually ravenous. The evening meal was the substantial one. We would have a small breakfast, a small lunch, and keep our energy up between meals by snacking on *ugali*, a mash made out of millet — like a solid piece of soft dough or porridge. It is very filling, eaten instead of bread. You can have it hot or cold, and I invented lots of things with it. I ate *ugali* for breakfast with scrambled eggs, with tinned sardines or salmon for lunch, with chicken stew or wildebeest curry for dinner. Sometimes I would slice off a piece of cold *ugali* and put it on a plate and pour some golden syrup on it — and that was *ugali* for pudding as well. We always had *ugali*. No one ever went hungry, because, if worse came to worst, you could have some *ugali* and gravy, or *ugali* and meat, or *ugali* and fish, or *ugali* and jam. Burton's remark applied as strongly to us as to the peoples he met: "Their food is mostly *ugali*, the thick porridge of boiled millet or maize flour, which represents the 'staff of life' in East Africa."

At this campsite, a cool wind blew all night. Nothing else disturbed the silence except the occasional call of a nightjar. The next morning we woke to see the full moon setting as the sun rose. The dawn was windy and cool; it had been a pleasant sleep and we were ready to get on with the crossing of the Rubeho Mountains. In this area, Burton's experiences were quite like ours, as he had camped in the Rubeho foothills near where we camped. Unlike us, however, he seemed compelled to make an impression on the natives in the area: "We left Márengá Mk'hali at 1 p.m. on the 3rd of September, and in order to impressionize a large and well-armed band of the country people that had gathered to stare at, to criticize, and to deride us, we indulged in a little harmless sword-play, with a vast show of ferocity and readiness for fight."

⋆ ⋆ ⋆

We left camp at 8:45 a.m. By then the sun was well up. We heard on the radio that there was fighting in Zaïre near the border of Rwanda and Burundi, near Lake Kivu and the large town of Bukavu a little north of where we were heading. We drew in Burton's route on the modern Tanzanian map, and decided not to follow it exactly, but to go north to Dodoma (the land of Ugogo) and then west.

As we moved into the Rubeho foothills we noticed more baobabs. When he encountered it, Burton described the baobab, or calabash-tree, of the interior: "The mbuyu — the baobab, Adansonia digitata, monkey-bread, or calabash,... is of more markedly bulbous form than on the coast, where the trunk is columnar; its heavy extremities, depressed by the wind, give it the shape of a lumpy umbrella shading the other wild growths."

When summarizing village life in East Africa he mentioned the scarcity and poor quality of the pottery he had seen before describing what was used instead:

> *In a country where pottery is scarce and dear, the buyu or Cucurbita lagenaria [which is the same plant as the European bottle gourd or calabash gourd] supplies every utensil except those used for cooking; its many and various adaptations render it a valuable production. The people train it to grow in the most fantastic shapes, and ornament it by tatooing with dark paint, and by patterns worked in brass tacks and wires; where it splits it is artistically sewn together. The larger kinds serve as well-buckets, water-pots, travelling-canteens, churns, and the sounding boards of musical instruments: a hookah, or water-pipe, is made by distorting the neck, and the smaller varieties are converted into snuff-boxes, medicine-cases, and unguent-pots. The fruit of the calabash-tree is also called buyu: split and dried, it is used as ladles, but it is too small to answer all the purposes of the gourd.*
>
> RICHARD F. BURTON
> ***The Lake Regions of Central Africa***

Gourds are still used by all tribes to hold water, milk, honey, and other liquids.

We met members of the Wagogo tribe (proof that we had reached Ugogo), and saw the typical settlements of flat-topped, thatched houses. We bumped our way a long distance down into the valley, then followed a meagre track through the mountains.

Schoolchildren near Mpwapwa.

Along the way, we noticed a plant with a milkweed-like pod that is valued by the Hadza tribe. The plant contains an intensely poisonous, sticky substance which the Hadza use to coat the points of their arrows and spears. It easily kills pigs, deer, wild boar, antelopes — and human beings. Thad recognized the plant and stopped to gather some. I was careful not to touch any part of it.

Burton referred to all his camps when crossing the Rubeho Mountains as "Rubeho." He spent five nights in the hills before he dropped into the plains, which he called "Ugogi." As he prepared to attack the pass, Burton could hardly bear to face the difficulties of the ascent. The sicknesses of many different types that assailed them throughout the trip had already begun to take their toll: "The great labor still remained. Trembling with ague, with swimming heads, ears deafened by weakness, and limbs that would hardly support us, we contemplated with a dogged despair the apparently perpendicular path ... up which we and our starving drooping asses were about to toil."

The air of the pass seemed to help Burton recover a little, although Speke's condition worsened and he needed to be carried as they proceeded: "By resting after every few yards, and by clinging to our supporters, we

reached, after about six hours, the summit of the Pass Terrible, and there we sat down among the aromatic flowers and bright shrubs — the gift of mountain dews to recover strength and breath.... At length a hammock was rigged up for my companion."

* * *

I stopped to take pictures of children and their schoolhouse. Surprisingly, a crowd gathered, including the village chief and the head of the school, whose permission I asked. However, just as I was about to take the photo, two politicians and two police officers who were passing in a jeep stopped and objected. Although I was the one taking the photograph, they began to threaten Pollangyo, who was with me. "You are selling our people for money," they told him, and accused him of holding up the poor of Africa to the ridicule of the rich by helping me to get my photographs. Pollangyo remained calm, however, and although one of my rolls of film was confiscated, we managed to get away. I gathered that we were lucky not to have been put in detention overnight.

Our next village was Mpwapwa, about two hundred kilometres from Mikumi on the red-earth road that stretched to the base of the distant hills.

Buying goat meat by the roadside.

There were village boutiques on either side of the road, selling vegetables, tomatoes, sugar cane, and yams. As we crossed the plains we saw women carrying brightly coloured plastic containers of water and bags of peanuts. The peanut, or "ground nut" as it is usually called in Africa, has a curious history. One of the chapters of that history is the story of the infamous British "Ground Nut Scheme" of the 1940s. This was a £25-million plan to cultivate 1.2 million hectares of peanuts in the Mpwapwa region and export them via a new port connected by a railway to the peanut fields — the port and railway to cost an additional £5 million. However, the scheme collapsed because the planners failed to take into account the realities of the soil and climate of the Mpwapwa region, and the difficulties of introducing mechanized cultivation. Perhaps they would have been more successful if they had read Burton. He begins his description of Ukaranga, the country between the Malagarasi Ferry and Lake Tanganyika, by writing: "Ukaranga signified, etymologically, the 'Land of Groundnuts'."

Eventually, at Mbande, we hit the main road to Dodoma, still eighty kilometres away. The road was well paved, but we still managed to get red dust on everything. My khaki clothes were covered in filth, my shoes were caked with the stuff, and I got a lungful of it every time I breathed.

Burton and Speke's route took them a little to the south of Dodoma. Along the way we passed some huge outcroppings of rock that Burton described: "a large crevasse in lofty rocks of pink and gray granite, streaked with white quartz, and pudding'd with greenstone and black horneblend.... Farther down the bed huge boulders ... rose, perpendicularly as walls, to the height of ... one hundred and twenty feet [thirty-seven metres]...."

Dodoma began as a settlement of thatched huts of the Gogo, a tribe that Stanley called, "masters in foxy craft." The settlement grew with the arrival of the railway at the beginning of the twentieth century. The railway stations became the centres of the towns that lined the old caravan routes. That is where the markets and shops were established. Dodoma dwindled considerably during the First World War, when thirty thousand people died of starvation in a famine caused by the misappropriation of food supplies by the Germans and the British. In the 1970s the Tanzanian government declared that Dodoma was to replace Dar es Salaam as the capital in the 1980s, but this still has not happened. "Idodomya," meaning "the place where it sank" and referring to an elephant that got stuck in the mud of a Gogo washing hole, is a phrase that gave the town its name on German maps. The name, like the elephant, stuck.

Dodoma's main modern importance came with the reform plans of Julius Nyerere, the father of Tanzanian independence. He used Dodoma as a pilot program for his concept of communal village life, which had three phases. First, Nyerere attempted to create self-reliant agricultural socialist villages whose residents held their property in common and worked together for the good of the village. Though remaining traditionally African in some respects, the villages were in large part modelled on Chinese communist villages. The African village unit was called the *ujamaa* (Swahili for "family" or "brotherhood"). When this scheme resulted in the enrichment of some farmers at the expense of others, a second phase began under which the state assumed direct control and attempted to resettle most of the people living in rural areas into planned villages with modernized services. But this latter scheme proved to be too expensive and also failed. Finally, the African villagers were encouraged by economic incentives to amalgamate small farms into larger units whose success would be determined by the dedication and hard work of those who lived there. The whole rural population was regrouped into these larger units through a compulsory policy which came to be known as "villagization." This process resulted in the elimination of traditional tribal rule, with predictable resentment. Villagization was ruthlessly enforced, and in the long run might still prove to be beneficial.

Villagization may have been partly responsible for my difficulty in matching Burton's place names to those on modern maps. I was beginning to fully understand what Rennie Bere meant when he wrote in *The Way to the Mountains of the Moon*, "Throughout Africa, of course, place-names have the disconcerting habit of moving with an individual or an event." The impact of villagization on tribal practices and the effect of widespread political change would also have influenced place names.

West of Dodoma, we took yet another rough, sandy road, this time headed towards Manyoni, a railway town and the centre of a tobacco-growing region, about 140 kilometres away. Wagogo herdsmen struggled to make a living in this desolate land, sometimes, according to Burton, resorting to extortion from the caravans: "In Ugogo," he wrote, "the merest pretext — the loosing a hot word, touching a woman, offending a boy, or taking in vain the name of the sultan — infallibly leads to being mulcted in cloth."

We stopped to camp at 5:00 p.m., and were asleep that night by 8:30.

We were up at 5:45 a.m. the next day, to the by now familiar sound of doves cooing and hornbills drumming. It was light early on the plains, and we roused ourselves as soon as the world started moving around us. In this early part of our journey, my mind was always on Burton and his struggling train of reluctant porters with all their complaints and mutinies. We were now entering Burton's Third Region, which he described as the flat table-land from the Wasagara Mountains to Tura in Unyamwezi, rising gently to the west.

We broke camp at 8:00 a.m. and set off westward towards Manyoni and Tabora. We passed numerous villages, and along the way were reminded that the Swahili word for "white man" is *mzungu*, which comes from *mzungu kati*, meaning "wandering around in circles, going nowhere." I was beginning to understand why.

Manyoni, when we reached it, appeared to be little more than a dusty strip of small hotels: Manyoni Inn, Royal Hotel and Inn, Caribuni Hotel, Central Line Hotel, Video Inn, Dara Inn. These "hotels" were really small restaurants or tea houses. We looked in the market for a *hengo*, a unique, long-handled knife used by the Wagogo. No luck.

We chugged and bumped along the dirt road through dense, brown thorn thickets, first in a southerly direction, then west. The road followed a relatively straight path very near the railway line. After the central railway leaves Dodoma, it drops down past the Bahi Swamp, then climbs the escarpment of the rift valley. It continues along the caravan route and through what is known as the Itigi Thicket before the land opens out into Myika country. The track finally exits the tsetse-ridden woods and slides into Tabora station.

Itigi, forty-two kilometres from Manyoni, is where Thad Peterson's missionary parents had arrived by railway in 1952, *en route* to the Iambi area,

A tramway is one thing that is needed for Africa. All other benefits that can be conferred by contact with civilisation will follow in the wake of the tramway, which will be an iron bond, never to be again broken, between Africa and the more favoured continents.

HENRY MORTON STANLEY
Through the Dark Continent

Dar es Salaam to Dodoma railway.

Another peculiarity of the Wanyamwezi is the position of the Wahárá or unmarried girls. Until puberty they live in the father's house; after that period the spinsters of the village ... assemble together and build for themselves at a distance from their homes a hut where they can receive their friends without parental interference.

RICHARD F. BURTON
The Lake Regions of Central Africa

Overleaf: Women carrying reeds for thatching.

where Thad was later born. There are still Christian missionaries all over Tanzania as well as in Uganda and Kenya.

Outside Itigi we continued running alongside the railway. Again there was dense thorn thicket on either side of the road and occasional herdsmen, but the population was much sparser along this straight road fifteen metres from the railway track, which cut through very flat land.

Between the first gradient of the Rubeho Pass and Tabora, Burton and Speke passed through thirty-three stations. Although hardly any of the place names that Burton mentioned appeared on our maps, many were recognized by the local inhabitants. When I first read Burton's *The Lake Regions of Central Africa*, I was struck by the whimsical literal translations he provided for place names. I was again reminded of this when we reached Kazi Kazi, a small railway station whose name means "work-work." I was never really sure whether this name implied colonial criticism of the natives or native criticism of the colonials.

Fifty-five kilometres beyond Itigi, we turned off the dirt road to look for Lake Chaya, where I had calculated our route would again join Burton's. However, the lake was totally dry — just a dry, cracked mud pan. This was disappointing, as sight of a body of water in this semi-arid region would have been a welcome relief. We decided to console ourselves with lunch, but no sooner had we set up our picnic on the bonnets of the Land Rovers when a swarm of bees descended on us. No stings, but they crowded around the food, and particularly the water. I immediately covered myself with Muskol — which seemed to do the trick.

I was aware that Burton had stopped somewhere here at a place he called Jiwe, which can mean "lake." We must have been on the north-eastern edge of the lake. Burton probably approached it from the south.

After lunch, and less than twenty kilometres farther on, we reached Karagasi. At the sight of date palms, I knew this was the old caravan route, and I felt sure we were on the actual Burton-Speke route to Tabora. From time to time I would see topographical features that matched Burton's descriptions. And there were familiar place names once in a while, such as Tura. Burton specifically named Tura as the last station of his Third Region

The Wazaramo tribe is rich in albinos; three were seen by the Expedition in the course of a single day. They much resemble Europeans of the leucous complexion; the face is quite bald; the skin is rough, and easily wrinkles in long lines, marked by a deeper pink; the hair is short, sharp-curling, and coloured like a silk-worm's cocoon, and the lips are red. The eyes have grey pupils and rosy "whites:" they appear very sensitive to light, and are puckered up so as to distort the countenance. The features are unusually plain, and the stature appears to range below the average. The people who have no prejudice against them, call these leucæthiops Wazungu, "white men."

RICHARD F. BURTON
The Lake Regions of Central Africa

and the first station of his Fourth Region, which he called the region of hilly tableland.

Only a short distance from Tura, we came across a red truck stranded on the road. Four youths stood menacingly on the other side. Breakdown? Ambush? Thad ordered Pollangyo to get the gun out. Although it turned out to be a genuine breakdown — a flat tire — our caution was not unjustified. Anything can happen on these side roads, as Burton found out near here when he was prevented from proceeding until he gave a bullock and a little cloth to a local chief:

A little farther on, we met three Sukuma maidens who had come a long way to get water. "Aren't you afraid of being eaten by the lions?" we asked. "No," they answered; "the lions are looking for animals, not people!" An interesting answer.

Thirty-five kilometres from Tura, late in the afternoon, we pulled off the road into a clearing. It was a beautiful spot for a camp. We were probably about two hours from Tabora, and the thought of being so close to one of the most important stops of the 1857 expedition made me feel very much part of the Burton-Speke journey. We noticed that the trees of the clearing had been "ringed" — that is, long, circular strips of their bark had been removed to make the "cannons" for the cylindrical honey hives we had seen before.

As we set up camp, we were again attacked by bees and flies. However, they seemed far less interested in stinging us than in gathering whatever moisture they could find. They clung to any wet surface — dishcloths, towels, anything. Then, as if on command, after sundown they all disappeared, leaving us in peace. Strangely there were no mosquitoes then either.

Pollangyo cooked up some *ndizi-mshale*. This was a favourite dish of his — bananas prepared as a stew and served up with some meat that Ali had cooked with tomatoes. This particular type of banana is much denser than potatoes and very filling. The word *ndizi* means "bananas," and the word *mshale* means "arrow." The fruit is thinner, straighter, and longer than the ordinary banana that is used for roasting.

Somewhere south-west of here Burton saw the "Mgongo T'hembo," or "Elephant's Back," which he said was "a long narrow ridge of chocolate-colored syenite, outcropping from the low forest lands around it." I speculated that these must be about fifty kilometres away and would be a spine-back ridge of mountains. We looked everywhere for the ridge but did not find it. Again, we were disappointed.

After dinner, Thad and I took a gun, a stick, a strong torch, and a *panga* (a heavy knife) into the bush to look for animals. In the pitch dark, we walked around the large clearing at the edge of the *miombo*. We saw a spring hare, which has a distinctive long black tail, limping across the clearing. We saw a nightjar, too, but nothing else. However, it was exciting being out on a game walk again. One never knows what one is going to run into. On a similar night walk in South Maasailand, Thad said that he had once walked into a pride of sixteen lions. This would certainly make your heart beat faster.

The next morning a pale golden sunrise lit the east, glinting through the feathery acacias across the clearing in front of our camp. The morning chorus began: doves, the chatter of innumerable quelea birds, and the buzzing and humming of the bees and tsetse flies.

We broke camp at 8:30 a.m. and set off, always keeping our eye out for the names Burton listed along his route: Tura, Kwale, Rubuga, Ukona, Kigwa, Hanga, and then Kazeh. Rubuga and Kigwa are on the modern Tanzanian map. On the way, we heard radio reports of an ebola outbreak in Zaïre. This viral infection ruptures cell walls, beginning with those of the internal organs, and turns the victim's body into a sack of bloody pulp.

On and on we went, sometimes passing from red-soil regions into areas of rich, black earth — ideal for growing cotton. Burton specifically mentions the cultivation of cotton at Ukona: "cotton-plots, carefully hedged round against the cattle, afforded material for the loom, which now appeared in every village." Then we came upon a sandy track winding through *miombo* (woodlands). The railway was some distance north of us, but this was definitely the old caravan route the two explorers had taken to Kazeh. Every now and then we passed a borassus palm — the tallest fruit-bearing palm in the country — planted by the old Arab slave traders. They really are enormous trees, and are distinctive for the cluster of fan-like fronds at the top of a thin, straight bare trunk.

We got lost again, about sixty kilometres from our last camp, and asked a village elder where we were. He confirmed that this was the subdistrict of Kigwa somewhere near the Burton route. Eventually we got to the town of Kigwa proper, then proceeded to Kinamagi. We began to see more settlements and more cultivated land. The Nyamwezi tribe inhabits this area. According to Pollangyo, they are very musical people and love singing. Mango trees lined the route, their branches laden with green fruit. We crossed the railway again coming up from the south, and then, at long last, arrived at Tabora.

✳ ✳ ✳

It had taken us five and a half days to reach Tabora from Bagamoyo. It took Burton and Speke nearly five months. We had driven 1,400 kilometres, though the distance from Bagamoyo to Tabora is about 680 kilometres in a straight line.

Burton, Speke, and Grant always referred to this town as Kazeh, though everyone else called it Tabora. Kazeh was founded by the Arabs about 1825 as a caravan depot. It eventually became the hub of the slave routes that spread north to Speke's "Great Lake" (Victoria), to Karagwe on its western shore, west to Lake Tanganyika, and south to the populous shoreline of Lake Malawi. Because Kazeh lay on the main route to the coast, it is not surprising that all the early explorers, including Livingstone and Stanley, journeyed through it.

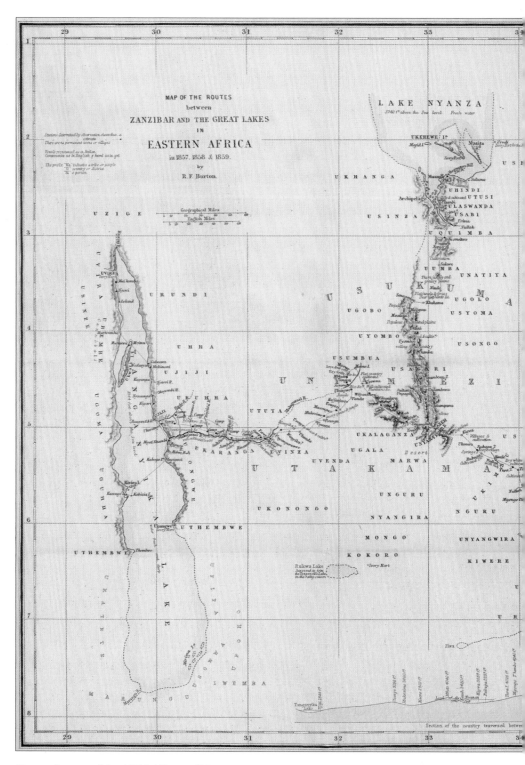

Burton's map of the 1856–59 expedition.

Preparing the next day's pomoni — traditionally women's work.

Burton described the expedition's flamboyant entry into the town. As usual the explorers took steps to impress the local population with their dignity and importance:

> *On the 7th of November, 1857 — the 134th day from the date of our leaving the coast — after marching at least 600 miles [960 kilometres], we prepared to enter Kazeh, the principal bandari of Eastern Unyamwezi, and the capital village of the Omani merchants. The Baloch were clothed in that one fine suit without which the Eastern man rarely travels: after a few displays the dress will be repacked, and finally disposed of for barter in slaves. About 8 a.m. ... when the line of porters, becoming compact, began to wriggle, snake-like, its long length over the plain, with floating flags, booming horns, muskets ringing like saluting-mortars, and an uproar of voice which nearly drowned the other noises, we made a truly splendid and majestic first appearance.*

> RICHARD F. BURTON
> ***The Lake Regions of Central Africa***

For the two explorers, Kazeh was a major milestone in their journey. They were ready for a rest. They stayed there for five weeks, dismissing much of

Locals consuming the honey-based wanzuki.

their caravan and hiring fresh porters before they resumed their trek towards Lake Tanganyika.

Both Burton and Speke were now quite ill, and both suffered from trachoma, an affliction that seriously impairs vision by causing lumps to form on the inside of the eyelids. Burton at this point seemed to be in worse shape than Speke, which may partly explain why he spent most of his time in Kazeh with the Arab traders (who were also slavers). Burton says these Arabs treated him with "open-handed hospitality and hearty good-will."

Speke, on the other hand, spent much of his time in Kazeh gathering information. He writes: "Captain Burton got desperately ill, whilst I picked up all the information that I could gather from the Arabs, with Bombay as interpreter." Implicit in this statement is a growing conflict between the active Speke and the more contemplative Burton. Burton and Speke had been sent to find one great lake, the one shown on Rebmann and Erhardt's map, which they had been shown in the Royal Geographical Society in London and a copy of which they had with them. The Arabs now told them that there were in fact three lakes: Nyassa (now called Lake Malawi) to the south, the Ujiji lake (Lake Tanganyika) to the west, and the "Sea of Ukéréwé" (Lake Victoria) to the north. With Bombay as his interpreter, Speke learned from Snay bin Amir and others that "the Kitangulé and Katonga rivers ran out of the Ukéréwé Lake (Victoria N'yanza), and that another river, which is the Nile, but supposed by them to be the upper portions of the Jub river, ran into the N'yanza." They also originally told Speke that no river flowed *out* of the "Sea of Ujiji," but they recanted when Speke insisted they must be wrong: "I made them confess that all these rivers ran exactly contrary to the way they first stated...." Speke wrote that, at this time, "... I felt so curious to find out, and so sure in my own mind that the Victoria N'yanza would prove to be the source of the Nile, I proposed going to see it at once, instead of going on to Ujiji. The route, however, to the northward was said to be dangerous ... and Captain Burton preferred going west."

So they went west, and Speke was not to have a chance to slake his curiosity until after they returned to Kazeh six months later. About the lake to the north, Burton would write, "... by his [Snay bin Amir's] distances and directions we were enabled to lay down the southern limits and the general shape of the Nyanza or Northern Lake as correctly — and the maps forwarded from Kazeh to the Royal Geographical Society will establish in fact — as were subsequently determined, after actual exploration, by my companion." Burton is being defensive here for on these maps he had, in fact, "adjusted" the distances, dimensions, and shape recorded by Speke. He wanted Lake Tanganyika to be the source of the Nile, but in the event was not able to either prove or disprove it. He accepted the fact of the three large lakes, but did not, like Speke, continue to quiz people for details about them. Information was there for the asking, and Speke was hungry for details and directions. On the trip to Lake Tanganyika, he came to think that what we now know is the eastern escarpment of the western rift valley was the eastern end of a great arc of mountains, the Mountains of the Moon of Ptolemy. Even so, or perhaps even more so, by the time they returned to Kazeh, Speke had become preoccupied with the idea that Lake Victoria might be the source of the Nile. Burton was equally convinced it was not.

⋆ ⋆ ⋆

We did not stay long at Tabora. For me, the main significance of our arrival there was that Ujiji on the shore of Lake Tanganyika now really felt within our reach. I was anxious to get going.

The arms are slender assegais with the shoulders of the blade rounded off.... Some have large spears for thrusting, and men rarely leave the hut without their bows and arrows, the latter unpoisoned, but curiously and cruelly barbed. They make also the long double-edged knives called sime, and different complications of rungu or knob-kerries, some of them armed with an iron lance-head upon the wooden bulge. Dwarf battle-axes are also seen, but not so frequently as amongst the western races on the Tanganyika Lake. The shield in Unyamwezi resembles that of Usagara; it is however rarely used.

RICHARD F. BURTON
The Lake Regions of Central Africa

Crossing the Malagarasi River.

We had a rushed lunch at the Tabora Hotel: Nile perch, chicken, and *ugali* — enough to satisfy our hunger. We left the hotel at 2:00 p.m. and headed for the market, near the railway station, to replenish supplies for the long journey to Ujiji.

About six kilometres after setting out, in nearby Kwihara, we visited a replica of the *tembe* (rectangular house) where Livingstone and Stanley stayed after their famous Ujiji meeting. It is a classic rectangular-shaped building with faded brick walls and floor of packed earth. The ailing Livingstone stayed here for five months, reading the Bible, catching up on his journal, and waiting for the supplies and porters that Stanley had promised to send him from Zanzibar. These eventually arrived in August 1872, and Livingstone left on his final journey.

Our next destination was Malagarasi and the river of the same name. Malagarasi was the final station in the Fourth Region of Burton's trek. Once he crossed the river, he was within ten stations of Ujiji and Lake Tanganyika. From Kwihara we took a narrow, rough road (just a footpath, really) through planted fields and poor settlements, then managed to pick up the main road again about six kilometres beyond Tabora. In Tumbi, a small village, we asked where we could buy some *wanzuki* — the local honey brew. We were too late, however, as it had all been sold. We did see one old lady preparing the next day's batch of *pomoni*, and she was happy to show us how she dried corn mash on mats.

We passed through the town of Ndono and, twenty kilometres beyond it, encountered another truck breakdown. We gave one of the passengers a ride to Urambo to get a spare wheel, and in return he promised to take us to buy some *wanzuki*. We filled up with more petrol (just in case), then went in search of our tipple.

Pandemonium! Crowds of women and men, well spliced on *wanzuki*, which was being served by the gallon. Everybody seemed to be having a lot of fun. We bought almost a gallon — several Pepsi-Cola bottles full were emptied into our gallon container — then headed westward on the main road to Malagarasi.

A little over 130 kilometres from Tabora we broke off from the main thoroughfare and pitched camp about a kilometre from the road. The flower of the terminalia tree has a very distinctive, rancid smell, which is supposed to attract flies. The odour is almost like that of bad butter or bad cheese. It was all around us. I decided just to get used to it. What else could I do?

While Ali cooked our dinner we drank the *wanzuki*. No wonder the local people were having such a good time. Thad and I poured ourselves two full beakers of the tan-coloured local drink — made with honey, yeast, and roots. It was an effervescent and very pleasant drink — thirst-quenching, if a bit too gaseous. It was slightly sweet — halfway between a beer and a wine. A bit like mead, perhaps. It had a definite kick, and I was quite light-headed after the third beaker.

We took showers, using our ingenious shower contraption. At 2:00 a.m. there was another kind of shower — rain. It lasted a short time, but long enough to wake us all. Pollangyo had a bad stomach, which he blamed on the meat that Ali had cooked.

✳ ✳ ✳

At sunrise (just before 7:00 a.m.), I realized that it was twelve days since I had arrived in Africa. We had travelled more than 2,100 kilometres since leaving Arusha, and had spent two nights in Bagamoyo and two nights in Zanzibar before starting our cross-country journey west to Lake Tanganyika.

Leaving camp at 8:30 a.m., we passed Usinde (Burton might have been a little north of here.), Ushokola, and Kaliua, a railway town. We did not seem to be running into any of the place names Burton mentioned, and I wondered whether we were still on the old caravan route.

Kaliua was a fair-sized town, and quite an old settlement. It seemed strange that it was not mentioned by Burton. We stopped and asked an elder in the village about some of Burton's names and he recognized some of them. Wilyankuru (in Burton's Region Four) was north of Urambo, where we had bought the *wanzuki*. The elder also knew of Usinge, possibly Burton's "Masenge."

The next town was Kasisi. The fields around it were more heavily cultivated than in other areas, and the land was cleared for almost a kilometre on either side of the road. Two-storey tobacco-drying kilns called *bani* dotted the landscape. The villagers here recognized more names from the Burton itinerary: Sengatti (Burton's "Songati") and Sorora. An elder also recognized Usagozi

End of the work day on the salt flats.

and Uganza. All these names were on Burton's list of stations in the Fourth Region, so we took this as confirmation that we were where we thought we were, even though the elder told us that Usagozi was north of our route.

Soon we left this settled area and re-entered *miombo*. It was beautiful country, but a very bad road. At one point, we ran over a black-necked spitting cobra. At Uganza, all signs of former settlements had disappeared. We picked up a woodcutter of the Mha tribe, and he recognized more names from the Burton itinerary: Mukozimo, Usenye, Rukunda, Wanyika, Unyanguruwwe, Ugaga.

Eventually, we returned to the direct route to the Malagarasi River, the final station of Burton's Fourth Region. We were now entering what is currently called the Kigoma Region, near Ujiji and the eastern shore of Lake Tanganyika. We broke off the road and into the flood plain of the Moyowasa — a tributary of the Malagarasi. Here, the lands were broad and flat and seemed to stretch endlessly to the horizon. In the distance we saw spur-winged geese and egrets sheltering under borrasus palms. We were actually on a peninsula with the Ugala River, another tributary of the Malagarasi, to the south of us. It was cooler on the flood plain.

The whole area used to be much more populated, but this all changed when Nyerere started his "villagization," moving people closer together to ensure better provision of water, schools, and health services. Now there are mango trees — a sure sign of settlement — but no more people. We had lunch and left the spot half an hour later.

Just after 3:00 p.m., we reached the Malagarasi River. We followed it for a while, driving off the road and across a wide plain, then down to the railway station, and, at 4:00 p.m., actually crossed the river. This was no easy task, and I wondered if it had ever before been crossed in jeeps or Land Rovers. We were lucky. The river was quite low and we were also fortunate to be shown the cattle ford, where the water was shallowest.

I had been secretly hoping to travel down the Malagarasi to Ujiji by raft or boat, but realized almost immediately that the river was much too low. We were told that there were fishermen with dugout canoes in the area, but they would go only short distances. There were crocodiles and hippos clearly visible in the river. It is well known that there are more deaths caused by hippos than by any other animal in Africa. Despite their placid appearance, they are extremely aggressive and attack boats and charge people on river banks. In the end we decided we would camp for the night and drive to Ujiji next day. In retrospect this was far more sensible than going by boat. What would we have done with our Land Rovers?

After crossing the Malagarasi we worked our way south a short distance along the river before making an early camp on a spot below a rocky hill over-looking the river. Three hippos snorted menacingly in the river below us.

✳ ✳ ✳

There was a thunderstorm at 4:00 a.m. Not just a little rain, but a heavy, noisy downpour. It did not last long, however, and I slept again until six o'clock. A tropical bou bou woke me, making its insistent, melodic call to its mate across the plain. These birds are famous for the beauty of their thrilling song and are mentioned in Persian poetry — something Burton no doubt knew about.

Early in February 1858, Burton and Speke reached the last station before Ugaga on the river: "[W]e resumed our march on the 2nd of February. The road, following an incline toward the valley of the [Malagarasi] river, in which bush and field alternated with shallow pools, black mud, and putrid grass, led to Unyanguruwwe, a miserable settlement, producing, however, millet in abundance, sweet potatoes, and the finest manioc."

Before fording the Malagarasi, Burton and Speke camped for the night. Then they made arrangements to secure a ferry.

> *The Sultan Mzogera had sold his permission to cross the river. The mutware, or mutwale, the lord of the ferry, now required payment for his canoes....*
>
> *The Lord of the Ferry delayed us at Ugaga, by removing the canoes, till he had extracted fourteen cloths and one coil bracelet.... On the 4th of February we crossed to Mpete.... [W]e came upon the "Ghaut," a muddy run or clearing in the thicket of stiff grass which crossed the stream. There we found a scene of confusion. The Arabs of Kazeh had described the canoes as fine barges, capable of accommodating fifty or sixty passengers. I was not, however, surprised to find wretched "baumrinden" — tree-rind-canoes, two strips of "myombo" bark,*

from five to seven feet [1.5 to 2 metres] in length, sown together like a doubled wedge with fibres of the same material.... When high and dry upon the bank, they look not unlike castaway shoes of an unusual size. We entered "gingerly."... The ferryman, standing amidships or in the fore, poled or paddled according to the depth of the stream.

RICHARD F. BURTON
The Lake Regions of Central Africa

On leaving his Fourth Region, Burton noted: "The fauna of Unyamwezi are similar to those described in Usagara and Ugogo. In the jungles quadrumana are numerous: lions and leopards, cynhyænas and wildcats, haunt the forests; the elephant and the rhinoceros, the giraffe and the Cape buffalo, the zebra, the quaqqa, and the koodoo wander over the plains; and the hippopotamus and crocodile are found in every large pool."

Then, in a more lyrical vein, he added: "The Land of the Moon, which is the garden of Central Inter tropical Africa presents an aspect of peaceful rural beauty which soothes the eye like a medicine after the red glare of barren Ugogo.... There are few scenes more soft and soothing than a view of Unyamwezi in the balmy evenings of spring."

By crossing the Malagarasi River, Burton and Speke entered the Fifth Region of their journey. The tone of Burton's remarks grew harsher. They were now deep in the interior, in mosquito-infested territory described by Burton as "a howling wilderness, once populous and fertile, but now laid waste by the fierce Watuta."

Our own experience of the area was much more pleasant. After a breakfast of maize porridge, eggs, papaya, and pineapple, Thad, Pollangyo, and I set out to explore along the Malagarasi. We came across some old bark canoes similar to those used for Burton's crossing. We also found a small fishing camp. The fishing looked promising, but we did not have time to linger. Great swirls in the water signified the existence of large fish — or crocodiles. There were a whole variety of birds: fish eagle, black-chested snake eagle, egret, red-necked spur fowl, wattled plover, nub-billed duck. The banks were thickly overgrown right down to the water's edge, making travelling by Land Rover extremely difficult. We managed five or six kilometres, but were absolutely massacred by tsetse flies. No amount of Muskol would keep them away. At about 9:30 a.m. we returned to camp, where Joshua and Ali had finished packing the second Land Rover.

As we headed back along the Malagarasi River, looking for a road to Ujiji, we passed isolated villages of small, thatched mud huts. A Sukuma villager in one settlement advised us that Ugaga, which Burton had mentioned, was ahead of us.

In the outlying areas, the roads are certainly not made for automobiles, and few cars are seen. Some people were curious and came to inspect the Land Rovers, but for the most part people kept to themselves and got on with their own business. In the East it would have been very different. There, if you stopped your car or jeep, twenty or thirty people would immediately crowd around you — looking, touching, questioning. The villagers in Africa, by contrast, tend to concentrate on their own affairs. Whenever we wanted information, we had to search for someone to ask.

About an hour after crossing the river, we had to stop to fix a flat tire. It was a very rudimentary road wandering westward through woodland. There should have been game, but we did not see any, though we did notice roan or sable antelope droppings on the road. We went on through Ilunde, a village now almost completely deserted, and crossed railway tracks again, going on to Charkuru and the valley settlement of Uvinza, a much larger town than most we had passed. This is where the salt works are that Burton describes:

> [T]he place in question is a settlement of Wavinza, containing from forty to fifty bee-hive huts, tenanted by salt-diggers. The principal pan is sunk in the vicinity of the river, the saline produce, after being boiled down in the huts, is piled up, and handmade into little cones. The pan affords tripartite revenue to three sultans, and it constitutes the principal wealth of the Wavinza: the salt here sold ... finds its way throughout the heart of Africa, supplying the lands adjoining both the Tanganyika and the Nyanza lakes.
>
> RICHARD F. BURTON
> *The Lake Regions of Central Africa*

We crossed the Rusugi River in order to visit the salt flats. The operation seemed quite organized, as it must also have been in Burton's time. The flats are a huge area where the salt can be seen drying. We were there towards the end of the day and watched lines of women carrying the salt in baskets on their heads, the day's production, to a central building for further processing.

There were rock outcroppings all over the place — good leopard country. Burton mentions this, but only in discussing the children dressed in leopard skins. Nowadays, if any villager is caught with a leopard skin there is a very severe penalty involving a long jail term.

We took a sharp turn to the west on a relatively new road, but because it did not appear on the modern Tanzanian map we could not be sure where it went. However, the villagers assured us that this was indeed the road that led to Kigoma and Ujiji. After lunch, which we had under a tamarind tree, the road began to descend sharply. I knew we must be going down to the big lake, and my excitement grew.

Then our route took us alongside the railway line to Kigoma. At one point, where the land was very hilly, there was no road at all, and we consid-

Fugitives were continually coming in throughout the night.

HENRY M. STANLEY
How I Found Livingstone

Overleaf: Boatloads of refugees forced to wait offshore at Kigoma.

ered shoving the two Land Rovers onto the railway tracks and driving to Kigoma that way. However, it was quite precipitous on either side and it would not give us much chance to get off the line out of the way of an oncoming train. So, instead, we just gunned the Land Rovers through the rough terrain. At Kalenga, two young boys tried to sell us a dead banded mongoose. I cannot imagine what they thought we would do with it. And then, at last, at 3:18 p.m., we reached Kidawe and caught our first sight of Lake Tanganyika.

It was overcast, and therefore I did not see the light shimmering on the waters of the big lake, as Burton had, but the experience was thrilling nonetheless.

Burton's description of his first sighting, on February 13, 1858, is almost ecstatic.

> *Nothing, in sooth, could be more picturesque than this first view of the Tanganyika Lake, as it lay in the lap of the mountains, basking in the gorgeous tropical sunshine.... Villages, cultivated lands, the frequent canoes of the fishermen on the waters, and on a nearer approach the murmurs of the waves breaking upon the shore, give a something of variety, of movement, of life to the landscape.... Truly it was a revel for soul and sight. Forgetting toils, dangers, and the doubtfulness of return, I felt willing to endure double what I had endured; and all the party seemed to join with me in joy. My purblind companion found nothing to grumble at except the "mist and glare before his eyes."*
>
> RICHARD F. BURTON
> ***The Lake Regions of Central Africa***

Burton's description of Speke's attitude here is also important. It is clear that the two men now had serious differences of opinion that would lead to later conflict. I could not help wondering whether Speke had already lost interest in Lake Tanganyika, knowing, from talking to people along the route, that it could not be the source of the Nile, as Burton still believed. Perhaps he was already on the alert for an opportunity to get away from Burton long enough to get up to Nyanza, the northern lake. His opportunity would come, but not before a gruelling assignment on Lake Tanganyika.

Descending from the hills, we drove into and right through the busy town of Kigoma, then six kilometres southeast to Ujiji. Ujiji is one of Africa's oldest market villages. It is a colourful, bustling, commercial centre. The majority of the population is from the Ha tribe, although Arab influence is seen in the architecture. Structures bear a strong resemblance to coastal homes, and this is especially evident in the carved wooden doors.

At Ujiji, Burton reflected on the economics of the slave trade, remarking that the town was "still the great slave-mart of these regions, the article being collected from all the adjoining tribes of Urundi, Uhha, Uvira, and Marungu.... [T]he trade realizes nearly 500 per cent, and will, therefore, with difficulty be put down."

Burton and Speke, the first Europeans to see Lake Tanganyika, arrived at Ujiji in February 1858, and immediately started exploring the waters of the lake. Twenty-three years later, in 1871, Livingstone also made his way to Ujiji, at that time the terminus for most caravans from the coast. It was here that the historic meeting between Stanley and Livingstone took place. Both the name of Livingstone Street and a 1927 plaque donated by the Royal Geographical Society commemorate the event. In Ujiji we headed straight to the Livingstone Memorial. It stands on the spot where Stanley met the famous explorer, but the beach and the lakefront have receded considerably. After a look at the memorial, I went down to the beach: boys were swimming, girls bathing and washing, women tending their children, men selling wares, boats being built.

The Livingstone memorial in Ujiji.

Just before 6:00 p.m., we went back to Kigoma and checked into the Railway Hotel. This old relic looks over the lake and some landscaped gardens. The rooms were hot and austere: a fan, a rudimentary electrical system, bars on the window above my bed, a piece of dirty cloth pulled over the window, which I drew back to let in the breeze off Lake Tanganyika. I could hear waves lapping outside the window. In fact, I was so entranced by the sound that I stood on the bed to see the lake and feel the wind. My main interest, however, was the mosquito netting. I decided it did not seem too bad.

As it turned out, I spent a sleepless night. A few "ladies of the night" plied their trade in a remarkably noisy fashion on the promenade between my room and the lakefront. They did not seem to stop their bargaining until well after midnight. Besides, I had been too optimistic about the quality of the mosquito netting. It was full of holes and offered little protection. And then there was the wind. Its velocity increased at about 3:00 a.m., creating pounding waves very much like ocean surf. Although by 6:00 a.m. the wind had subsided and it was much quieter, everything was very different from the *miombo* where we had been camping. I preferred the bush.

* * *

We spent a necessary day in Kigoma, servicing the cars, doing laundry, getting supplies — and hearing stories about the refugees in south-western Tanzania who were pouring in from Rwanda and Burundi. Even in Kigoma there were refugees, a growing crowd of people who had made their way across Lake Tanganyika from Zaïre, seeking escape from the political turmoil in that country.

Dog day in Kigoma.

Saturday is dog day in Kigoma. People bring their dogs to a pound where the animals are dipped in a strong disinfectant solution to get rid of the fleas and lice. It was a totally mad scene, humans making much more noise than the dogs.

When we drove down to the Kigoma harbour to negotiate for a boat to explore the eastern coastline north of Ujiji and Kigoma, we encountered a crisis in the making. Many boatloads of refugees had arrived the night before from strife-torn Zaïre. It was a pitiful scene. The refugees had been ordered to stay on their boats and not to land; hundreds and hundreds — maybe even thousands — of people in longboats kept offshore by armed guards with machine-guns. The guards were there to prevent the refugees from setting foot in Tanzania until they had official refugee status.

There were dozens of villagers on the beach, talking, bartering, jostling, craning for a better view. I mingled with the crowds, hoping to take photographs, but was not very popular with either the villagers or the refugees. I did not blame them. Those who had come from Zaïre were fleeing the conflict between the ruling dictator, President Mobutu, and the rebel leader, Laurent Kabila. The refugee situation was greatly worsened by conflict between warring factions of Tutsis and Hutus, which had resulted in the further flight of hundreds of thousands of Hutus from neighbouring Rwanda.

The refugees are the result, not the cause, of the strife — the result of political upheaval and of genocide, stemming in turn from colonial interference in Africa, from the transition to undemocratic forms of independence, and from tyranny and greed.

Refugees are big business in Africa. The Western world is being held to ransom by the various countries to which refugees flee. Tanzania, for example, will not always admit the refugees unless Western countries pay the government for costs and administration. When payment is assured, a certain number are allowed in and given refugee status. It is not a simple humane act. It is a business deal. Only when the money is actually paid do the white United Nations vans come into play to transport refugees, to set up the camps, to provide medical services, and so on. The host countries make enormous financial demands on the Western countries. Some of this money trickles down to the refugees. Most of it, however, usually goes to the people organizing food and shelter for them. The refugees were being held offshore not simply because of lack of space. It was financial blackmail.

After a time, I moved off and wandered around the bustling Kigoma market. It had everything for sale, from watches to vegetables: rubber goods, chemicals, outboard motors, automotive parts, sticks, brightly coloured plastic, cloth. Most of the merchants seemed to be of Arab origin, and of course I thought again of Burton and the Arab traders.

Thad and I noticed one Parakuyu Maasai woman selling "potions" at the side of the road and thought of Burton. Curiosity demanded that for 4,000 shillings, we buy some *dawa ya kiume* (medicine for maleness). This was a whitish powder mixed with two shades of brown powder and made from the bark of the *ormerurai* tree. This is its name in Maa, the Maasai language. In Swahili it is called the *urale* tree. The potion was supposed to be an aphrodisiac. Instructions: 1$\frac{1}{2}$ heaped teaspoons in black tea. Add sugar if necessary. Take this mixture before eating, morning and evening, for four days. The good results were guaranteed to last for two months. We asked some questions about the tree and the different colours of powders. All the powder is taken from different parts of the same tree — some from the bark and some from the roots.

The Parakuyu Maasai woman then also gave us a long twig from the *Acacia nilotica* tree. In Maa it is called the *ol-kiloriti* tree. Instructions: Take half of the twig, and soak it in a cup of water for one hour. When the twig gets soft, chew on it. Do not swallow it. Get the juice out of the twig and spit out the pulp. After that, drink the rest of the juice. This must be taken together with the powder potion already prescribed. The *ol-kiloriti* twig is also used in meat-eating ceremonies by the Maasai. It is cooked with soup and helps a lot with the digestion of meat.

Back at the hotel before noon, we planned an early lunch before setting out on our expedition along the coastline. However, it looked gloomy, with heavy rain clouds over the lake. Burton called Ujiji the "place of storms," and a real one seemed to be brewing. We had been warned that severe storms with huge waves arise without notice on the lake and can make conditions very dangerous.

The east side of Lake Tanganyika around Kigoma is fairly flat, but as you journey a little farther north the shore slopes precipitously and the water is very deep. This is a narrow, rift-valley lake. The wind whipping across the water causes the dramatic waves. We waited until the danger of a storm had passed before beginning our exploration.

While we waited we found out more about the refugee situation. Bujumbura is in Burundi, at the north-east corner of Lake Tanganyika. The army there is controlled by the Tutsis, who are waging a bitter civil war with the majority Hutus. It was possible, therefore, that the refugees we had seen were Hutus from Burundi who had fled initially to Zaïre and now were seeking a new haven in Tanzania. On the other hand, they may have been refugees from Zaïre's own civil war, or a mixture of both. We never found out.

Zaïre is just across the lake from Kigoma and Ujiji. One can see the hills on a clear day. We had heard that the flames of civil war in Zaïre had been fanned by ethnic Tutsis in Rwanda (the country north of Burundi) as part of a plan to distract international attention from events in Burundi. This could not have been accurate, although it later became clear that Tutsi sympathies were very much with the Kabila forces and the anti-Mobutu movement. The refugees we saw later, south-west of Lake Victoria, were from both Rwanda and Burundi, and were mostly Hutus.

We waited patiently for well over an hour for the boat that was to take us up the east coast of Lake Tanganyika. Because of the refugee situation, the boat's departure from Kigoma harbour was delayed by bureaucratic wrangling. However, it eventually reached us, and we cruised northward, stopping at seven different fishing villages: Kalalangabo, Kagongo, Kigale, Kananie, Mtanga, Ngelwe, and finally Kazinga. Although Burton and Speke did stop at and visit fishing villages, the names in Burton's diary are different. There were boatloads of refugees waiting offshore at every village we saw. All were Hutus, and all had arrived from Zaïre. It really was a pitiful sight. The police were everywhere, searching the refugees for guns and ammunition. If not confiscated by police, weapons are traded for money or provisions, usually to rebel Tanzanians. Arms are also sought by refugees planning to return to Burundi to seek revenge against the Tutsis. Once searched, the refugee boats were allowed to go to Kigoma. There they were checked again, and their occupants were registered as refugees, but only after the required guarantees from the international community. Refugees cannot settle in Tanzania anywhere but in the refugee camps. It was heartbreaking to see tired, sad-eyed, dejected

"Polypharmacy" is not the fault of the profession in East Africa, and the universal belief in possession tends greatly to simplify the methodus modendi. The usual cathartic is the bark of a tree called kalákalá, which is boiled in porridge. There is a great variety of emetics, some so violent that several Arabs who have been bold enough to swallow them, barely escaped with life.

RICHARD F. BURTON
The Lake Regions of Central Africa

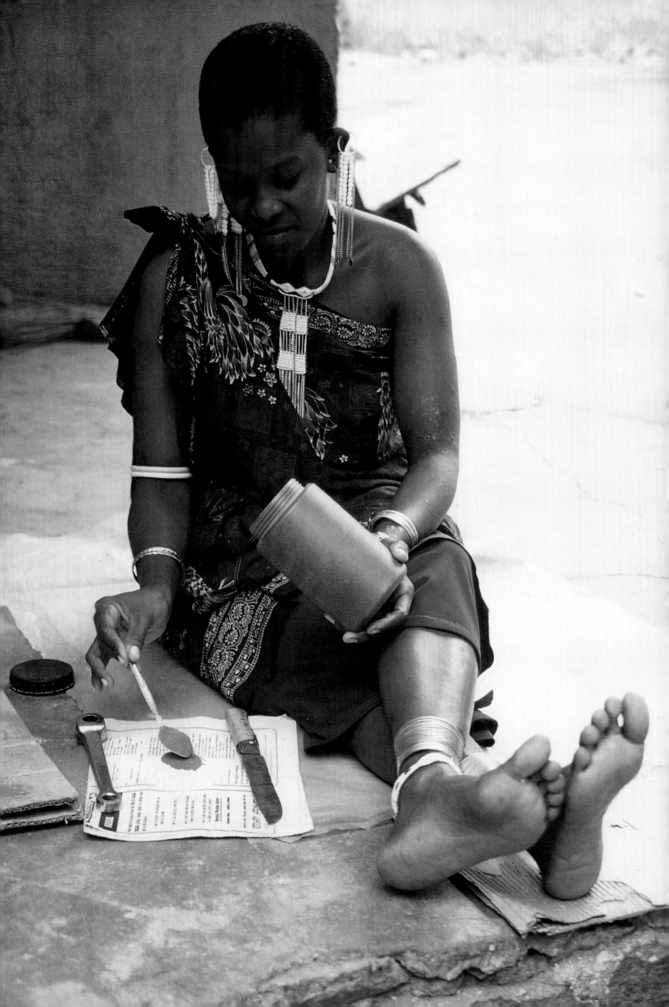

families with small children huddled amid their possessions: mattresses, bundles of clothes, bicycles. Everything — people and goods — piled into the slender open boats.

✳ ✳ ✳

Burton said of the people of this region, "The lakists are an almost amphibious race, excellent divers, strong swimmers and fishermen, and vigorous ichthyophagists [fish eaters] all." The boat, a twelve-metre open-shell cargo boat called a *mutumbu*, was driven by an outboard motor and had a brightly coloured green and yellow hull. Across the bow on the inside were painted the words *Mpaji ni mungu*, "God gives all." The boat was manned by boatmen of the Waha tribe. In the fishing village of Mtanga, the crew demanded that we buy some *kayoga*, the traditional drink of the Waha. This is a local brew made from bananas,

*Waha boat and inscription
"God gives all".*

and it was, we quickly realized, much stronger than the others we had tried along the way. The Waha boatmen soon lost their reserve. They welcomed the *kayoga* and instantly began having a good time, entering and leaving the harbours with increasing confidence and many taunts, jibes, and jokes.

Our trip up the coast took four hours and went as far as the Burundi border. Because of the refugees, there was a disturbing quality to our explorations. There was an uneasiness to Burton and Speke's experiences at Lake Tanganyika, too. It was there that their unlikely partnership began to founder, dashing forever any hope that they would identify the source of the Nile together.

The Wajiji are a burly race .... The women ... are held in high repute .... The head is sometimes shaved; rarely the hair is allowed to grow; the most fashionable coiffure is a mixture of the two; patches and beauty-spots in the most eccentric shapes .... Women as well as men are fond of binding a wisp of white tree-fibre round their heads, like the ribbon which confines the European old person's wig.
RICHARD F. BURTON
The Lake Regions of Central Africa

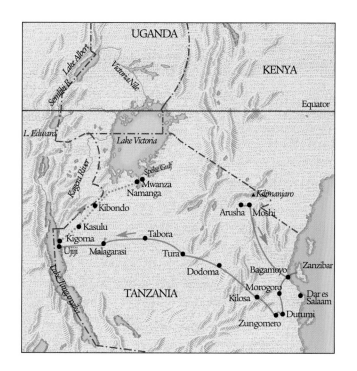

Nga Myanza:
Lake Tanganyika to Lake Victoria

Thus men do geography!

RICHARD F. BURTON
The Lake Regions of Central Africa

5

Nga Myanza:
Lake Tanganyika to Lake Victoria

Burton and Speke arrived in Ujiji on February 14, 1858. "The direct longitudinal distance from the coast is 540 geographical miles, which the sinuosities of the road prolong to 955." Today, Bagamoyo and Ujiji are about five metres farther apart than they were then because of the spreading of the eastern rift valley. "The total time," Burton says, "was seven and a half months." Though he found the scenery *en route* "exceedingly beautiful," at first sight Ujiji did not impress Burton: "About 11 a.m. the craft was poled through a hole in a thick welting of coarse reedy grass and flaggy aquatic plants to a level landing-place of flat shingle, where the water shoaled off rapidly. Such was the ghaut or disembarkation quay of the great Ujiji ... a few scattered huts, in the humblest bee-hive shape, represented the port-town."

Illness continued to plague Burton and Speke as they prepared to set out on the lake, but later Burton decided their time at Lake Tanganyika had improved their health. He imputed almost magical qualities to the lake water, reporting that it was pure and sweet, yet rumoured to be incapable of quenching thirst. The water was also believed to have an exceptional ability to corrode metal and leather. I personally did not test any of these theories, as Lake Tanganyika is one of the worst bodies of water for bilharzia.

Before coming to Africa, I had learned just how dreadful bilharzia can be. Bilharzia, or schistosomiasis, is caused by the bilharzia worm, a parasite that thrives in the blood of birds, snails, humans, and other mammals. It was named after the parasitologist Theodor Bilharz, a contemporary of Richard Burton.

At last my experience in [being stared at] enabled me to categorise the infliction .... [Is] the stare curious or intelligent,... generally accompanied with irreverent laughter regarding our appearance.

RICHARD F. BURTON
The Lake Regions of Central Africa

I could only see a sea horizon; and on inquiring how far back the land lay, was assured that ... there was an equal expanse of it east and west.... The quantity of mosquitoes on the borders of the lake is perfectly marvellous; the grass, bushes, and everything growing there, are literally covered with them.

JOHN HANNING SPEKE
What Led to the Discovery of the Source of the Nile

Previous page: Sunrise over Lake Victoria.

The larvae are harboured by snails, who serve as intermediate hosts. Humans are infected when they bathe in — or even come into contact with — water infested with the snails. These larvae enter through the skin; migrate through the blood vessels; and mature in the infected person's bowel, bladder, and the large veins that carry blood to the liver. They deposit eggs in these organs. Many of the eggs are passed out in the faeces; others lodge in the liver, bladder, genitals, lungs, and even the spinal cord. A person might notice a skin eruption at the point at which the larvae have entered his body. Fever, diarrhoea, bleeding, and even cirrhosis of the liver can follow. Perhaps the most debilitating symptom is an all-encompassing lethargy that saps the victim's energy — for the rest of his or her life. An estimated eighty million Africans are infected with bilharzia. Toxic drug compounds with severe side effects are used to treat the disease, but treatment is usually available only outside of Africa, and while it may halt the progress of the disease, it cannot reverse the damage.

Eager as I was to explore Burton and Speke's Lake Tanganyika, I wanted no part of the sicknesses they had suffered: "At first the cold damp climate of the Lake Regions did not agree with us.... All energy seemed to have abandoned us. I lay for a fortnight upon the earth, too blind to read or write except with long intervals, too weak to ride, and too ill to converse. My companion, who when arriving at the Tanganyika Lake was almost as 'groggy' upon his legs as I was, suffered from a painful ophthalmia, and from a curious distortion of face, which made him chew sideways, like a ruminant."

His ill health notwithstanding, Burton was eager to explore the lake: "But work remained undone; it was necessary to awake from this lethargy. [I was] determined to explore the northern extremities of the Tanganyika Lake, whence, according to several informants, issued a large river flowing northward...."

In order to carry out their explorations, Burton and Speke needed a suitably substantial boat, and Burton sent Said bin Salim, their caravan guide, in search of a large dhow he had heard about. According to Burton, he instructed Speke to put together a crew and outfit the dhow for what Burton called "a month's cruise." In Speke's version of events, however, he undertook this excursion because Burton was too ill to do so. Speke claimed that "Captain Burton threw obstacles in my way at first," and implied that it was his own decision to explore the lake while Burton lay in camp. This explanation was, of course, after the fact, and perhaps Speke intended to show himself as a man of action, unlike Burton, who was often a man of inaction.

Speke set out alone to reconnoitre the lake, but it was a miserable trip with a very disappointing result. Burton, meanwhile, remained in camp, "eating and drinking, smoking and dozing."

Speke's exploration of the upper part of Lake Tanganyika netted a lot of trouble and very little knowledge. Despite his face-saving claims to the contrary, Speke did not seem at all eager to explore this lake. I am certain the information he got from the Arabs had convinced him that the lake to the north, the "Nyanza," held the key to the great mystery of the Nile's source — not Lake Tanganyika. I think Speke was just following orders when he went on this mission without Burton and was anything but enthusiastic.

Speke was away for twenty-seven days, and it was one of the worst experiences of his trip.

> At night a violent storm of rain and wind beat on my tent with such
> fury that its nether parts were torn away from the pegs, and the tent
> itself was only kept upright by sheer force. On the wind's abating, a
> candle was lighted to rearrange the kit, and in a moment, as though by
> magic, the whole interior became covered with a host of small black
> beetles.... One of these horrid little insects awoke me in his struggles to
> penetrate my ear, but just too late: for, in my endeavour to extract him,
> I aided his immersion. He went his course, struggling up the narrow
> channel, until he got arrested by want of passage-room. This impedi-
> ment evidently enraged him, for he began with exceeding vigour, like a
> rabbit at a hole, to dig violently away at my tympanum.... Neither
> tobacco, oil, nor salt could be found: I therefore tried melted butter; that
> failing, I applied the point of a penknife to his back, which did more
> harm than good; for though a few thrusts quieted him, the point also
> wounded my ear so badly, that inflammation set in....
>
> JOHN HANNING SPEKE
> *Journal of the Discovery of the Source of the Nile*

Speke suffered from the effects of this experience for the next six or seven months, and it certainly affected his work on the lake. When he finally returned, Burton was furious that he had accomplished nothing and regarded him with contemptuous humour: "I never saw a man so thoroughly moist and mildewed."

Continuing in a contemptuous tone, Burton criticized the "orthography and syntax" of Speke's diary. The diary was published in *Blackwood's Magazine* in 1859, accompanied by a map which Burton felt revealed Speke's lack of integrity as a geographer.

> I must confess, however, my surprise at, among many other things,
> the vast horseshoe of lofty mountain placed by my companion in the
> map attached to that paper near the very heart of Sir R. Murchison's
> Depression. As this wholly hypothetical, or rather inventive feature —
> I had seen the mountains growing upon paper under my companion's
> hand from a thin ridge of hill fringing the Tanganyika to the
> portentous dimensions given in Blackwood's Magazine ... — wore a
> crescent form, my companion gravely published, with all the pomp of
> discovery, in the largest capitals, "This mountain range I consider to
> be THE TRUE MOUNTAINS OF THE MOON." Thus men do
> geography! and thus discovery is stultified.
>
> RICHARD F. BURTON
> *The Lake Regions of Central Africa*

These words of Burton's, published in 1860, imply that Speke altered his "on-site" drawings to support an unfounded hypothesis. But even by March 1858, when the "mildewed" Speke returned to camp, relations between the two men were strained.

Despite their growing disillusionment with each other, however, they had to carry on. The Arabs had seemed certain that a river flowed north out of Lake Tanganyika, and if they were correct, the problem of the Nile's source might be solved. Burton, therefore, as his 1860 account tells us, "began to seriously seek some means of exploring the northern head of the Tanganyika."

On April 10, 1858, Burton and Speke set out together on the lake to search for the northern river. They travelled in canoes. "The paddling," Burton said, "is accompanied by a long monotonous melancholy howl...."

They travelled past Bangwe Bay, camped at Kigari, and after six hours of rowing reached "another dirty little fishing-village called Nyasanga." On April 14, they came to "Wafanya, a settlement of Wajiji mixed with Warundi." They were approaching an area inhabited by cannibals: "the Tanganyika ... is divided into two stages by the Island of Ubwari.... Mariners dare not disembark on Ubwari except at the principal places; and upon the wooded hill-sides wild men are, or are supposed to be, ever lurking in wait for human prey."

By April 23, they were among the Wabembe. "They prefer men raw," Burton commented, "whereas the Wadoe of the coast eat him roasted." Thad Peterson reminded me that the Wadoe tribe that Burton mentions was probably the same as the Ndoe tribe that Professor Kajeri in Kaole belonged to.

On April 26, they were in Uvira and had reached "the northernmost station to which merchants have as yet been admitted." Two days later, Burton says, "all my hopes — which, however, I had hoped against hope — were rudely dashed to the ground." This was because Burton had received a visit from three native Africans, who told him that the Arabs were wrong.

> [T]heir well-made limbs and athletic frames ... were set off by ... a profusion of broad massive rings of snowy ivory round their arms, and conical ornaments like dwarf marling-spikes of hippopotamus-tooth suspended from their necks. The subject of the mysterious river issuing from the lake was at once brought forward. They ... unanimously asserted, and every man in the host of bystanders confirmed their words, that the "Rusizi" enters into, and does not flow out of the Tanganyika. I felt sick at heart.
>
> RICHARD F. BURTON
> *The Lake Regions of Central Africa*

[G]azelle eyes, oval face, high thin nose, and fine lips.

JOHN HANNING SPEKE
Journal of the Discovery of the Source of the Nile

164

Of course, Burton and Speke had to conclude that Lake Tanganyika could not possibly be the source of the Nile. This was far more difficult for Burton than for Speke. In fact, it sometimes seemed that Burton never gave up his original belief that the Nile began here. However, in *The Lake Regions of Central Africa*, published in 1860, he wrote: "A careful investigation and comparison of statements leads to the belief that the Tanganyika receives and absorbs the whole river-system — the net-work of streams, nullahs, and torrents — of that portion of the central African depression whose water-shed converges toward the great reservoir." His "careful investigation" did not reveal that the Lukuga River flows out of Lake Tanganyika near the mid-point of its western shore at present-day Kalemie, about 120 kilometres south of Ujiji. The Lukuga joins the Lualaba River, which is a major tributary of the Zaïre (Congo) River.

It was not until Livingstone and Stanley explored Lake Tanganyika thirteen years later that they were able to confirm positively that the Ruzizi River flowed into the lake at its northern end, not out of it. But for Burton, there was now nothing but the journey home: thirty-three days on the lake just to get back to Ujiji and then the long return trek to the coast. They had only enough supplies to get them to the coast, not enough to let them explore the south end or western shore of the lake. Burton and Speke, disaffected and disappointed by their findings on Lake Tanganyika, headed for Kazeh again.

In Kazeh, Burton was faced with important responsibilities. He had to re-furbish the caravan for the long portion that remained of the return journey to the coast. And he had to compile and organize the scientific observations he had made so far. Speke, on the other hand, was anxious to investigate the Arabs' claim that a "Nyanza" even larger than Tanganyika could be reached by heading north from Kazeh. Appearing to have rather more important matters to attend to, Burton willingly approved Speke's plan to look for this northern lake.

That Burton was comfortable in Kazeh, there can be no doubt. His Arab friends welcomed him with delicacies. "There," he says, "a large metal tray bending under succulent dishes of rice and curried fowl, giblets and manioc boiled in the cream of the ground-nut, and sugared omelets flavored with ghee and onion shreds, presented peculiar attractions to half-starved travelers." He also welcomed conversations with the Arabs, as much for the sheer pleasure of conversing with them in their own language, something Speke could not share, as for the information they could impart about the lands on either side of the caravan route.

Burton seemed to need a break from his "companion," who, it turned out, had a slightly different view of the reasons why Burton stayed in Kazeh and sent him alone on the adventure that made him famous: "Burton in the meantime stays here to get things in order for our journey seawards, a good arrangement, for rest seems to do him a power of good.... Burton has always been ill, he would not set out in the dew and has a decided objection to the sun...." Reading between the lines, one gets the feeling that Speke, the man of action and explorer, was chafing under the yoke of Burton the scholar and anthropologist.

On the surface, however, it would seem that the two men, though differing in minor ways in their opinions, were in full agreement that Speke should explore "Nyanza" alone. And so, in this almost casual way, Burton missed his chance to share in the discovery of the century.

✳ ✳ ✳

After a terrible night in Kigoma, disturbed by local revelry, with music blaring well into the early hours of the morning, we packed the Land Rovers and left the old Railway Hotel soon after breakfast. We planned to head for Mwanza on Lake Victoria, not taking the route that Burton and Speke took through Kazeh, but our own, more direct route north-eastward through refugee country. Before we got on our way, though, we had a moment of panic when we thought we had lost Thad's map of Tanzania on which we had marked both our route and Burton and Speke's. To my great relief, we eventually found it jammed between two books in Thad's plastic book tray — his library. It would have been an awful sweat to redo my research into the place names on Burton's map as well as our own.

As we prepared to leave the area, I was again struck by the steepness of the hills bordering Lake Tanganyika. The land falls off sharply, creating deep water quite quickly. Others, including Burton, wrote about this. Beyond Kigoma harbour, as you head north towards Burundi, past the little fishing villages, the sides of the lake are rocky and precipitous.

Lake Tanganyika is the archetypical rift-valley lake: long, narrow, and deep. It is 680 kilometres long and 72 kilometres across at its widest point. With a depth of 1,430 metres, it is the second-deepest lake in the world, after Lake Baykal (1,742 metres deep) in south-eastern Siberia. Its surface, 775 metres above sea level, is far too low for Lake Tanganyika to be the main source of the Nile. If it had an outlet that flowed directly into Lake Albert (altitude 619 metres), then it could be a source. However, between the two lakes stand Lake Edward and the Virunga Mountains, a late, volcanic addition in the western-rift-valley processes. The raising of these mountains divided an ancient lake, cutting off Lake Tanganyika to the south from Lakes Edward (910 metres above sea level) and Albert to the north. The Virunga Mountains are the site of Lake Kivu, at 1,459 metres the highest lake in East Africa, higher even than Lake Victoria (1,135 metres). It is from Lake Kivu that the Ruzizi River drains into Lake Tanganyika.

Leaving Ujiji and Kigoma, we headed for Kasulu, travelling east for a time on the red-dirt road through villages, *miombo*, bamboo thickets, banana plantations, and mango groves. It was Sunday, and in most of the villages we saw women — all very well dressed — on their way to church. Upwards of 75 per cent of the congregations seemed to be women. The Sunday

Sunday service. Most of the congregation is female.

church-going appeared to be an opportunity for a social gathering. Even in the middle of nowhere, on the narrow, dusty, roads, in front of all the little churches, people gathered to chat before or after the service.

Ninety-three kilometres from Kigoma, we reached Kasulu. There, to add to my knife collection, I bought a woman's small sickle — designed for cutting grass — from a Waha tribeswoman.

We then headed north for Kibondo, but somehow missed a turn-off and had to ask directions. We ended up on a helter-skelter cross-country ride on a very rough track before we found the right road. The main route north to Mwanza runs parallel to the Burundi border. We took a short-cut through banana, fig, and guava plantations.

Because of the political unrest in the region, we had our guns with us. One was a 1960 Winchester .375, with a bolt action which can hold five bullets; but with only one cartridge in the chamber it is really only a sport rifle. We also had a six-shot, .38-calibre American police service revolver. I had no idea how any bandits or guerrillas might be armed. Thad reminded us all of the advice we had been given. "Don't slow down. Travel at about eighty kilometres an hour. Have your guns ready. And stop immediately, if you see stones across the road, or any other barricade. Stop and turn around. Don't try to get through." We had managed to confirm that no trouble had been reported recently in the areas we intended to visit, but with the influx of refugees, anything could happen. It was best to be prepared.

We stopped for a lunch of cold *ugali*, chicken, cheese, tomatoes, papaya, and black coffee. About a hundred kilometres from Kasulu we reached the

Malagarasi River again, at a spot north and west of where we had first forded it. This time we crossed on a bridge. We were now on a much different route from Burton and Speke's. I was getting ready to put Burton aside and to begin seeing the African journey through other eyes.

Travelling north-east through little hilltop villages, we passed Busunzu, inhabited by the Waha tribe. Then through Mukugwa, where there is a United Nations Christian refugee settlement, and past the Moyowasia–Kigosi Game Reserve. Just before the town of Kafura we bought two enormous mushrooms from a couple of young boys on the road. These were for dinner. I had heard that African mushrooms had strange qualities. I tried to put my mind at ease by noting that they looked like European mushrooms I had safely eaten before — *cèpes*.

We passed through Kibondo late in the afternoon, and kept going on to Kumkugwa, where we bought some *kayoga* banana brew and also some more *wanzuki*. The local brews seemed to overferment and not last long. At Kasanda, we found ourselves in the highlands, the back edge, as it were, of the eastern escarpment of the western rift valley. This area, south-west of Lake Victoria, is quite well populated. Thatched houses of red mud sit among eucalyptus, banana, and mango groves. Below us we saw an enormous plain stretching north-east towards Lake Victoria. Clouds were forming and it looked as if it would soon storm. I could see rain ahead of us in the valley below.

We reached Kakonko at 5:25 p.m. — just a few hours' drive from the lake. It was raining, and we had to find a campsite. We had found nothing by 6:00 p.m., and so we just turned off the road into *miombo*. It was very wet. We just managed to pitch the tents before dark — a muddy, difficult job. Out of the blue, Joshua made several pertinent observations about the day's journey from Kigoma. He noted that the people were very, very dark, much darker than in the rest of Tanzania. He also pointed out that all the goats seemed to have twins, and sometimes even triplets. This was curious. And the local people seemed somewhat afraid of cars, and people driving cars. When we stopped, the children ran off into the fields or the thickets. The fact that there is not much automobile traffic in the area may account for the wariness. (Or maybe people feared something more specific, which we were to learn about the next day.) Joshua also noticed — as I did — that more than half the people we saw were children. According to census data, about 50 per cent of the Tanzanian population is under the age of sixteen, 75 per cent under thirty-three.

In shape they differ, some being simple cones, others like European haystacks, and others like our old straw beehives. The common hut is a circle from 12 to 25 feet in diameter; those belonging to the chief are of considerable size.

RICHARD F. BURTON
The Lake Regions of Central Africa

Overleaf: Village of beehive huts with a boma of sticks.

With the help of some petrol, we finally got our fire going and started cooking dinner. Somewhere before he reached the Malagarasi River, Burton talked about an isolated village where the people ate only mushrooms. We talked about this as we cooked one of the mushrooms we had bought. The mushrooms were so enormous we used only one, and it, together with cooked bananas, leftover chicken, onions, and tomatoes — washed down with *wanzuki* and *kayoga* — made a good evening meal. All of us ate the mushroom, although there were some jokes as to who would survive the night. The *wanzuki* was sweet with a bit of a kick. We drank quite a lot of it, and had a good night's sleep.

We left camp at 8:00 a.m. Before we had travelled ten kilometres down the road we reached a police barricade, where we were warned, "Proceed cautiously, this next stretch is dangerous." Rwandan refugees had been setting up road-blocks and causing trouble between here and Bukoba, 240 kilometres away, on the lake. The previous March, a bus had been stopped and two guards killed. In October, only a month before our trip, there had been another ambush attempt. We had to accept an armed police guard for sixty kilometres. Our guard, a Sukuma tribesman, had a semiautomatic rifle manufactured in China. As we turned off the winding, dusty, pothole-riddled road onto a much better paved road, Joshua radioed me from the other Land Rover, "This is a nice road — but I'm not putting on my seat belt yet. I want to be able to get out quickly if I have to!"

Our guard pointed out the exact spot around a tight corner where the two armed guards had been killed, and another spot on the paved road (also round a bend) that was a dangerous point. Danger aside, this was beautiful country. Lush green patches of *miombo* were nestled against a wide escarpment with rock outcroppings. We did not encounter many people — only the occasional cyclist carrying bundles of sticks.

Sukuma armed escort.

At Lusahanga we turned right off the main road onto a bumpy, red-soil track. Here we met another roadblock and more police cars, and dropped off our escort.

Surprisingly, given the warnings we had received, our drive was relatively uneventful. For a time, we drove through the bandit area in convoy with a truck, a bus, and another armed guard. At first, we were behind the two larger vehicles, then between them, and eventually we led the convoy before we turned off onto a small track between banana plantations and headed for Geita and the main road to Mwanza. Here, about thirty kilometres south of the lake, we travelled east, descending to a plain that provides views over an enormous wide horizon. We saw a few settlements consisting of beehive-shaped thatched houses, but there was still no sign of the great lake.

Still heading east we passed Isambara, set among fields of cassava, banana, papaya, and acacia. The houses here were mud with thatched sloping roofs. We entered the Mwanza region, which was slightly more populated. A roadside sign caught my eye: "Buck Reef Gold Mining Company." There is gold mining all through the country south and south-east of Lake Victoria. The mines have produced a profitable yield for decades. Geita is a gold town; however, it was not gold dust we found there, but red dust all over everything — eyes, ears, nose, mouth. As we made our way through increasingly populated areas, we tried hard to avoid getting behind other vehicles, particularly vans or trucks that kicked up clouds of dust.

We heard news on the radio that yet another thousand refugees had arrived in Kigoma from Zaïre. Dar es Salaam had given no instructions about what to do with these refugees, and Kigoma was in a state of chaos. We had missed it by a few hours.

As we entered the outskirts of Mwanza, we saw no more reed baskets, gourds, or bark containers. We were back now in the world of plastic. It took a moment's adjustment to realize that this was the self-same area where John Hanning Speke had arrived in August 1858, and had left convinced that he had solved the riddle of the Nile's source.

Speke had set off with a small contingent, including Sidi Bombay, on July 9, 1858. The journey north from Kazeh to Mwanza was not a particularly difficult one, but by this time Speke was growing tired of the whole Burton expedition and finding it boring. "There is literally nothing to write about in this uninteresting country. Nothing could surpass these tracks, jungles, plains for dull sameness.... the country is one vast senseless map of sameness."

On August 3, Speke reached the summit of a hill. Looking down he saw water and realized that this was the great northern lake the Arabs had told him about. He was amazed that "the vast expanse of the pale-blue waters of the N'yanza burst suddenly upon my gaze. It was early morning. The distant sea-line of the north horizon was defined in the calm atmosphere between the north and west points of the compass."

In a moment of either foolhardy speculation or brilliant insight, Speke decided that what lay before him was indeed that much-sought-after prize — the Nile's source: "I no longer felt any doubt that the lake at my feet gave birth to that interesting river, the source of which has been the subject of so much speculation, and the object of so many explorers."

Any human being would be bursting to tell such good news to another, and Speke hastened back to Burton at Kazeh. But when he got there, he did not tell Burton at once. Instead, surprisingly, he slept on the matter and told Burton the next day, probably because he suspected Burton would receive his news with mockery, disbelief, and contempt. Perhaps his travels with Burton had prepared Speke for the reaction he would get. Burton wrote: "We had scarcely ... breakfasted, before he announced to me the startling fact that he had discovered the sources of the White Nile. It was an inspiration perhaps.... The fortunate discoverer's conviction was strong; his reasons were weak...."

From this moment on, the relationship between Burton and Speke changed significantly. Before this, though they had had their differences,

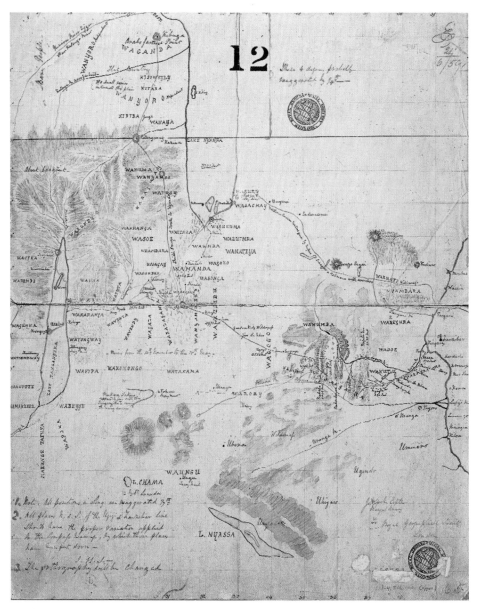

Speke's map of the Burton–Speke expedition, 1856-59.
Map courtesy of the Royal Geographical Society.

My first occupation was to map the country. This done by timing the rate of march with a watch, taking compass-bearings along the road, or on any conspicuous marks — as, for instance, hills off it — and by noting the watershed — in short, all topographical objects.... Occasionally there was the fixing of certain crucial stations, at intervals of sixty miles or so, by lunar observations, or distances of the moon either from the sun or from certain given stars, for determining the longitude, by which the original-timed course can be drawn out with certainty on the map by proportion.

JOHN HANNING SPEKE
Journal of the Discovery of the Source of the Nile

they had acted as two professionals engaged in an endeavour in which one man, Burton, was the superior and the other, Speke, the subordinate. Now they were equals and rivals. From that fateful morning, Burton and Speke were embroiled in a struggle — sometimes overt, sometimes not — for acceptance by the Royal Geographical Society, and the public, of their different views about the source of the Nile.

Despite the evidence that Lake Tanganyika could not be the Nile's source, Burton did not totally abandon the possibility. However, he chose not to argue his case against Speke. Instead, he attacked Speke as a geographer — even going so far as to "rearrange" the Mountains of the Moon on the map in order to diminish the validity of Speke's discovery. Speke took Burton's attacks in a gentlemanly fashion, but he had a plan in mind for his own vindication. Speke wrote:

> *Captain Burton greeted me.... [I] expressed my regret that he did not accompany me, as I felt quite certain in my mind I had discovered the source of the Nile. This he naturally objected to, even after hearing all my reasons for saying so, and therefore the subject was dropped. Nevertheless, the Captain accepted all my geography leading from Kazé to the Nile, and wrote it down in his book — contracting only my distances, which he said he thought were exaggerated, and of course taking care to sever my lake from the Nile by his Mountains of the Moon.*
>
> JOHN HANNING SPEKE
> ***Journal of the Discovery of the Source of the Nile***

Burton vetoed any possibility of exploring the Nyanza further and the two explorers set out to travel the hundreds of kilometres back to the coast. According to Burton, at the end of their trip Speke promised to wait for Burton's return to England before revealing any of their findings. If this was the promise, it was not kept. The day after his return to London, Speke told his version of what had been accomplished to Sir Roderick Murchison, the president of the Royal Geographical Society. The result was fame for Speke and profound resentment by Burton. The enmity between them — and Burton's public expressions of doubt about Speke's claims — continued for years. But Speke's confidence in his theories brought him enthusiastic support. It would not be long before he set off again in pursuit of his own dream.

✳ ✳ ✳

As I approached Mwanza and the scene of Speke's momentous first sighting of the lake, I reflected on everything that went on between Burton and Speke.

In the early part of their journey, with all its frustrations, I think the two of them, despite all their sickness, were working towards the same goal. However, Burton was not the single-minded explorer that Speke was.

Water hyacinths clogging the shore of Lake Victoria.

Whenever the two explorers encountered Arab settlements, Burton would selfishly spend time on things and people that had little to do with the journey. Speke, on the other hand, seemed totally focused on his goals, but when a goal had to be abandoned, his preferred recreation was hunting big game. He had ample opportunity to speak to the Arab traders at Kazeh. He had the use of a translator, and the slave traders would have been a particularly rich source of information about the geography of Africa. Arab traders had known the eastern shore of Lake Victoria for many years before Speke questioned them about it in 1858. They had also reached Karagwe and Bunyoro, on the western shore, in the late 1830s. They certainly told Speke about the lake. That was why he went. Speke simply had a stronger belief in the importance of this mass of water than Burton did.

Anyone who has climbed to the top of Isamilo Hill, as I eventually did, and looked down on the great expanse of water that is Lake Victoria, will understand Speke's instantaneous response and his unshakeable belief in

its significance. It is a phenomenal sight. Its vastness, when seen from that high point of land, is stunning. It is the second-largest freshwater lake in the world — as big as Ireland. (Lake Superior is the largest.) Even though I was far better prepared for the sight than Speke could have been, I was, like Speke, overcome by it. It was no longer a surprise to me that Speke could make that tremendous leap of faith. Faced by its majesty, anyone would accept that this was a lake of vital geographical importance.

✳ ✳ ✳

My first glimpses of Lake Victoria were towards the north from the left-hand windows of the Land Rover as we drove up from Kigoma. We did not get to Mwanza that first day, but stopped at Namanga on an inlet just west of Mwanza. A ferry makes the four-kilometre crossing from Namanga to Mwanza. Speke, too, saw Lake Victoria, or at least the inlet, before he got to Isamilo Hill. He caught a glimpse of the same gulf from the east four days before reaching Mwanza. It would not be possible to get directly to Mwanza and Isamilo Hill from Kazeh without first crossing, or at least going along-side, this quite large inlet. When Speke arrived at the centre of Mwanza, which was then only a small village, and climbed Isamilo Hill, he would have seen Lake Victoria to his north and the large inlet behind him to the south-west.

Mrs. Gaetje, a charming Swiss lady in her mid-seventies, and her son own the Namanga ferry that runs twice a day to Mwanza and back. She also owns a beautiful small lodge right on the edge of Lake Victoria and adjacent to the ferry dock. The lodge was built in 1952 entirely by Africans and has a very old-world colonial atmosphere. The beautifully landscaped gardens boast a profusion of tropical plants, including frangipani, hibiscus, fig trees, flame trees, mangoes, ferns, and oleander. There were small groves of pomegranate and orange trees. Everything was planted in the early 1950s. Amazing! There were birds everywhere: a pair of fish eagles, hadada ibis, weaver-birds, striped kingfishers, and many others.

We introduced ourselves to Mrs. Gaetje and talked her into letting us pitch our tents on her lawn. This was too good an opportunity to miss. She told us that her late husband, who was German, began the ferry service. She has lived on the shores of Lake Victoria since 1953. The Gaetjes had come to Africa in 1938 and began dairy farming. When the Second World War broke out and her husband was put in a detention camp, she carried on. After the war, they worked in Geita — he in the gold mines, taking people back and forth in a van. The business grew, and eventually they ferried people to and fro between Mwanza and Namanga. Despite the Tanzanian program of nationalization, the family still owns the ferry. However, Mr. Gaetje died twenty years ago, and the ferry is now run by the son. That evening we had drinks with Mrs. Gaetje overlooking the bay and the town of Mwanza. The charming experience gave me a taste of German colonial life. Mrs. Gaetje loves the country and the people. She was very philosophical about her rather difficult life, saying, "We always worked."

We had two or three hours free before sunset. Our tents were pitched right at the water's edge. Water hyacinths floated in front of us, and across the inlet we could see Mwanza, a vibrant African city that seemed to grow even as we watched it. I sat there on an inlet of a huge and beautiful expanse of water and thought about the role this mighty lake had played in the great explorations of the past and the answers to the riddles it still held in its watery depths.

* * *

The next morning, at 6:00 a.m. exactly, the fish eagles screeched their mocking cry. It was a wonderful way to wake up. A hadada ibis also made its hideous shriek as it flew across the bay in front of our camp on the water. A few minutes later, we were treated to a spectacular sunrise. At first, a few glimmers of golden light; then the huge, red ball rose over the hills behind Mwanza. Apart from the occasional fishing boat, the scene was

Waiting to board the Namanga ferry.

undisturbed. Little egrets and kites silhouetted themselves against the rising sun. An idyllic spot. This would be a good way to start every morning. No other sounds. Just the birds and the water lapping quietly on the shores of Lake Victoria.

There are three main Tanzanian ports on Lake Victoria: Musoma on the east shore, Mwanza on the south shore, and Bukoba on the west shore. All can be reached by ferry. Our initial plan was to go by the local ferry to Mwanza, return for the night, and then to drive around the south-west shore of Lake Victoria towards Bukoba, which we hoped to reach the following day.

Thad, Joshua, and I headed for Mwanza, while Ali and Pollangyo stayed behind to look after the tents. We managed to get to the ferry terminal well before 9:00 a.m., but already the crowds were so thick that we were not sure we could get on. There were five buses waiting. The ferry, with us on it, eventually left at 9:30 a.m. The day got hotter and hotter with each minute. Mwanza is now Tanzania's second-largest city, after Dar es Salaam. Its name means "to the lake," and it comes from *nga myanza* in Kisukuma, the Sukuma language. The Sukuma are the main tribal group in the city, which is now a busy port and centre for agriculture.

The ferry was packed with buses, petrol tanks, vans, land cruisers, jeeps, fuel tankers, cars — and people. The people pressed up against the front of the ferry, along the sides and against the rails. They favoured brilliantly coloured clothing: shirts, T-shirts, *kangas* (dresses) of red, violet, indigo,

Bismarck Rock, outside the Mwanza ferry terminal.

blue, green, yellow, and orange. It was as hot as hell — and getting hotter. People took refuge in the shade of the buses. We would be heading eastward into the sun and into the glare.

A year or so earlier, one of these ferries went down just outside Mwanza, and twelve hundred people were killed. How do they gauge the weight? There seemed to be no organized method. I wondered how much this decrepit old ferry boat could carry.

The engines started with a low rumble, and the ferry moved hesitantly forward and slowly entered Lake Victoria, a floating mass of metal and people. The engines vibrated; the passengers waited patiently. I could not believe that they could get this huge, heavy weight away from the slender landing pier and out onto the lake, but somehow the craft stayed afloat. We felt a bit of breeze at last as we slowly chugged into a little bay just west of Speke Gulf. We travelled northward first, out among a bevy of fishing boats, turned until the bow pointed back towards the ferry terminal, then headed east to Mwanza — apparently stern first. The journey across the gulf took about an hour. When we arrived in Mwanza at about 10:30 a.m., another teeming mass of people waited at the pier.

Mwanza was a very busy, densely populated town. And hot. We drove out of town on the worst possible road — rutted, half-paved, with slums and stores on either side. All around us were huge outcroppings of rock — in the water, sticking out of the soil, and sheltering the shanty-town dwellings we passed in the poorer end of town — the remnants of immense, ancient glacial action. The city seemed to be sprawling beyond its boundaries. Clearly it was expanding at an enormous rate, and every section of it we saw was hot, dusty, and crowded. Overhead, fish eagles circled constantly — again and again sounding their high-pitched, mocking laugh.

Our first chore in Mwanza was to find a place to leave our guns and radios. It was illegal to take them into Uganda where we soon planned to be. We tried without success to locate a missionary friend of the Petersons. Eventually, we left the radios at Forté's Safaris and decided to take the guns with us to Bukoba, where, if possible, we would leave them with the police. This was safe, wise, and legal. But then we changed our minds again and decided to leave the guns with the police in Mwanza. We would pick them up when we got back there — whenever that might be.

In the early afternoon after we had picked up a few more provisions, we took the 2:30 p.m. ferry back to Namanga. It was a much faster journey.

We ate our campfire dinner that night overlooking the flickering lights of Mwanza in the distance. Frogs croaked below us in the water. Crickets chirped in the warm dusk. We ate tilapia fish (known locally as *ngege* or *mbira*) grilled in silver paper — as well as rehydrated vegetables and *ugali*. Always *ugali*. There was a heavy wind, with whitecaps on the lake, and for a while we thought there was a storm brewing, though eventually it passed over harmlessly. Still, I was glad we were not going out that night on a ferry to Bukoba. All of us realized that the next day would be the beginning of a new chapter — our journey around the south-west tip and up the west side of Lake Victoria, trying to follow the route taken by Speke and Grant in 1861.

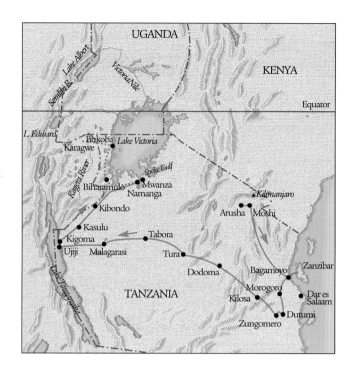

In the Court of Rumanika: Bukoba

Sir Roderick ... knowing my ardent desire to prove to the world, by actual inspection of the exit, that the Victoria N'yanza was the source of the Nile, seized the enlightened view that such a discovery should not be lost to the glory of England and the society of which he was president; and said to me, "Speke, we must send you there again."

JOHN HANNING SPEKE
Journal of the Discovery of the Source of the Nile

6

IN THE COURT OF RUMANIKA:
BUKOBA

The debate caused by Speke's discovery could clearly only be settled by further exploration. The Royal Geographical Society offered to pay for another expedition, to be headed by Speke, and when Speke heard of James Augustus Grant's recent return home to Scotland from India, he chose Grant as his fellow adventurer in June 1859.

Speke and Grant had a great deal in common. They were the same age. They had become friends while in the army together in India, where Speke had given Grant advice about shooting. "You must have a thorough confidence in yourself and instrument or you will never excel," he wrote to Grant in 1855.

He could not have chosen a more dedicated, loyal, obedient lieutenant. Grant was completely content to do whatever Speke asked — so much so, that one sometimes wonders about the closeness of the relationship between the two men. In his study *Empire and Sexuality: The British Experience*, Ronald Hyam places Speke on his list of high-profile asexuals, men who are fundamentally uninterested in the erotic. Hyam also suggests there may also have been a certain boyishness about Speke that was by no means

The first greetings of the king, delivered in good Kisŭahili, were warm and affecting, and in an instant we both felt and saw we were in the company of men who were as unlike as they could be to the common order of the natives of the surrounding districts.... Having shaken hands in true English style, ... the ever-smiling Rŭmanika begged us to be seated on the ground opposite to him, and at once wished to know what we thought of Karagŭé ....

JOHN HANNING SPEKE
Journal of the Discovery of the Source of the Nile

King Cosmas Rumanika Ndagara IV

The now famous Victoria Nyanza, when seen for the first time, expanding in all its majesty, excited our wonder and admiration. On its shores are beautiful bays, made by wooded tongues of low land ... running into the lake, with very often a rounded detached island at their apices. The low islands of Sesseh lie on the western shore of the lake.

JAMES AUGUSTUS GRANT
A Walk across Africa

Previous page: Haya tribeswoman on the western shore of Lake Victoria.

unattractive in heroes of the empire. Alan Moorehead, in *The White Nile*, also remarks on the slavish devotion that Grant gave to Speke, but mentions also that Grant was a brave and accomplished soldier as well as a competent artist and scientist.

Grant was loyal to a fault, and took orders from Speke that a man of more independence would not have taken. But it is possible that this was more the result of his army training than of an unnatural affection towards Speke. It was ingrained in Grant to take orders. Burton was also an army man, but he was unruly and unpredictable. Grant, like Speke, tended to devote himself single-mindedly to the job at hand.

In December 1859, Speke and John Petherick, of the British diplomatic corps, developed a plan for which they got Sir Roderick Murchison's approval: Petherick would ascend the Nile, first to Khartoum, and then to Gondokoro, a small Austrian mission station at the southern edge of the Sudd, aiming to be there by an agreed-upon date. There he was to meet Speke and Grant, who would be travelling north from the Victoria Nyanza, and have with him the supplies and boats necessary for them to travel down the Nile to Cairo.

On April 27, 1860, Speke, Grant, and officials of the Cape Colony sailed from Portsmouth on the H.M.S. *Forte* bound for the Cape. From Cape Town, Speke and Grant then embarked for Zanzibar on the slave-hunter H.M.S. *Brisk*, arriving in Zanzibar on August 17.

A little over a month later, on September 25, 1860, they sailed from Zanzibar to Bagamoyo, from where they were to take the old caravan route to Tabora (Kazeh). The Royal Geographical Society's instructions stated that the expedition should go around the Victoria Nyanza, find the source of the Nile, and trace its course to Gondokoro, trying to reach it by December 1861. The explorers' report, first publication of which the Society reserved to itself, was to give a general but accurate description of the country, including all bearings necessary to fix the exact route on a map. Grant was to use photographs and drawings to record the journey, and Speke was to collect zoological specimens.

With perhaps more inspired hope than good sense, Speke seems to have based the route for this expedition on the experiences of Arab and Swahili merchants to whom he had spoken in Kazeh when he was there with Burton in 1858. Snay bin Amir, from whom he had first heard about Lake Victoria, told how he had "travelled up its western flank to Kibuga, the capital of the kingdom of Uganda." Snay said he had travelled north–north-west from Kazeh, through Usui, to a kingdom, called Karagwe, whose northern border was the Kitangulé River. He had then travelled north and crossed the Katonga River to reach a second kingdom, Uganda. Perhaps most importantly, he repeated rumours that "large sailing-craft ... navigated after the fashion of ocean mariners ... frequent the lake (meaning the Nile at Gondokoro)." Other merchants said that the Kivira River (which Speke took to mean the Nile) flowed out of the lake five days' march east of

Kibuga, and that there was a third kingdom, called Unyoro, north of Uganda, which they had not been allowed to enter.

They eventually reached Tabora on January 25, 1861, but were delayed there for more than seven weeks by flooding, which blocked their route and prevented them from getting grain and porters. Speke took advantage of the delay to learn more about the kingdoms west and north of the lake — and about their rulers. The next stage of their journey took them north towards Victoria Nyanza, but Grant was so stricken with fever that he had to remain camped at Ukuni, while Speke went ahead and searched for porters. Speke reached Mihambo, in the large Uzinza district shown on Grant's map (and on modern maps) south-west of Lake Victoria, in late July. There he was detained by King Lumeresi, who controlled the area. Lumeresi's demands for *hongo* (extortionate expenses) drained Speke of all his resources, but he was saved by the timely arrival of Grant in late September. They were allowed to proceed north into the Usui territory controlled by King Suwarora, another *hongo* artist. It took them a month to reach the northern border of Usui. They entered the territory of Karagwe on November 15, 1861.

To the west and north-west of Lake Victoria, there were at that time three separate and distinct kingdoms, of which Karagwe was the southernmost. Each of the kingdoms had a different geography, climate, level of social sophistication, and degree of political control by its king. Karagwe had a relatively cool, moist climate, endless grasslands on which animals grazed, and steep cliffs descending into lake country. This kingdom was ruled by Rumanika, a gentle king, at least by comparison with the rulers of the other two kingdoms.

The former kingdom of Karagwe is now the most northwesterly part of Tanzania — a short panhandle bordered on the east by Lake Victoria, on the west by Burundi and Rwanda, and on the north by Uganda. It was to this area and the city of Bukoba that we were now headed. As we travelled westward from Mwanza around the southern end of the lake and up its western flank I realized with some relief that I was sloughing off Burton for the first time and going on a new adventure with a different person — Speke. I was retracing the steps of a different character, with a different aim. This time I was much less concerned with the people — their characteristics, emotions, religions, and so on — all the things which intrigued Burton. Despite my awe of Burton and fascination with his character, I felt a definite empathy with Speke — a hungry adventurer who wanted to get on with his quest: find the kingdoms, see the kings, find the outlet of Lake Victoria, and assure himself that it was indeed the source of the Nile. This was exciting stuff for me.

I put myself completely in the explorers' shoes on this second journey. It was as if I were Speke. I could understand the man's mind. What he had planned to do was to go around the western and northern boundaries of Lake Victoria until he found the exact location at which the water flowed out of it. How did he know where to go? How did he know the outflow was likely to be at the north-east corner of the lake? Obviously he was told. He gathered information wherever he could, at every step of his journey. This was the key to Speke's success. I am now convinced he had excellent information and that he was a good researcher. He was also no longer hampered by the peculiarities and ambitions of Burton.

Now I, too, was liberated from the need to plough through mounds of research about Burton's places, names, statistics, characteristics, opinions, and explanations. Burton's anthropological observations, his knowledge, his curiosity — these provide a feast of information. But I was glad, really, that I was no longer looking at every face, every unique characteristic of a village. It was much simpler now. I had fewer preconceived ideas and therefore could experience things more immediately. I felt I was entering new lands in much the same way that Speke had done.

We drove the four hundred kilometres to Bukoba in one day from our campsite on the shores of Lake Victoria at Namanga. Our route took us along the southern bend of the lake and straight north across the somewhat dangerous Kagera region — through which flows the Kagera River, an important piece in the Nile puzzle. Along the way, we had our usual share of adventures.

This westernmost part of Tanzania must be very difficult to protect. As one rounds the south-west corner of Lake Victoria and travels northward into the Kagera district, approaching Rwanda, the only track is a narrow, desolate road through *miombo*. Rwandan refugees, usually persecuted Hutus who have come across the Tanzanian border, shelter here. These are people who have not been given refugee status. Through necessity, some have become bandits, and they live an isolated existence. They have no money, but are usually armed. They go after literally anything they can get: food, vehicles, clothes, guns — particularly guns.

Near Biharamulo, we were halted by a police barrier and proceeded from there with two guards armed with sub-machine guns — one for each of our Land Rovers. The Rwandan refugee bandits will take considerable risks to get transport — and indeed anything else they can sell. This is roadside ambushing of the worst kind. These bandits will kill because they have nothing left to lose. However, possibly because we clearly had armed guards with us, we were left alone.

We were to encounter checkpoints all along our route, and the military always subjected us to stringent questioning: "Where are you going? What are you doing? Where did you get the Land Rovers? Why are you in this area? Have you got any guns?" Earlier, in order to avoid hassles, we had not declared the weapons we were carrying, but during this particular part of the journey we could say truthfully that we were unarmed. We

Guard escort with sub-machine guns near Biharamulo.

Roan antelope in miombo south of Bukoba.

had left the guns behind at Mwanza because we knew we could not take firearms into Uganda. At the Biharamulo checkpoint, when the officers offered us an armed escort for hire, we had little choice but to accept. We agreed to pay whatever they demanded. We chatted them up and gave them extra money to make sure they were on our side. There had been several ambush attempts in the past two days, and the guards insisted that they would be needed all the way to Bukoba. I remembered that Burton, Speke, Grant, and the Bakers had to pay to pass through a tribe's territory, and had often been charged above market value for mules, or porters, or boats. It seemed that some things had not changed much in 140 years.

On this part of the trip, we also went off the road to the site of a game camp where Joshua had worked thirty years before. This was the first time he had been back. The camp was still there but looked deserted. When he had been here, Joshua told us, there had been lots of game: elephant, lion, buffalo, giraffe, topi (jimela), and water buck. Speke also writes about plentiful game. Now, however, there is hardly any game, and what remains is very difficult to see. Refugees, apart from setting ambushes, also kill game simply to survive. Joshua told us the story of an assistant game scout he worked with who had died of a black mamba bite. He had not noticed the bite at all until someone saw the two holes in his leg and blood oozing down. He was dead within twenty minutes.

We were shown the site of an ambush — an obviously bad spot. Logs had been placed across the road. The guards told us that no guard ever wanted to go in the first car in the morning. This is the most dangerous time. The guards also showed us a culvert where there had been a hold-up a week before. The logs were still there at the side of the road.

We saw some roan antelope. This was the first time I had ever seen these beasts. The guard enigmatically said: "Even me. I've never eaten one of those!"

As well as being a bad bandit region, the area along the lake south of Bukoba is one in which AIDS is prevalent.

As we continued north through mountainous terrain, we were sometimes at an elevation high enough to catch glimpses of Lake Victoria. Speke, however, did not go to Bukoba but travelled some distance inland from the lake. He did not set eyes on Lake Victoria until about one hundred kilometres north of Bukoba, opposite the Sese Islands.

As we neared Bukoba, we passed more cultivated areas and saw huge shade trees that the guards and local people call *miumula* trees. At one point, a gap in the trees allowed us a wonderful view of the wide expanse of the lake, with islands scattered here and there. A woman of the Haya tribe stood on a rock in the foreground. Closer to the city, we saw a woman by the side of the road selling green grass for thatching. The road along the edge of the lake led through lush country, but here, as elsewhere, there are no longer any cattle. The rinderpest disease wiped them out almost completely in the 1890s. In that same epidemic, buffalo, greater kudu, eland, and warthog were all reduced to a fraction of their former numbers.

Coming into the city, we passed coffee bushes, banana trees, oil palms (*michikichi*), yellow bamboos, pines, and even small tea plantations. The last stretch of road was particularly rough, and I was glad when we reached Bukoba late in the afternoon.

Bukoba is situated on a hill overlooking Lake Victoria's western shore. It takes its name from a tribe that later merged with the Wahaya. Bukoba first captured the attention of Westerners through the work, in the late 1880s and 1890s, of Dr. Eduard Schnitzer, who became known as Emin Pasha. Schnitzer chose Bukoba as the site of a railway station to serve the needs of the robusta coffee trade, an industry he helped to found. Robusta coffee (*Coffea canephora*) trees grow wild in the forests of Uganda and much of West Africa. The Baganda and related tribes grew it for chewing and for use in the blood-brotherhood ceremony.

We parked and walked around the waterfront of downtown Bukoba until sunset. This is a quiet, unhurried town — a lakeside port, obviously influenced by the Muslim traders, but now mainly supported by agriculture. The wealthier inhabitants live mostly on the outskirts or in the country, not the town itself. There was none of the ruthless hustle and bustle of the fast-growing Mwanza.

We stayed in the tiny, rundown Upendo Hotel, right in the middle of town. The sounds of the African city were all around us. People chattering, crows cawing, dogs barking, and the inevitable hadada ibis shrieking their mocking call. We had an early vegetarian dinner, again with *ugali*, over which

Thad Peterson and puff adder, one of the most venomous snakes in Africa.

we discussed plans for the next day's journey into what had been the kingdom of Karagwe. We intended to find the exact location of King Rumanika's stronghold on the Kagera River. As far as we were able to discover, this stronghold was in the town of Mabira, which was only sixteen kilometres from the border of Rwanda, so there was some danger of trouble from the refugee bandits.

In Bukoba we called in at the Regional Cultural Office and met the regional officer — Mr. S.J. Erassi. He was extremely courteous and eventually arranged for the regional arts and research officer — Mr. G. Kabululu — to accompany us to Bushangaro, the actual site of King Rumanika's palace. Speke called it Bweranyange (or Weranhanjé), which means "white bird," presumably the cattle egret. We also planned, if we had time, to visit the site of the hot springs where Rumanika spent considerable time. We were told that the old king's descendants are still known to be in the area. After Tanzanian independence in 1961, these chieftains ceased to have any political status or power. Nevertheless, they are still respected as tribal leaders by their people.

* * *

Nearing the border of Karagwe, Speke saw, "in the far distance ... a line of cones, red and bare on their tops, guttered down with white streaks, looking for all the world like recent volcanoes...." They were. He had seen the M'fumbiro Mountains — probably the peaks of Karisimbi (4,507 metres) and Mikeno (4,437 metres), which are distinctly cone-shaped.

Speke and Grant entered Karagwe, Rumanika's kingdom, near Lake Urigi (now Lake Burigi), about fifty kilometres west of Lake Victoria. Lake Burigi drains north into the Muish Swamp, which in turn feeds the Mwisa River, a tributary of the Kagera River. As they travelled north along the 1,500-metre high N'yamwara ridge, the Kagera River would have been about fifty kilometres away on their left (to the west), flowing north in this stretch.

Near the border, the explorers were welcomed by representatives of the king, who said that, if they stayed in any village in his country, they were to be fed there at the king's expense, "for there are no taxes gathered from strangers in the kingdom of Karagŭé." A pleasant change from their treatment in the last twelve months.

Speke noted that the soil of the kingdom of Karagwe was rich and red, like the soil of Devon, and he was pleased when Rumanika sent presents to him on his arrival: sheep, fowl, and sweet potatoes. All Speke offered in return was a few yards of red blanket, but this was graciously accepted with no demand for any greater gift.

In contrast to the misery he suffered during so much of the trek with Burton, Speke was in nearly a euphoric mood on the way to meet the king. "[W]e found we had attained the delightful altitude of 5000 odd feet. Oh, how we enjoyed it! every one feeling so happy at the prospect of meeting so soon the good king Rŭmanika. Tripping down the greensward, we now worked our way to the Rozoka valley, and pitched our tents in the village."

Whether he was elated at the prospect of meeting a king with a good reputation, or energized by the altitude, or a little high on *pombe* (ever-present then, as now), it is hard to find Speke more jolly than this.

On November 25, they came in sight of Rumanika's palace at Bweranyange (Speke's Weranhanjé), which had been the capital of Karagwe since the time of the possibly legendary King Ruhinda (*c.* A.D. 1500), from whom the people took their name, Wahinda. It remained the capital until the time of the German administration. It was situated on the eastern shore of a little lake that Speke and Grant each claimed they had named "Little Windermere," insisting that there was no native name for it. However, we now know that the natives called it Lake Rwebishonga and now call it Lake

Mujunju. This lake is about forty kilometres west of Lake Victoria on the same latitude as the middle of the Bumbiri Islands, which would be about twenty kilometres south of Bukoba. "Little Windermere," Speke noted, "gets drained into the Victoria N'yanza through the Kitangulé river."

The meeting with "the ever-smiling" Rumanika went exceptionally well. "The king was plainly dressed in an Arab's black choga, and wore, for ornament, dress-stockings of rich-coloured beads, and neatly-worked wristlets of copper." The king's brother and sons were also present, the young princes "squatting quiet as mice." The language spoken during the meeting was Kiswahili — that is, Swahili. The king used the word *wazungu,* the plural of *mzungu,* to mean "white men," the same usage as today. When Speke offered to take one or two of Rumanika's children to have them educated in England, the king was in favour of the idea, saying that the boys would return with "a knowledge of everything." They spoke about this possibility more than once, but when the explorers left for Uganda the boys did not go with them. Perhaps Rumanika had an inkling of what lay in store for them and was willing to wait for more regular contact with Europeans.

Like so many of the natives the explorers encountered, King Rumanika could not imagine why Speke and Grant would want to spend so much money travelling. He thought that men of wealth should just sit down and enjoy what they had. Speke's answer to this is a perfect blend of the objectives of exploration: the scientific and the commercial. Discovery is of equal importance to tourism and trade. Speke told Rumanika: "To observe and admire the beauties of creation are worth much more than beads to us. But what led us this way we have told you before; it was to see your majesty in particular, and the great kings of Africa — and at the same time to open another road to the north, whereby the best manufactures of Europe would find their way to Karagué, and you would get so many more guests."

Speke spent some time describing one curious feature of Rumanika's family: "I had heard ... that the wives of the king and princes were fattened to such an extent that they could not stand upright." In order to check on this, Speke visited the king's brother and was struck "with the extraordinary dimensions, yet pleasing beauty, of the immoderately fat fair one his wife. She could not rise; and so large were her arms that, between the joints, the flesh hung down like large, loose-stuffed puddings." Speke noticed a large number of milk-pots hanging from poles, and probably was not surprised when the king's brother told him that the obesity of his spouse was "all the product of those pots: from early youth upwards we keep those pots to their mouths, as it is the fashion at court to have very fat wives." Of another, Speke noted that, "her features were lovely, but her body was as round as a ball."

For the most part, however, Speke kept his mind on the task at hand. He again observed "in the distance some bold sky-scraping cones situated in the

Overleaf: The thousands of blue plastic roofs of Chabalisa refugee camp in Karagwe.

country Rŭanda, which at once brought back to recollection the ill-defined story I had heard from the Arabs of a wonderful hill always covered with clouds, on which snow or hail was constantly falling." This must have been another sighting of the M'fumbiro Mountains (also called the Virunga Mountains).

Of course, I already knew from my research that the Kagera River is one of the main feeder rivers of Lake Victoria. But Speke, with only the tales of traders and locals and the evidence of his own eyes to guide him, did not think this: "The Kagéra was deep and dark, of itself a very fine stream, and, considering it was only one — and that, too, a minor one — of the various affluents which drain the mountain valleys into the Victoria N'yanza through the medium of the Kitangŭlé River, I saw at once there must be water sufficient to make the Kitangŭlé a very powerful tributary to the lake."

Gaetien Kabululu, the regional arts and research officer accompanying us, confirmed that the Kagera River is an important "supply" river for Lake Victoria. Several rivers feed into it. It starts in the highlands on the border between Burundi and Rwanda. It is more than 480 kilometres long. The rivers that flow into it include the Ruvuvu (in Burundi) and the Ngono (which flows north into it from the Mulemba district of Tanzania).

The current Rumanika, the direct descendant of the king whom Speke met, is the chief of the Hinda tribe. By asking as we went, we were able to find our way to his territory, an area rich in metal deposits that were at one time locally processed. At the town of Kyaka, I first saw the Kagera River. We were allowed to photograph the river but not the bridge — which was guarded by armed military personnel. I could see a very strong current, a current that Gaetien Kabululu said continued right into the middle of Lake Victoria. The current of the Kagera, in fact, can actually be seen several kilometres out into the lake, cutting across the north-west corner towards the point where water flows out of the lake to become the Nile. When Idi Amin was in power in Uganda, he tried to wrest from Tanzania the territory north of the Kagera River. There is little doubt that it is a significant body of water, both geographically and politically.

We entered the Karagwe district in a downpour and made our way up into the hills as red streams of water flooded the rough, winding road. We were in *miombo* among tall euphorbia trees, eucalyptus trees, and banana plantations, as well as muhumulo trees, also called *Maesopsis eminii*. We stopped for lunch overlooking a deep, misty valley, then continued our winding journey towards where Bweranyange had been, about 1,500 metres above sea level. It grew colder and we were soon above the clouds, which partly obscured our view of the valley below.

There were two main refugee camps in

Refugee camp signpost, Karagwe.

The Kagera River near Kyaka.

Karagwe district, holding a total of 150,000 refugees. (There are another 500,000 refugees in Ngara district south of Karagwe.) We drove by Chabalisa Camp No. 1 and Chabalisa Camp No. 2, where, we were told, all the refugees are from Rwanda. They have official refugee status and have been in these camps since 1994. We were looking at a vast valley filled with what appeared to be postage stamps of blue plastic — thousands and thousands of shacks roofed with blue tarpaulins. It was a truly shocking sight. I could see the dejected faces of the people in the crowd as we negotiated muddy streets winding among hills covered with huts. The poverty and sense of hopelessness were overpowering. Occasionally, they are able to get a little work in the banana fields, either for cash or for food. Very few of the refugees speak Swahili. When Rwanda gained its independence from Belgium in 1965, the northern portion of the former Ruanda-Urundi not only changed the spelling of the country's name to Rwanda, but also chose to make the Bantu language, "rungaRwanda," sometimes called "Kinyarwanda," its official language, along with French.

* * *

Following an extra search we reached the village of Nyakaiga, home of King Cosmas Rumanika Ndagara IV. He is the sixth-generation direct descendant of the King Rumanika whom Speke and Grant met in 1861. After many, many questions and misdirections, we did eventually find the king — in itself, an amazing discovery. After some introductory conversation, he took us to the site of the old palace. There was absolutely nothing there — just the site and a marvellous view over the countryside below. The king criticized the district commissioners, who were still with us, for not helping him build a museum on the site. He also reminded us that Speke had offered to send some of the chief's children to England to be educated. "That wouldn't have been a good idea," our host commented. "Then they would have become Englishmen!"

Once we had seen the site of the old palace, we drove three kilometres to a local bar in Nyakaiga and talked with the king for nearly two hours.

I found King Rumanika a very outspoken man, with strong opinions. He knew something about both Speke and Stanley, and about his ancestor's meeting with the two explorers. Both Speke and Stanley had made the arduous journey into the hills to meet the king, as we had done — and it was an arduous journey, even in Land Rovers. Despite Speke's encouraging words about opening the kingdom to international travellers and trade, no tourists visit the land of Rumanika. This was entirely new territory to me.

The current King Rumanika is far from wealthy. He has a dream to build a museum to commemorate his ancestors on the site of the old palace, but he has often been disappointed by people who have promised help and then failed to deliver. He showed us a few traditional huts, where people prayed for healing or for rain. I agreed with him that a small museum or monument to the old kings, perhaps in the form of more huts on the location of the old compound, would be a good idea. I also promised to discuss the matter with the Royal Geographical Society in London. Rumanika understood all too well that Speke's visit to his ancestor was really the first colonial exploration of the area. "Look what's happened since," he reminded me. He does not want it forgotten, and I cannot blame him. Rumanika, though poor, is a proud man, a leader with the respect of his community. He *is* a king. He has begun the preservation of his past in a humble way, and I sincerely hope that some day he will be able to realize his plans for the reconstruction of the palace.

Rumanika, still referred to as His Excellency, is a handsome, serious man, probably in his late fifties. He retains a regal manner, although time and circumstances have robbed him of the life of easy, good-humoured grace enjoyed by the royal family when Speke visited. Julius Nyerere's attempts to reduce the power of tribal leaders has been effective, although it was not possible totally to erase tribal honour and customs.

I felt that, like Speke, I was a revered guest of Rumanika, and we spent quite a lot of time together. Actually finding King Rumanika and talking to him was a delight and an honour for me. At the right moment, I asked him what he thought about the rumour that Speke may have sired a son during his visit to these kingdoms. I became aware of this when I read that Speke's accounts of his exploits in Buganda were severely edited before publication in *Blackwood's Magazine* and that he had been intimate with a girl named Meri. This union may have resulted in a child, whose existence Speke kept secret. "Ah, yes," Rumanika answered, "this could easily have happened. Either here or in Buganda. This was considered a good practice in establishing relationships. However, it is likely that the child was either brought up outside the area or did not survive. It was acceptable for people to sleep together — the king's wives and children might sleep with the same people." His own father had married several times, he said, and one of the wives was a white woman. The tribal elders allowed the marriage but insisted that the white wife be kept away from the area. When Rumanika's father wanted to be with her, he had to go outside the kingdom. This was the only way he could have a relationship with this woman. She was not allowed to be one of his queens or have any position of power in his kingdom. Eventually, they were divorced. Had Speke had a son, it would have been unlikely that he would have been allowed to live in the kingdom or marry into the tribe.

We had driven 163 kilometres from Bukoba to see the king (*mfalme* in Swahili). The journey had been well worth it. We left Nyakaiga at 6:00 p.m. It was far too late to get all the way back to Bukoba, or indeed make the journey to the hot springs, so we decided to spend the night in the town of Karagwe. But where would we sleep? Before looking for accommodation, we had dinner at a tiny local roadside restaurant: fried tilapia and an omelette. We met a Czech water engineer who asked us what we were doing in the area. "Looking for the source of the Nile," we replied.

"Oh, that's easy. The Kagera River. I have flown over it and Lake Victoria in the rainy season. The silt comes right down the river, across the lake and into the Nile and what was once Ripon Falls," he responded.

That night I restudied what Speke had said about the Kagera. "To-day we reached the Kitangulé Kagéra, or river, which, as I ascertained in the year 1858, falls into the Victoria N'yanza on the west side," he wrote. This statement interested me for two reasons. First, Speke says he found out about the course of the Kagera on his initial trip to Lake Victoria. A little more reading refreshed my memory. On returning to Kazeh in June 1858, after the rather disheartening trip to Lake Tanganyika with Burton, Speke had heard Snay bin Amir say: "On crossing the Kitangulé river, I found it emanating from Urundi (a district of the Mountains of the Moon), and flowing north-easterly." Second, he was using the word "Kagéra," as it seems Wahinda did, to simply mean "river."

"I looked down on the noble stream with considerable pride," Speke goes on. "About eighty yards broad, it was sunk down a considerable depth below the surface of the land, like a huge canal, and is so deep, it could not be poled by the canoemen; while it runs at a velocity of from three to four knots...."

I found it curious that he would use the word "pride." I read on.

> *I say I viewed it with pride, because I had formed my judgment of its being fed from high-seated springs in the Mountains of the Moon solely on scientific geographical reasonings; and, from the bulk of the stream, I also believed those mountains must attain an altitude of 8000 feet or more, just as we find they do in Rŭanda. I thought then to myself, as I did at Rŭmanika's, when I first viewed the Mfŭmbiro cones, and gathered all my distant geographical information there,*

> *that these highly saturated Mountains of the Moon give birth to the Congo as well as to the Nile, and also to the Shiré branch of the Zambézé.*
>
> *I came, at the same time, to the conclusion that all our previous information concerning the hydrography of these regions, as well as the Mountains of the Moon, originated with the ancient Hindŭs....*
>
> JOHN HANNING SPEKE
> ***Journal of the Discovery of the Source of the Nile***

At this time, Speke's understanding was based on what his guides in Karagwe told him. According to him, they referred to the M'fumbiros, lying due west of their country, as the Mountains of the Moon.

Speke acquired geographical information not only from Arab traders and Africans.

> *[In Zanzibar] Colonel Rigby now gave me a most interesting paper, with a map attached to it, about the Nile and the Mountains of the Moon. It was written by Lieutenant Wilford, from the "Pŭrans" of the Ancient Hindŭs. As it exemplifies, to a certain extent, the supposition I formerly arrived at concerning the Mountains of the Moon being associated with the country of the Moon, I would fain draw the attention of the reader of my travels to the volume of the "Asiatic Researches" in which it was published. (Vol. iii. of A.D. 1801.) It is remarkable that the Hindŭs have christened the source of the Nile Amara, which is the name of a country at the north-east corner of the Victoria N'yanza. This, I think, shows clearly, that the ancient Hindŭs must have had some kind of communication with both the northern and southern ends of the Victoria N'yanza.*
>
> JOHN HANNING SPEKE
> ***Journal of the Discovery of the Source of the Nile***

Speke put faith in the map given to him by Rigby in September 1860. Like so much of the information about the source of the Nile, this map is controversial. Lieutenant Wilford later withdrew the conclusions of the original article because doubt was cast on their authenticity by reports that the maps and other "ancient documents" making up the *Puranas* were fraudulent, a hoax perpetrated by a Hindu writer who created the documents himself.

I am still not entirely convinced that this map was a fake. As Stanley said, they had it right in the past. Whatever knowledge Speke got out of the conversations and old documents, it had much more influence on him than it appears to have had on others — Burton, for example. Obviously, Speke paid a great deal of attention to old writings, maps, and other information he got from the caravan traders. He certainly had a great deal of confidence that he could locate the exact source of the great river. On this trip with Grant, he went all the way across to Tabora, across the south-west of Lake

Victoria, then up into the Kagera region and Rumanika's kingdom before even getting a glimpse of the lake. How could he possibly know where he was going? My own travels confirmed for me that it is very difficult to see the lake while taking a route even quite close to the western side of the lake. Speke therefore had to have considerable advance knowledge in order to find his way. I think that those who insisted the *Puranas* map was a fraud may be wrong. Despite inaccuracies, it was well known that for centuries there were other ancient maps that showed great masses of water in the centre of Africa with rivers flowing out of them into one great river. It may well be that the ancient Hindus had the same knowledge.

✳ ✳ ✳

As we left Rumanika's kingdom I readied myself, in much the way Speke had, to enter the next kingdom, which in Speke's time was Buganda, reigned over by the twenty-five-year-old Mtesa. The journey there would take us into what is now Uganda. Rumanika had warned Speke that Mtesa was very different from himself. Grant, in the meantime, had contracted an infection in his leg, and Rumanika warned that nobody who was ill would be allowed to enter Buganda. Nor, Rumanika warned, would Mtesa allow in men who were wearing trousers — or donkeys who were not.

Speke would have explored more in Karagwe, but all that he did was subject to the scrutiny of the king. Not having the same problem, I was free to move on and did so. There was a lot of ground to cover. But I deeply regretted not having the time to explore fully the tributaries of the Kagera.

On January 7, 1862, a delegation arrived in Karagwe with presents for Rumanika from the *kabaka* (king) of Buganda, Mukabya Mtesa, and an invitation to the explorers to enter his kingdom. Speke and Grant had been at Rumanika's court for only six weeks, but they were already overdue for the rendezvous with Petherick in Gondokoro, seven hundred kilometres to the north. So, on January 10, Speke set off north and became the first European to be allowed to enter and eventually to pass through this part of Africa.

✳ ✳ ✳

We stayed in a very modest roadside guest house in Kayanga, a town in the Karagwe district. It was the only place we could get and it was awful. My room was a small cement construction two and a half metres square. The only furniture was a bed. Nothing was very clean, including the one-hole toilet. We had to draw our own water for washing and going to the lavatory. Luckily, had a lock on it. Psychologically it made me feel safer, although the flimsy wooden door would not provide much protection and failed to provide a sound barrier between me and a number of guests who had decided to talk through the night.

The town itself was very busy. The influx of refugees had brought a second influx of people who were providing aid. It was cold at this altitude, but the air was clear. Quite a different atmosphere from the seaside ports and lowland cities on the lakes.

* * *

In one of our discussions, Gaetien Kabululu talked further about the Kagera River. Some of his comments confirmed gruesome reports we had heard that dead bodies thrown into the Kagera River in Rwanda had found their way downstream into Lake Victoria. At one time, nets had to be placed strategically in several places across the Kagera River because the Nile perch in the lake were feeding on the dead bodies. Not surprisingly, the price of Nile perch had dropped dramatically.

"The brutal genocide in Rwanda was terrible," Kabululu said. "Men, women, and children — speared together — floating down the river into Lake Victoria. All on the Kagera River. Lots of people. An awful sight. Very brutal. Very cruel. Terrible!"

Gaetien Kabululu, regional arts and research officer, Bukoba.

As for the suggestion that the Kagera had some claim to be called the source of the Nile, he asserted quite confidently that it was. "I have no doubt that [the Kagera River] is the main source of the river Nile. Not only from the air — where you can see the different colour and the big current — moving very fast — to form the Nile. Also in the steamer in the lake — you can feel the current of the Kagera where you cross its flow. The boat shivers. Boat captains have to be very careful when crossing. They slow speed and cut across diagonally — otherwise there will be trouble. It is a strong flow of water. Some other rivers flow into Lake Victoria — but the Kagera is the main source. At any time you cross the Kagera current — on the lake — you know you are on the Kagera — anywhere up to the Nile."

There was added confirmation from Joshua: "In the old days they say they used to ring a bell when boats in Lake Victoria crossed the Kagera current — warning passengers about the rough water. The Kagera's current is very strong. They say they can see it."

I wondered why Stanley and Speke had not made more of the Kagera as a source of the Nile.

The next day, before we headed back to Bukoba, we had a brief meeting with a district cultural officer, Boaz Kaitaba, who showed us a whole array of artefacts (spears, drums, anvils, spear holders) made from iron smelted in the Karagwe district. We also met the district council chairman and the district executive officer. They welcomed us, but also quizzed us quite pointedly about our visit and the reasons for our interest. When I told them that

Local chemist's store, Kagera district.

we were very grateful for Gaetien Kabululu's help in seeing King Rumanika, the district executive officer curtly corrected me: "We don't call them kings anymore."

As we pulled onto the road, I remembered a comment of Speke's about his passing a plain where "Rumanika keeps his thousands and thousands of cows." When Thad Peterson had asked the current Rumanika the previous day why he had no cows, he had replied, "There are no herd-boys anymore. They are all off to school. And then there are thieves. It is all too much trouble." This was ironic, since the land here was quite good for raising livestock. In most parts of East Africa it is impossible to keep cattle or other livestock because where there is *miombo* there are tsetse flies to plague the animals and spread disease. The Maasai, whom we visited later, can raise cattle because their land is savanna and not *miombo*.

Sometimes in our travels, we amused ourselves with trivialities. I taught Joshua a match game. I set out three piles of matches: five, four, and three, and told him that the object was to take any number out of any single pile, but to make sure that your opponent was forced to take the last match. (Mathematicians and logicians will recognize this as the game called Nim.) We had hours of fun until Joshua eventually, by recognizing my opening move, realized the trick to winning.

On our trip back to Bukoba, we passed the Kagera again. Below the road the slow, brown, winding river coursed its powerful way towards Lake Victoria. Over a century ago, the river would have been much bigger. The water level in many of the lakes, including Victoria and Tanganyika, has dropped considerably since the mid-nineteenth century. I had noticed this first in Ujiji. Heavy rainfall from 1961 to 1965 had greatly swollen all the Central African lakes, but now the levels were low again. Was deforestation of the Ruwenzoris and the Lake Victoria basin affecting the water catchment?

We arrived back in Bukoba in time to check into the Upendo Hotel again for a rest and clean-up before a late lunch. Later that afternoon I dallied in the market among the long stalls where people sold grain, flour, rice, and other food, as well as new and used clothing, *kangas* (women's dresses), pants, glasses — a wide assortment of wares. We found a kiosk where a young Muha tribeswoman sold herbal potions. We quizzed her for quite a while, and for 2,000 Tanzanian shillings ($3.50 U.S.), bought a mixture of five dried barks for arthritis, called *dawa zamaergi*. Directions: Boil one heaped teaspoon in one cup of water. Take three times a day. Keep taking it indefinitely. For 5,000 shillings, a second potion was purchased, *hamu ya mume*. This mixture, made of ground-up roots from four different trees, was advertised as a powerful aphrodisiac. Directions: Boil one heaped teaspoon of powder in one cup of either black tea or black coffee. Take two times a day for four days. Important: do not sleep with your partner during this four-day period.

The young Muha woman guaranteed that both these potions would work, saying, "If the last mixture does not work — come back and I will give you another, stronger mixture."

✳ ✳ ✳

We heard on the evening news that there were now as many as ten thousand refugees in Kigoma on Lake Tanganyika — all Hutus, some from Rwanda, but most from Zaïre. But the refugee camps were designed to accommodate only about three hundred people. By now, I was sure, there would be absolute chaos in the port, where another thousand refugees were waiting in boats for permission to land.

Before dinner that night, we drank *ruibisi* — the traditional banana brew of the Bukoba district. It was easy to digest, and not too strong. We seemed to finish an entire petrol can full of the concoction, and by dinner time were feeling quite light-headed. King Rumanika had been drinking *kanyogi* — neat. This 60-proof, clear liquor, which is produced by Tanzania Distilleries Limited in Dar es Salaam, has its own distinctive flavour — somewhere

[T]he longer I lived with him the more did my admiration and reverence for him increase.

HENRY MORTON STANLEY
How I Found Livingstone

Joshua Mbewe and his son Ali.

206

between vodka and gin.

Over dinner with S.J. Erassi, the regional cultural officer, the conversation turned to the subject of cannibalism. For once, I was not the one who introduced the topic. I had tried to discuss this a few times during the journey, but found people extremely unwilling to talk about it. Mr. Erassi told us quite seriously that the Bugabo tribe in this area had definitely practised cannibalism at one time. However, he refused to comment on their current practices. The Bugabo are a subtribe of the Haya — one of the tribes living in the Bukoba region.

One dish the people in Bukoba definitely still eat is grasshoppers. I was forcefully reminded of this the next morning. During certain times of the year, hordes of grasshoppers swarm across the land. Thousands fly into the lights and are trapped, then fried and sold. They are a great delicacy in the area and extremely expensive. Joshua caught one and gave it to me, inviting me to try it. Instead I had two samosas for breakfast with leftover coffee. I was anxious to get cracking. We left Bukoba before 8:00 a.m. and headed north to the former kingdom of Mtesa. This was the second kingdom visited by Speke, who went without his fellow explorer. Grant, his leg agonizingly sore, remained behind as something of a captive guest in the court of Rumanika.

There was no want of food here, for I never saw such a profusion of plantains anywhere.

JOHN HANNING SPEKE
Journey of the Discovery of the Source of the Nile

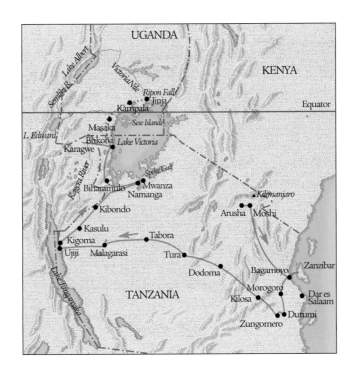

"The Nile Is Settled":
Into Uganda

We were well rewarded; for the "stones," as the Waganda call the [Ripon] falls, was by far the most interesting sight I had seen in Africa. Everybody ran to see them at once, though the march had been long and fatiguing, and even my sketch-block was called into play. Though beautiful, the scene was not exactly what I expected; for the broad surface of the lake was shut out from view by a spur of hill.... Still it was a sight that attracted one to it for hours ... as interesting a picture as one could wish to see.

JOHN HANNING SPEKE
Journal of the Discovery of the Source of the Nile

7

"THE NILE IS SETTLED": INTO UGANDA

Buganda, the kingdom of Mtesa in Speke's day, is now part of Uganda. Like other African nations at the time of European exploration, Buganda had an established political structure revolving around the absolute power of the *kabaka* (king). Sir Edward W.F. Mutesa II, or "King Freddie" — a direct descendant of the kings of the nine-hundred-year dynasty that included Mtesa I, whom Speke met — was crowned *kabaka* as a teenager. He quickly departed for London, England, then went to study at Cambridge, where he became something of a *bon vivant*. In 1948, he returned to Africa and assumed his throne in the *kibuga* (royal city) adjacent to Kampala. Mutesa II was not generally respected by his people, who may have felt that he did not take the fate of his nation seriously. This changed when he began to demand independence for Buganda. His demands did not please the ruling British, who first pressured him to return to London and then eventually stripped him of his remaining powers as a monarch. Undaunted, he returned to Africa and became the first president of Uganda when it gained its independence in 1962. In 1966, Prime Minister Obote overthrew Mutesa II. "King Freddie" once more sought refuge in London, where an assassin felled him in 1969. He was buried at the royal tomb on Kasubi Hill early in the 1970s.

In 1993, Ronald Mutebe, the son of Mutesa II, and English-educated like his father, became *kabaka*. However, the National Resistance Army (NRA), headed by Yoweri Museveni, was now the ruling political power in the

A woman ... retires from the hut to the jungle, and after a few hours returns ... carrying a load of firewood on her head.

RICHARD F. BURTON
The Lake Regions of Central Africa

Wood gathering on the north-west shore of Lake Victoria.

The palace or entrance quite surprised me by its extraordinary dimensions, and the neatness with which it was kept ... and fenced all around with the tall yellow reeds of the common Uganda tiger-grass ....

JOHN HEMMING SPEKE
Journal of the Discovery of the Source of the Nile

Previous page: Mtesa's palace in the kibuga at Kampala.

country. Under Museveni, the country appears to be regaining some of the stability and prosperity it enjoyed before the violence it suffered under its post-independence rulers, especially Idi Amin, who seized power in 1971. In an extraordinary move, in 1995 Museveni reinstated the position of *kabaka*, although with limited powers.

Winston Churchill once called Uganda "the Pearl of Africa." It is a fertile country, consisting of a high plateau two thousand metres above sea level, flanked by the Ruwenzori Mountains, which form its western border. The rainy seasons are March to April, and October to November. Most of the country enjoys moderate temperatures. Coffee is a major crop of Uganda. The ravages of Amin's brutal rule, including economic chaos and the physical destruction of the landscape, have gradually been repaired since the late 1980s. Christianity and Islam are the main religions of Uganda today, but the tribal past has not been forgotten. Forty tribes still exist in Uganda, and of those the Baganda is by far the largest.

✳ ✳ ✳

The route we followed was probably very similar to that taken by Speke and Grant 140 years ago. From Bukoba, we retraced our steps north-west to Kyaka, recrossed the Kagera, and headed towards the Uganda border. This route took us through beautiful, productive, well-populated stretches along the red road. Of course, we had to go through Customs and Immigration when we reached the border, and this involved the usual long process of questioning before we were allowed into the country.

✳ ✳ ✳

Speke's walk from Rumanika's capital to that of Mtesa took him six weeks. He and Grant were already overdue for their rendezvous with Petherick (supposedly by now hanging on in Gani, the territory south of Gondokoro, with boats to take them down the lower Nile).

Less than one week into their journey, Speke and his party reached and forded the Kitangulé River, which is now called the Kagera. About ten days later, on January 28, they crossed yet another of the papyrus-choked watercourses that Speke called "rush-drains," climbed a hill, and he saw the Victoria Nyanza for the second time in his life — this time from a point opposite the Sese Islands. Within a few days the travellers crossed the Katonga River. Two weeks later, they reached the Mwerango River, and Speke was delighted to find that it flowed northward: he had entered the watershed of the Nile.

He proceeded, full of confidence that he would soon reach his goal. To Speke, meeting with King Mtesa was an integral part of his plan. Speke's habit of learning about the Nile by talking directly with those who knew about it was nowhere clearer than in his hopes for conversation with the king. "I had a great deal to tell him about, as he was the father of the Nile, which river drained the N'yanza down to my country to the northward." On February 20, 1862, he came in sight of Mtesa's capital — near present-day Kampala.

After a number of frustrating preliminary dealings with the emissaries of Mtesa's court, Speke was finally invited into the presence of the king. Speke's attitude was that he should appear "rather as a prince than a trader, for the purpose of better gaining the confidence of the king." To that end, he put on his best clothes, but he felt he suffered in comparison to his hosts.

> *They wore neat bark cloaks resembling the best yellow corduroy*
> *cloth, crimp and well set, as if stiffened with starch, and over that, as*
> *upper-cloaks, a patchwork of small antelope skins, which I observed*
> *were sewn together as well as any English glovers could have pieced*
> *them; whilst their head-dresses, generally, were abrus turbans, set off*
> *with highly-polished boar-tusks, stick-charms, seeds, beads, or shells;*
> *and on their necks, arms, and ankles they wore other charms of wood,*
> *or small horns stuffed with magic powder, and fastened on by strings*
> *generally covered with snake-skin.*
>
> **JOHN HANNING SPEKE**
> ***Journal of the Discovery of the Source of the Nile***

Speke took great care in arranging the procession that solemnly marched towards the palace. Of course, the Union Jack came first. Twelve men dressed in red flannel cloaks (and probably sweltering) formed the honour guard, their bayonets fixed at the end of their sloping guns. The rear of the procession was made up of the rest of Speke's men, each bearing a gift, the exact articles duly noted and including firearms, cloth, "best beads," a gold chronometer, and a complete set of cutlery.

Speke was very impressed with the entrance to the palace, especially "by its extraordinary dimensions, and the neatness with which it was kept." The compound held countless "gigantic grass huts, thatched as neatly as so many heads dressed by a London barber, and fenced all round with the tall yellow reeds of the common Uganda tiger-grass...." And he was amazed at the effort that went into the reception that awaited him. It seemed as if the whole kingdom had turned out to greet him: groups of the king's wives, officers to open each gate he entered, courtiers, little turbaned pages, bulls, dogs, goats, cocks, hens, and musicians playing on stringed instruments like the harps of Nubia.

There was a moment's discomfort when the king's officers asked Speke and his men to sit on the ground in the sun to await the pleasure of the king. Speke refused. Diplomatic manoeuvrings then occurred, during which Speke established, by a show of indignation, that he would not sit upon the ground to await the pleasure of the king. As a great concession, apparently, Speke was then given permission to sit on a chair — a privilege until then

Speke meets Mtesa, 1862.

reserved solely for Mtesa himself. Speke privately gloated at this triumph, but when he returned to the court, he "advanced, hat in hand."

The initial meeting between Speke and Mtesa occurred on February 20, 1862. It consisted of a long period during which the two simply stared at each other, Speke beneath his umbrella, a device that roused the laughter of the court. The explorer had plenty of time to notice the king's appearance. He saw a handsome, tall, well-formed man of about twenty-five with hair cut short except for a high, cockscomb-like ridge at the top. Mtesa wore a beautiful beaded necklace of elegant multicoloured patterns. He had other fine jewellery: a bead bracelet, a wood and snakeskin charm. Brass and copper rings alternated, one for each of his fingers. Above his ankles, a wide "stocking" of beads decorated each leg halfway to the calf. Everything he wore was tasteful, elegant, and neat, as were his habits. He carried a square of gold-embroidered silk and used it to hide his mouth when he laughed or to wipe it when he drank — which he did copiously. He was surrounded by his spear, his shield, his white dog, and his women.

When they had stared at each other for an hour, the king retired to eat, but offered nothing to Speke, who waited until he was once more granted the royal presence. First the king showed Speke a hundred of his wives, then he asked what messages had been sent by Rumanika. When Mtesa was told of "Englishmen coming up the Nile," he said that he had heard about that, too. Speke then offered him a gold ring "made after the fashion of a dog-collar." When Speke finally attempted to discuss his plans for exploration, however, the king turned the conversation to the subject of guns: "What guns have you got? Let me see the one you shoot with."

Though disappointed, Speke recognized that Mtesa could not be rushed. "I then said, 'I had brought the best shooting-gun in the world — Whitworth's rifle — which I begged he would accept....'"

A second meeting took place on February 23, when Speke was again invited to Mtesa's palace. It appeared that the king intended a presentation of gifts, but the proceedings were interrupted by rain. After the rain had stopped, Speke was again summoned into Mtesa's presence. There he found the head of a black bull lying in front of the king, and four live cows walking around the court; the king commanded Speke to shoot the four cows.

Borrowing the revolver he had given the king, Speke shot all four "in a second of time," but the last one did not die at once. Instead, it turned on Speke, who used a fifth bullet to kill the animal. The court burst into a great round of applause. To Speke's amazement, "the king now loaded one of the carbines I had given him with his own hands, and giving it full-cock to a page, told him to go out and shoot a man in the outer court; which was no sooner accomplished than the little urchin returned to announce his success, with a look of glee such as one would see in the face of a boy who had robbed a bird's nest, caught a trout, or done any other boyish trick. The king said to him, 'And did you do it well?' 'Oh, yes, capitally.'"

This display of ruthlessness put something of a damper on things. "I had not been able to speak one word I wished to impart about Petherick and Grant," Speke complained, "for my interpreters were so afraid of the king they dared not open their mouths until they were spoken to." Speke made a number of attempts to get Mtesa to send for Grant and to communicate with Petherick, but Mtesa was far more interested in the entertainment value of having a cow-shooting white man amuse the court.

Eventually, after much time, Speke was able to send for Grant, whose convalescence was progressing well enough to allow him to leave Rumanika's court in Karagwe. Grant travelled by land, rather than by water as Speke had hoped, arriving on May 27. "How we enjoyed ourselves after so much anxiety and want of one another's company, I need not describe," Speke says. "For my part, I was only too rejoiced to see Grant could limp about a bit, and was able to laugh over the picturesque and amusing account he gave me of his own rough travels."

✳ ✳ ✳

We had to register our cars at the border town of Mutukala. Special licences were needed to enter Uganda. We also got our passports checked. A whole crowd of money changers descended on us, offering appalling rates of exchange. We got a little change for our American dollars (but not our English pounds). It was wiser to wait until we reached Kampala.

After Customs we made our way along the red road, noticing pine and albizia trees as well as the more usual banana plantations and mangoes. We drove through wide plains with hills in the distance. This is the territory of the Waganda tribe. The women's dresses here were longer than in Tanzania, but still colourfully patterned. We noticed the unusual long-horned Ankole cattle as we made our way north to Masaka, and we saw cyclists again, taking advantage of the paved road. As usual, the area became more populated as we headed towards the city. The landscape was a clutter of cars, telephone lines, tin-roofed houses, brick walls, and more mango trees and banana plantations.

Masaka today bustles with people, but it was reduced to near rubble in 1979, when the Tanzanian army occupied the town in its successful bid to oust Idi Amin. The buildings are mainly concrete. Fuel stations line the road: Equip, Total, Esso, Shell. Coca-Cola signs are much in evidence. Many people wore Western dress. Homes had tiled roofs and well-tended gardens. There were plenty of shops, and the streets were jammed with motorbikes, including motorcycle taxis. Khaki-clad police with black hats and belts struggled to impose some order on the traffic. As we sped through the town, Thad bore down on the cinnamon he was chewing. I noticed that he nearly always chews cinnamon when driving. A new habit. I remember when he used to chew tobacco, a habit I gather it took years to break.

Not far from Masaka, we saw Lake Victoria again, with the Sese Islands in the distance. This high spot of land, with a view of the lake suddenly bursting out below us and the islands breaking the horizon, was probably almost exactly where Speke saw the great lake again.

We soon became snarled in a jam of cars and bicycles. A truck laden with bananas belched poisonous black diesel fumes into the air. The landscape, however, was lush, and we began to see papaya trees. At a place called Lukaya, we saw an enormous muhumulo tree in the centre of town, its lower branches filled with weaver-birds' nests and its trunk surrounded by white pelicans.

We swept down onto flatter land — plains, scrub country, with bushes and acacia trees dotting the landscape. In the distance, it appeared to be raining, but the road we travelled on was dry. We crossed the Katonga River, and then, at 2:05 p.m., the equator. It was the first time that Joshua had ever been in the northern hemisphere. The land remained flat for a few more kilometres; then very slowly we began to climb to the hilly country around the north-west shore of Lake Victoria.

There were signs for churches, monasteries, convents, and church schools all along the road — familiar denominations such as Seventh-Day Adventist, Lutheran, Church of England, and Catholic, as well as many I had never heard of. There is no doubt that Christianity was used as a tool to colonize and to build the British Empire, to maintain the balance of power, as well as to replace "heathen" morality with "civilized" Western ways. In the great growth days of the empire, the missionaries played an enormously important role and promoted Christianity very adeptly. Africa provided a receptive audience.

There are churches all over Africa. Although Christianity is generally prevalent, a great many churches are splinter groups that have broken away from the Roman Catholic Church, the Church of England, and the other traditional denominations. The need for Christianity, and the need for

Schoolchildren south of Masaka.

religion in general, has clearly not diminished, even in our sophisticated, increasingly secular world. In my travels I have often been asked to comment on religious practices I have observed. Burton's obsession with religion was one of the things about him that inspired my interest and holds it to this day. I have observed many cultures, and those that have tried to stamp out religion have usually failed in the attempt. Religion is needed. In Africa it appears to play a vital role. Christianity is the fastest-growing religion in Africa — largely because of the proliferation of breakaway groups. Perhaps the new sects reflect the desire of Africans to Africanize the forms of Christianity brought to their land by Europeans.

Of course, Christianity existed in parts of Africa for many centuries before the incursions of the Europeans in the mid-nineteenth century. The Coptic Church, for instance, has flourished in Egypt and Ethiopia from before the middle of the fifth century. But it was the expansion of Christianity brought by the nineteenth-century missionaries that really challenged the hegemony of Islam and changed the face of religion on the continent. Now the pendulum may be swinging back, as the renewed vigour of Islam in several African countries again alters the balance of power throughout the continent.

* * *

Around 3:00 p.m. we reached the outskirts of Kampala, the capital of Uganda. Kampala is a reborn city after being nearly destroyed by wanton violence and ruthless looting in the war against Amin, almost twenty years ago. It is clearly back on its feet, now, with a population of about 775,000. We soon found ourselves among wall-to-wall stores, slums, and then the

Nateet Market. Garbage was strewn on both sides of the road, and we were made all too aware of the city smells. Within an hour we checked into the Grand Imperial Hotel, one of Kampala's oldest hotels and certainly its most imposing — now completely renovated.

The climate of Kampala, near the north-western corner of Lake Victoria, is affected by its close proximity to the lake. High temperatures, combined with abundant rainfall, ensure a rainforest lushness of vegetation in the city and its environs. Industry, agriculture, fishing, and animal husbandry provide the economic base for the area. Kampala was the centre for the British administration of Uganda during the colonial era.

The Grand Imperial Hotel is indeed grand. It is as good as any hotel in the East. It was the only time on the trip that we stayed in a decent hotel, and it was good to have a break from camping and the roadside lodges. We needed a rest. Ripon Falls, the Bakers' trek, Livingstone, Stanley — all lay before us. This was not nearly the halfway point of the journey, but it was a welcome intermission, and a chance to catch up on reading and research. At the hotel, I sent out some filthy clothes to be washed, showered to remove the caked red filth and grime of the rough road, and then soaked in an enormous bath for at least forty-five minutes.

Grand Imperial Hotel, Kampala.

Our plan was to head for Jinja the next day, hoping to see the outlet that Speke had declared to be the source of the Nile. Then we would proceed to Murchison Falls, where the Nile empties into the north end of Lake Albert, only to flow almost immediately towards the nearby outlet at the beginning of the Albert Nile.

We met Bart Young, a friend of Thad Peterson's, for drinks and dinner in the dining room of the hotel. He had bad news about Murchison Falls. Young, a Texan working for the Uganda Department of Wildlife, had been in Kampala for about a month. A little over a week before our dinner, sixteen Ugandans had been killed by Islamic militants from the Sudan. This was in the Murchison Falls area and inside the Ugandan border. The Sudanese were very well armed and apparently still in the region. The Ugandan army had been put on alert. The militants were apparently retaliating for gun running through Uganda by supporters of the Christian faction in the Sudan. This was unwelcome and alarming information, although we were already aware that the area was prone to violence and bloodshed.

Bart Young also told us that Kampala had its own problems. Two white expatriate Ugandans who had returned on a visit had recently been killed. He made no bones about the fact that it was now impossible to go to northern Uganda. Islamic rebels were situated from the Kaidepo National Park in the north-east, along the border with Sudan, all the way to Lake Albert. Going to Murchison Falls, towards the north-west, was possible but chancy. He suggested we contact Wolfgang Zimmerman, the German technical adviser for Murchison Falls National Park.

Next day we were greeted by newspaper accounts warning us about the rebel Islamic faction along Uganda's northern and north-western border. Our guide for the day was Ben Katumba, a former soldier in the Uganda National Liberation Army which fought against Amin's troops in 1978 in a bid to topple the regime. "The northern situation is very worrying," Katumba told us. "However, the danger is really on the north side of the river now, and not on the south side. I was in Murchison Falls last Thursday, and it is okay. You just cannot cross the river on the ferry. But you can go up to the falls on the launch. You can also go to the top of the falls — which is very interesting. Joseph Kony is the leader of the rebels. He's of the Acholi tribe in northern Uganda, which borders the Sudan. I think he is Catholic. The rebels are mainly Catholic. But now they are aligning themselves with the Sudan Islamic rebels. General Omar Bashir is the head of state in the Sudan where the country is fighting its own war, Muslims versus Christians. John Garang, the leader of the Christian rebels, is definitely a Catholic. Garang is being supported by foreign powers, including Uganda. Bashir seems to be financed and assisted by Iran."

There were certainly obstacles ahead of us. Nevertheless, we eagerly set out for Ripon Falls. At least we were free to make the attempt. Speke had faced a major obstacle that we did not. He first had to escape from the clutches of Mtesa.

★ ★ ★

Despite the fact that Grant had still not yet fully recovered from his leg ailment, the two men were eager to resume their mission. Speke had definite plans for continuing his investigation of the watershed in the area, but he was baulked by Mtesa: "A plan of the lake and Nile, which I brought with me to explain our projects for reaching Karagué and Gani, engaged the king's attention for a while; but still he would not agree to let anything be done." Gani, to the north, was the land of the Wagunya. It was north of Bunyoro, the third kingdom, ruled by King Kamrasi, but south of Gondokoro. The rumoured expedition of Europeans from the north was supposed to have an outpost there.

Grant had given Mtesa a compass. Although the young king could not figure out how to use it, he was diverted by it and would not pay attention to the explorers' plans. Speke wanted from Mtesa what he had wanted from everyone he had met in Africa — information about the source of the Nile. He knew better than to risk his life in getting that information. He played Mtesa's game. I found it interesting to learn that in modern Swahili the word *mtesa* means "persecutor." Perhaps the king's name took on this meaning for Swahili speakers, like the traders from the Zanzibar coast, because of his treatment of his own people and of visitors.

Speke and Grant tried all kinds of tricks to get away from Mtesa, which they finally managed to accomplish by making an appeal to the *kabaka*'s pride. Speke told him that he wanted to understand the flow of the Nile so that he could open a direct line of commerce between Buganda and England. Mtesa responded to this enthusiastically and with full understanding of the implications of freer trade. He said he was tired of having everything come to him by way of Rumanika. He told Speke that he wanted visitors (and, by implication, the goods that they carried) to come to him directly. Reasoning in this way, he finally granted the explorers leave to proceed, but not before demanding, in his edgy way, to know whom Speke liked better — him or Rumanika. Speke answered in perfect candour when he said, "I liked Rumanika very much because he spoke well, and was very communicative; but I also liked Mtésa, because his habits were much like my own — fond of shooting and roaming about; whilst he had learned so many things from my teaching, I must ever feel a yearning towards him."

On July 7, 1862, after four and a half months in the Ugandan court, Speke and Grant set out on their journey to Kamrasi's capital with an escort of Bagandans and a herd of cattle, a gift from Mtesa, to provide food along the way. They walked north for five days, covering nearly fifty kilometres. Each day, after some hours of travel, the director of the escort, a man named Budja, would choose a village as their stopping place for the night, usually one whose leader had recently been seized by Mtesa. The escort would then pillage the houses, taking everything they could. On the fifth day, it became apparent that there would be a delay of several days in order to collect the cattle. Speke strolled off with his rifle. Messengers found him and told him that one of his men, Kari, had been murdered by some villagers when he had been enticed into a plundering escapade with some of the escort. In his honour, Speke named the village Kari, and so it appears on Grant's sketch map of the expedition.

On July 16, still at Kari, Speke shot two zebras. Because of the grazing territories of the various zebra species, there is little doubt that these must have been what came to be called Grant's zebras (*Equus granti*). This was only one of the new species that were identified from specimens sent back to England. On December 5, 1861, Rumanika had presented Speke with the carcass of an antelope, the sitatunga or water-tragelaph. On the expedition's return home, based on several heads and skins they brought back with them, this antelope was given the scientific designation *Tragelaphus spekei* (later changed to *Limnotragus spekei*) in Speke's honour. The sitatunga is an aquatic antelope that inhabits the papyrus swamps north and west of Lake Victoria. Its long, splayed-out hoofs enable it to move freely on the surface of boggy swamps but make walking on drier ground more difficult. Its hunters take advantage of this in the dry season. Earlier still, when they were in Unyamwezi, Grant and Speke collected specimens of the more common dry-grass-country antelope which came to be identified as Grant's gazelle (*Gazella granti*).

Woodcut based on Speke's sketch of Ripon Falls, 1862.

On July 18, a consultation took place between the two men that changed the fate of each, for Speke, certain in his own mind that he was headed directly for the Nile's exit from the lake, ordered Grant to go on a separate mission. Grant agreed, apparently without any objection, giving up for all time any claim to being a discoverer of the Nile's source. Speke attributes this decision to concern about Grant's leg injury and the necessity for speed. Others attribute it to Speke's ambition to claim the discovery as his alone, in much the same way as he had done in his dealings with Burton:

> [A]s it appeared all-important to communicate quickly with
> Petherick, and as Grant's leg was considered too weak for travelling
> fast, we took counsel together, and altered our plans. I arranged that
> Grant should go to Kamrasi's direct with the property, cattle, and
> women, taking my letters and a map for immediate dispatch to
> Petherick at Gani, whilst I should go up the river to its source....
>
> JOHN HANNING SPEKE
> ***Journal of the Discovery of the Source of the Nile***

So, on July 19, the whole troop walked north together for five kilometres. Then Grant went west "to join the high road to Kamrasi's," and Speke went east, heading for Urondogani, a village on the Nile, where he thought boats would be provided to him on Mtesa's authority. He spent four hours crossing another rush-drain, the Luajerri River (now called the Sezibwa), which was supposed to rise in the lake and fall into the Nile.

Two days later, on July 21, Speke reached the Nile itself and reported, "Here at last I stood on the brink of the Nile; most beautiful was the scene, nothing could surpass it ... flowing between the fine high grassy banks, with

Ripon Falls submerged in the Owen Falls Dam reservoir.

rich trees and plantains in the background, where herds of the nsunnu and hartebeest could be seen grazing, while the hippopotami were snorting in the water, and florikan and guinea-fowl rising at our feet."

Having reached the river some distance north of the lake, Speke then proceeded south up the Nile, constantly in awe of the beauty he saw. "The whole was more fairy-like, wild, and romantic than — I must confess that my thoughts took that shape — anything I ever saw outside of a theatre."

Finally, on July 28, 1862, Speke reached "the extreme end of the journey." Here, the explorer saw what he was later to call Ripon Falls:

> *Though beautiful, the scene was not exactly what I expected; for the broad surface of the lake was shut out from view by a spur of hill, and the falls, about 12 feet deep, and 400 to 500 feet broad, were broken by rocks. Still it was a sight that attracted one to it for hours — the roar of the waters, the thousands of passenger-fish, leaping at the falls with all their might; the Wasoga and Waganda fishermen coming out in boats and taking post on all the rocks with rod and hook, hippopotami*

*and crocodiles lying sleepily on the water, the ferry at work above the
falls, and cattle driven down to drink at the margin of the lake, —
made, in all, with the pretty nature of the country — small hills,
grassy-topped, with trees in the folds, and gardens on the lower slopes
— as interesting a picture as one could wish to see.*

*The expedition had now performed its functions. I saw that old
father Nile without any doubt rises in the Victoria N'yanza.*

JOHN HANNING SPEKE
Journal of the Discovery of the Source of the Nile

✳ ✳ ✳

My own first sighting of the Nile was at Owen Falls, where there is now a dam.
Today, the Nile above Owen Falls no longer rushes down in a torrent as it did
when Speke saw it, because the dam's reservoir has raised its headwaters and
swallowed Ripon Falls from view. The Nile here is now a contained power.

All that anyone talked about near the Nile was the water-hyacinth
problem. The world's second-largest freshwater lake is being choked by the

Ripon Falls plaque, with the Speke Memorial visible on the west bank.

water-hyacinth plant (*Eichornia crassipes*) which threatens to destroy the fishing industries of Uganda, Kenya, and Tanzania, the three countries which border the lake. Trade is disrupted, too, because ships are unable to dock in ports that have been overrun by the plant. As well, the water hyacinth's uncontrollable spread may be contributing to an increase in outbreaks of such deadly diseases as malaria, bilharzia, and cholera.

It was difficult here to see the actual river because of the water-hyacinth plants. These weeds grow on the surface and have completely obliterated any sight of water above the dam. Looking down from the dam, all one sees is a mass of water hyacinths — a vast carpet of green for hundreds of metres. However, as you round the north-east corner of Owen Falls and go south through Jinja, up the river towards Ripon Falls, you can see the Nile on the right (that is, to the west) — a massive, mighty river slowly wending its way northward. Here the water hyacinths are mostly by the banks. Through the palm trees I could see the thin line of islands that mark what once was Ripon Falls, but is now only a powerful downward wave — extremely dangerous for swimming because there is a steep drop and the water just sucks the unsuspecting swimmer into the reservoir's watery depths.

According to Speke, it is at this spot that the Nile really starts. A sign indicates that here the Nile "starts its long journey," but says nothing about anyone's having "discovered" it. Ugandans are now extremely sensitive about claims that any European "discovered" the Nile. Across the river on the west bank is the Speke monument — a recently constructed simple obelisk.

Speke's theory was that Lake Victoria drains over Ripon Falls and becomes the mighty river Nile. Another powerful argument, however, is that the Kagera River, which cuts across the north-western corner of Lake Victoria and exits at Ripon Falls, is the source of the Nile. Nevertheless, it is true that Ripon Falls is the only continual effluent of Lake Victoria, the start of the Victoria Nile. This is where Speke felt he finally had confirmation that he had found the source of the Nile.

The Nile, even here, has a majesty about it. It is clearly life-giving. Everything about it on either side is lush and green. People are fishing, boating, growing things. Seeing the Nile first at Owen Falls had not been particularly exciting. The real thrill was walking along the banks of the river speculating where Speke might have first seen the falls. He actually saw them from the western bank, the other side of the river, where the new monument now stands. However, we chose the eastern side, where we could get nearer to the water and the falls themselves.

Speke almost got to stand where we were standing now. He was dissatisfied with his sketches of the falls and had been told by a local official that the lake was visible from the hill he had been sketching. "[W]e proposed going there; but Kasoro [who had been appointed by Mtesa as their guide]... resisted this, on the plea that I never should be satisfied. There were orders given only to see the 'stones,' and if he took me to one hill I should wish to see another and another, and so on. It made me laugh, for that had been my nature all my life...."

When we left Ripon Falls, we retraced our route north through the town of Jinja and stopped for a drink at the Sunset Hotel overlooking the Nile. The railway curves around the edge of the small bay, now completely clogged with water hyacinths.

Continuing north again, we reached Bujagali Falls, downriver from Owen Falls. Our guide, Ben Katumba, told us about a man called Budhagali who lives in the region of Bujagali Falls. Budhagali claims that he is the rightful owner of the falls. He also practises witchcraft. Many locals believe in his power and are quite afraid of him. Some years ago Budhagali was a tribal leader in the area.

✳ ✳ ✳

On the return trip to Kampala, we turned off to Namugongo, where there is a shrine to Christians persecuted and burnt on June 3, 1885, by the new king, Mwanga, the teenaged son of Mtesa I, who had died the previous year. Apparently, Mwanga did not like people praying to someone higher than him, so he killed them. The Christians were wrapped in slender reeds and burnt alive.

Back in Kampala, we spent three-quarters of an hour looking around the small but very interesting National Museum. Of particular interest to me was a diorama illustrating "The Drainage History of Uganda." Documentation accompanying this display explained that the drainage system of Uganda was affected over millions of years by great topographical changes caused by earthquakes and the shifting of vast geological masses. The display introduced me to the ideas of the effects of plate tectonics on the Nile: the formation of the rift valleys and their lakes, the tilting of the land, the flow of rivers being reversed, the creation of Lake Victoria, and the geologically recent connection of the central African lakes to the lower Nile.

Suddenly everything started fitting into place. The intricacies of the Nile headwaters were caused by the dynamic geological activity of millions of years. While it is natural for us to think that the landscape as we know it has always been that way, in fact it is constantly changing. The diorama in Kampala emphasized the fact that the Nile has had huge changes over time, especially at its source in the central lakes basin.

This geological understanding would have made the complexities of the Nile's source much less mystifying for the early Victorian explorers. I had always been confused as to whether the two lakes, Victoria and Albert, were in fact the sources or the reservoirs of the Nile. The information I

Nile beer advertisement and children.

gained from the diorama solved most of the puzzle for me. The lakes are the reservoirs. And the rivers — the Kagera feeding Lake Victoria, and the Semliki feeding Lake Albert — are the two main sources of the waters of the lakes. Taking this view made me much more aware of the importance of the Ruwenzori Mountains. At this point I began to focus much more intensely on their role in the Nile story.

* * *

We took the opportunity to visit the Kasubi Tombs, not only because they are an important monument in the history of Uganda, but because they provided a direct connection between Speke's journey and ours. The tombs are on the site of Mtesa's original palace. It was Suna II, Mtesa's father, who chose that site for the palace. The site became a mausoleum when Mtesa died in 1884, shortly after meeting Stanley. Mtesa was buried in this palace's courtyard, and from that time on, members of the royal family of Buganda were interred in or near the palace site. The current site also includes a large cone-shaped hut, originally built for Mtesa and now restored. It is reputed to be the largest grass-thatched hut in Uganda.

Kampala, like Rome, is reputed to be built on seven hills. For at least the last century and a half, the *kibuga*, the capital of the Bagandans' *kabaka*, was built on a hilltop for ease of defence and, if necessary, escape from attack. When a king died, his successor would build a new *kibuga* on another hill, but it was always in central Buganda, close to the lake (hence, usually within the bounds of what is now Kampala). Mtesa moved his capital quite frequently during his reign, perhaps as many as ten times. During Speke's stay in 1862, it was at Banda-Balogo, which Speke called Bandawarogo. When Stanley visited Mtesa in 1875, it was on the hill called Rubaga, where the Rubaga Cathedral now stands. By 1877, Mtesa was using two *kibugas*, Rubaga and Nabulagala (Kasubi). After his death in 1884, the new *kibuga* was built on Mengo Hill and remained there.

⋆ ⋆ ⋆

Immediately after seeing the outflow at Ripon Falls, Speke summed up his observations in his diary. He was aware that the watershed at the Nile's source was vast and complex. He concluded, however, "from this southern point, round by the west, to where the *great* Nile stream issues, there is only one feeder of any importance, and that is the Kitangulé [Kagera] river...."

Nothing mattered to Speke at this point except "the established fact that the head of the Nile is in 3° south latitude, where, in the year 1858, I discovered the head of the Victoria N'yanza to be."

In keeping with the great traditions of exploration, Speke named Ripon Falls after "the nobleman who presided over the Royal Geographical Society when my expedition was got up," and also honoured the French Geographical Society by calling "the arm of water from which the Nile issued" Napoleon Channel, because in 1860 the French society had awarded him a gold medal for discovering Lake Victoria.

After seeing Ripon Falls, Speke would have been eager to get home with what he considered to be indisputable proof of the validity of his great find. But to continue north to Gondokoro as planned, the expedition would have to travel through the third kingdom in this area, Bunyoro, ruled over by the dour King Kamrasi.

Speke and his small party embarked in five boats from Urondogani on August 13, but two days later had to abandon them and the plan to travel by river to the capital of Bunyoro, and set off overland. After a month's separation from Grant, Speke encountered him returning from Kamrasi's kingdom. The king had been suspicious of the explorers, but Grant's withdrawal had reassured him, and he now indicated that they were welcome. They marched into Bunyoro, reaching the capital on September 9, but were not able to meet the king until nine days later. Nothing happened there to match the graciousness of Rumanika or the erratic hospitality of Mtesa. "Nothing could be more filthy than the state of the palace," Speke wrote, "and all the lanes leading up to it: it was well, perhaps, that we were never expected to go there."

After a period of being trapped in Bunyoro, Speke and Grant were allowed to set off again towards Gondokoro. Gondokoro (near present-day Juba) was about 280 kilometres to the north. On November 9, they left Kamrasi's kingdom and travelled by canoe down to the Karuma Falls. The river was not completely navigable, as they had hoped, so they had to continue on foot, reaching what is now Nimule on December 3. They remained there

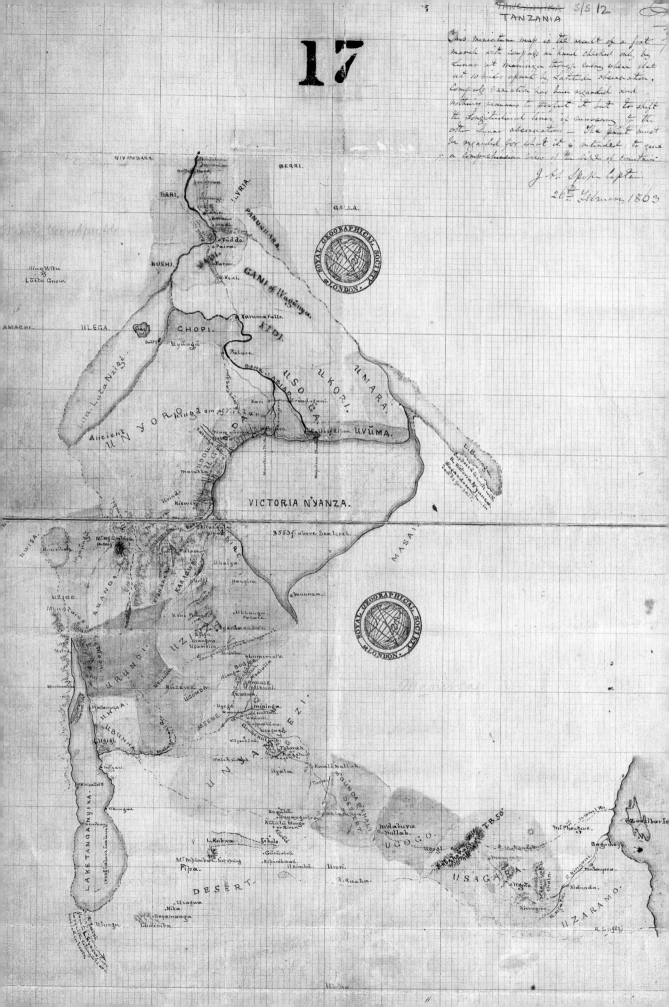

for some weeks, setting out again for Gondokoro on January 11, 1863.

Speke and Grant had been told that three white men had arrived by boat at Gondokoro. When they arrived there themselves on February 15, they expected to meet Petherick, despite being fourteen months overdue, with reinforcements of vessels and supplies. Instead, to Speke's great surprise, he ran into someone quite different:

> Walking down the bank of the river — where a line of vessels was moored, and on the right hand a few sheds, one-half broken down, with a brick-built house representing the late Austrian Church Mission establishment — we saw hurrying on towards us the form of an Englishman ... the next moment my old friend Baker, famed for his sports in Ceylon, seized me by the hand.
>
> JOHN HANNING SPEKE
> *Journal of the Discovery of the Source of the Nile*

For Speke, I am sure, the great adventure was now finished. In his diary he wrote, "I had now seen quite enough to satisfy myself that the White River which issues from the N'yanza at Ripon Falls, is the true or parent Nile," and on the way home to England, he cabled London from Khartoum with the message: "Inform Sir Roderick Murchison that all is well, that we are in latitude 14°30' upon the Nile, and that the Nile is settled."

I am sure Speke was sincere in believing that the Nile was "settled." But he spoke from incomplete information. He had certainly added enormously to Europeans' knowledge of the eastern branches of the White Nile's feeder waterways. But he had not yet verified his theories by exploring the length of the Victoria Nile from Ripon Falls to where it entered the north end of Lake Albert. And he had only a hazy notion, based on anecdotal evidence, about the whole western part of the system that included Lake Edward, the Semliki River, and Lake Albert.

With hindsight, we know that Speke had fitted in a huge piece of the puzzle of the Nile's sources. At the time, however, in England there was so little certain knowledge about the lake region of Africa that some continued to give

This miniature map is the result of a foot march with compass in hand checked only by Lunar at Maninga though every where else at 10 miles apart by Latitude observation. Compass variation has been regarded and nothing remains to perfect it but to shift the Longitudinal lines if necessary to the other Lunar observations — The colour must be regarded for what it is intended: to give a comprehensive view of the size of countries.

JOHN HANNING SPEKE
Speke's inscription on Grant's map, dated 26th February, 1863.

Grant's map of the Speke–Grant expedition, 1860–1863.

Map courtesy of the Royal Geographical Society.

credence to rival theories. Burton's theory, for example, that Lake Tanganyika might still prove to be part of the Nile system still had its believers.

To give a public airing to some of these theories, the British Association for the Advancement of Science sponsored a debate between Burton and Speke, to take place on September 16, 1864, in Bath, England.

On September 15, in the afternoon before the debate was to occur, Speke, the man who had so skilfully handled a gun in the court of Mtesa that he shot four cows in seconds, died of a self-inflicted gunshot wound as, apparently, he carelessly pulled his hunting firearm towards him while trying to climb over a loose-stone fence. His death would never be satisfactorily explained. He was widely respected for his skill as a hunter. He had been brought up with guns in Somerset, where his estate was. He had been a big-game hunter all his life, in both India and East Africa, and it was surprising indeed that a man with his experience would have a hunting accident.

Some people have pointed out that the timing of the debate with Burton was singularly disadvantageous for Speke. When Speke returned to England after the expedition with Burton, he was a hero, and Burton, though leader of the expedition, received little acclaim. Despite their agreement to wait until both could report their findings, Speke had selfishly claimed credit and glory before Burton even arrived home. But after Speke returned from his journey with Grant, public opinion soon turned against him. People had begun to doubt his claims. He had little in the way of scientific evidence to support his views, and he was about to pit himself against a master debater. Although Burton's theories were wrong, his intellectual gifts and eloquence might well have prevailed in an argument with Speke. There will always be speculation that Speke was unwilling to face his antagonist. But accidents do happen. Speke was a man of courage and determination — and a man who loved life. I think his death was an accident.

The entire nation was stunned by Speke's death. Burton is reported to have wept. One does not even want to think about the effect on the devoted Grant. Speke was only thirty-seven years old. He never married, and, despite his great achievement in Africa, he never became the household name that the other Nile explorers became.

The more I learned about Speke, the more I came to appreciate, understand, and even sympathize with him. I came to judge him on his own merits and not solely through others' eyes. His character lived for me in Africa. As I struggled over the territory he covered with Burton on the long trek from Bagamoyo to Ujiji; as I stood beside the waters first of Tanganyika and then of Victoria; as I spoke to Rumanika's descendant and later stood on the site of Mtesa's palace; and as I eventually looked out over the waters of Ripon Falls, I acquired a clear appreciation of this man and what drove him to his accomplishments. He was a man of purpose. He was a conscientious follower of orders, and a commander who was unquestioningly obeyed. He was clever; he had a sense of humour; and, judging from how he behaved in the courts of the African kings, he was more than skilled in the arts of public relations and diplomacy.

He had terrible flaws, too, of course. One of these flaws may have been a need to grab the limelight at all costs. He had certainly usurped Burton's prerogatives following their journey together. And, whether by accident or design, he had ensured that Grant would have a minimal share of the glory from the second trip to Lake Victoria. I found it somewhat ironic that such an avid seeker of fame should, in the end, have failed to secure the prominent and admired position in history that he probably deserves.

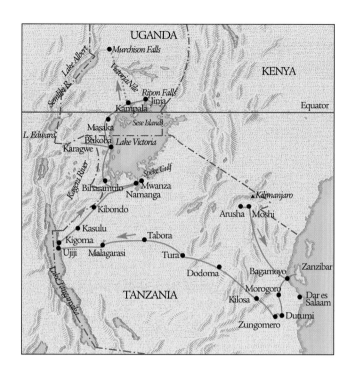

Baker of the Nile:
Kampala to Murchison Falls

[H]ere was the reward for all our labour — for the years of tenacity with which we had toiled through Africa. England had won the sources of the Nile! Long before I reached this spot, I had arranged to give three cheers with all our men in English style in honour of the discovery, but now ... I looked down upon the great inland sea lying nestled in the very heart of Africa, and thought how vainly mankind had sought these sources throughout so many ages, and reflected that I had been the humble instrument permitted to unravel this portion of the great mystery when so many greater than I had failed.

SAMUEL WHITE BAKER
The Albert N'yanza: Great Basin of the Nile

8

BAKER OF THE NILE: KAMPALA TO MURCHISON FALLS

Samuel and Florence Baker had already been travelling in Africa for two years when they met Speke and Grant in Gondokoro on February 15, 1863. In that time they had seen the Atbara before and during its flood, they had traced virtually all the sources of the Blue Nile, they had made the acquaintance of Arab traders and Abyssinian rebels, and had many other remarkable experiences. In some ways, however, their adventures were just beginning.

Speke and Baker had met while on a P. & O. steamer from Bombay to Aden in 1854. Now, the friends and their companions exchanged news: the Bakers telling of the recent death of Prince Albert, the Prince Consort, and of the outbreak of the American Civil War; Speke and Grant describing their journey, its hardships and successes. In Speke's opinion there were only minor matters to clear up about the sources of the Nile. Speke told Baker that Rumanika's people spoke of another lake, the Little Luta Nzigé ("dead locust"). What role did this lake play? Also, did the "Somerset" River (his name for the river flowing out of the Victoria Nyanza, named in honour of the English county where he lived) flow into the Luta Nzigé? Could his speculation that the "Somerset" River was connected with the Nile flowing into the Sudd at Gondokoro be confirmed?

Speke and Grant sailed off to Khartoum in the Bakers' boats. Samuel and Florence prepared to head south. It would take them a year to reach the Luta Nzigé lake; and another year to get back to Gondokoro. They were able to answer some of the questions and even find an important element of the Nile system that none of the previous explorers had heard of — Murchison Falls. We now know that they came close to, but did not find, other key pieces of the puzzle.

We were not going to retrace the Bakers' path. Instead, we planned to go north from Kampala until we hit the Victoria Nile, follow its descent past Murchison Falls to Lake Albert, and then trace the lake's eastern shore to the most likely point where the Bakers came upon it. The difficulty in trying to

We were now above the Murchison Falls, and we heard the roaring of the water beneath us to our left.

SAMUEL WHITE BAKER
The Albert N'yanza: Great Basin of the Nile

Previous page: Camping above Murchison Falls, just a few metres from the Nile.

tell the story of the two journeys, the Bakers' and ours, was that we were going to see the landmarks in the reverse order. Also, we were going to see some of the things that the Bakers had missed.

* * *

After our second night in Kampala, we checked out of the Grand Imperial Hotel. We were lucky in our choice of hotel. We heard a gruesome story from Bart Young about what can happen at a different kind of establishment: "You have to know where to go to eat. There is lots of good local food, but be careful. One night I went out with a friend in the Wildlife Department to have dinner in a Chinese restaurant. It was very late and we were very hungry — and there was no one else in the place. I should have realized that meant something. I ordered shredded pork and rice and a vegetable. As I was hungrily devouring the shredded pork, I bit into something quite hard. When I dug the thing out of my mouth, I realized that it was the claw of a dog! We immediately lost all interest in food."

We checked again with Bart and with the Murchison Falls authorities that morning about the safety of the area we were headed for, south-west of the falls. The word we received was that, although the area was definitely dangerous, we could minimize the danger by not going north of the river. Over the past weekend, an estimated two hundred rebels had entered Uganda from Sudan.

We left Kampala along the Kampala Road, then the Bombo Road, and headed north. Monday-morning crowds carried out the usual business of an African city as we passed through the outskirts full of shops, furniture sellers, coffin sellers, motorcycles, taxis, signs, fruit and vegetable markets — and decrepit cars: all white and all caked with red dust. All the men in this busy crowd seemed to be in Western dress, the women in *busuutis*, their national dress. We saw women carrying children, and other women carrying sticks for firewood and hut-building. People riding bicycles carried enormous bundles of charcoal, beans, maize, and other produce. Within a few kilometres, however, we found ourselves back among banana plantations, pasture land for cattle, and maize fields. Stretches of eucalyptus trees, palms, and elephant grass alternated with cassava and coffee crops. The earth was still that startling shade of red. We passed several brick kilns, and guessed that the red earth was used to make the bricks. When we filled up with diesel in a UPET (Uganda Petrol) station, a white-headed vulture looked down disgustedly at us. I realized the road we were on went to Gulu, where the rebels were. Even three hundred kilometres away, they were too close for comfort.

The Oris rebels were camped at the north-west end of Murchison Falls National Park. Their plan was to cross the Albertine Nile, join the Kony Olli Langy Group, which was camped near Karuma and Paraa — at the north-east and north-west edges of the park, respectively — on the Victoria Nile. Both Karuma and Paraa are actually on the river. We had no idea what we were

Abandoned Russian T-155 tank.

heading into, but we kept going, stopping to buy tomatoes, onions, bananas, rice, and a few other supplies — just as a precaution.

We met no other traffic, but just kept between the twin red ribbons of earth that bordered the straight, grey, paved road. Occasional potholes kept us alert. I found the absence of traffic ominous.

As we continued north-west to Lake Albert, through an avenue of tall trees that looked like pines, the landscape became more arid. It also appeared much more rural, with fewer settlements. I wondered if this paved road was built on "the highroad to Kamrasi's" that Speke had referred to.

At Nakasongola, the road suddenly veered north-west past rock outcroppings. It was still practically deserted. Not quite what I had expected. But it was a very good road and I liked the atmosphere. It was good to be back in the bush again — in dry savanna country, among acacia trees. I felt exhilarated. I was chastened somewhat, however, when we passed a derelict army tank at the side of the road, abandoned, no doubt, by Amin's forces when they fled. This one was a T-155 Russian tank — presumably Libyan-financed. Amin had found asylum with Gaddafi in Libya when he was first ousted.

With maps spread wherever I could put them, including my lap, I studied our route, knowing we were nearly at the end of the paved road. I anxiously kept an eye out for a particular bridge which heralded a turn-off westward — towards the safety of Masindi. Thad Peterson, who drove while I tried to navigate, grew increasingly tense. "For God's sake help me find this turn-off!" he cried. "If we don't find the damn bridge and get to Masindi, we'll be in Karuma with the rebels!" I knew exactly how he felt.

Planning to avoid the rebels east of the Nile.

We found the bridge over the eastward-flowing Kafu River. This is another of the rivers that used to flow west before the land rose and tilted, thousands of years ago. After we crossed the Kafu River we stayed on the main road north running parallel to the Victoria Nile. I wanted to keep the river between me and potential trouble, although it would have been interesting to look in at Masindi Port, close to the site of Kamrasi's capital. We turned off to Murchison Falls, taking a rough track through gorgeous open savanna country. Acacia trees dotted the landscape. What a contrast to the busy metropolis we had left only three hours earlier. I felt relieved to be in the freedom of the open spaces and away from the hubbub of crowded Kampala. We crossed a tributary of the Kafu, flowing west to join the river. I recalled that the Bakers had followed the Kafu on their way to Luta Nzigé.

* * *

Samuel Baker must surely be regarded as the great Victorian swashbuckling explorer. In fact, he embodied many of the values the Victorians held most dear, including the privilege of being exempt from having to do anything so mundane as work for a living. As the son of a man who was a bank director, railway magnate, and shipowner, Baker was wealthy enough never to have to worry about money. His family had made its fortune mainly in Jamaica and Mauritius, and for Baker the money was virtually inexhaustible. But this did not mean that the energetic Baker was inclined to be idle or live a life of luxurious ease. On the contrary, he was gifted with a personality that perfectly blended the adventurous with the practical.

Samuel White Baker was born in London, on June 8, 1821. Quite early in his life, he designed several guns and had them made to his specifications. When he was seventeen, he had become so familiar with guns that he was telling every military man who would listen to him that the British army should issue rifles rather than smooth-bore weapons to its soldiers.

In 1843, he married Henrietta Martin, a childhood friend, and travelled with her first to Mauritius, to the Baker family's estate, then to Ceylon in 1848, where he settled for a time, founding the town of Nuwara Eliya. The Bakers returned to England in 1855, where both fell ill. Hoping to recover, they took a restorative trip to the Spanish Pyrenees. However, Henrietta contracted typhus and died on December 29, 1855.

Baker, at a loose end, wandered aimlessly, first visiting his brothers serving in the Crimea in 1856, then in the Balkans with Duleep Singh, the Maharajah of Punjab, in 1858–59. He managed the construction of a railway connecting the Danube to the Black Sea in 1859–60. In February 1859, he met Florence Ninian von Sass, the woman who was to become his second wife. A beautiful, blonde Hungarian refugee, Florence literally owed Baker her life. She had been taken captive by Turks and was being sold as a slave in the Turkish market of Widdin. Baker bought her on sight, and they became inseparable.

Baker said of himself that he required constant change. This freedom of spirit was perfectly captured in his so-called marriage to Florence — a liaison which would have been totally scandalous in England. It is said that Baker and Florence underwent some sort of legalization of their union in Hungary before they left for Africa, but I am absolutely sure that in Victorian England no man or woman would have considered them legally married. Theirs was one of the great love stories. They were devoted to each other. Not only did Florence unquestioningly follow Baker everywhere, she dressed in trousers, refused to scream even when threatened by wild animals, chastised an African king when he demanded that she remain in his court without her husband, and even allowed her fair skin to tan as brown as a bean while her Victorian sisters stayed at home behind screens to protect their skin from firelight.

Even in the heart of Africa, Florence always idolized Baker. Years after their trip, she told her stepdaughter how lucky she felt to have a man who "had foreseen and provided for the difficulties by having a large supply of good tools — such as spades, hoes, billhook, etc. And he always went many, many miles ahead in a small rowing boat to sound the depth of water and to explore the miserable and fearful country generally."

About 1858, Baker became interested in African exploration. When his plans for an expedition to the Limpopo River came to nothing, he set out to investigate the Nile sources, beginning, in 1861, with the tributaries of the Blue Nile in Abyssinia (now Ethiopia). In mid-June 1862, after a year in

Abyssinia, the Bakers reached Khartoum at the junction of the Blue Nile and the White Nile. While there, they received a telegram from the Royal Geographical Society asking them to travel south to Gondokoro in search of Speke and Grant, who had not been heard from in more than a year.

Baker agreed. He would find Speke and Grant, or the source of the Nile, or both.

It was 1,600 kilometres from Khartoum to Gondokoro. To get there the Bakers had to navigate the Sudd, a vast, matted, tangled swamp infested with crocodiles and mosquitoes. It nearly killed them. Yet they made a relatively quick trip, taking only forty days. They set out in December 1862 and arrived in Gondokoro at the beginning of February 1863.

Gondokoro was a small settlement at a place on the Nile where the free-flowing rapids of the mountain river (the Bahr el Jebel) gave way to the giant swamp. It was a frontier town, full of raucous, hard-drinking traders. South of Gondokoro was unknown territory. Somewhere in that uncharted region, Speke and Grant were presumed to be wandering — if they were still alive. Thus it was much to Baker's amazement that, on February 15, 1863, he looked up and saw the two explorers coming towards him.

> *I had been waiting at Gondokoro twelve days.... Suddenly on 15 February, I heard a rattle of musketry at a great distance, and a dropping fire from the south.... My men rushed madly to my boat, with the report that two white men were with them who had come from the sea! Could they be Speke and Grant? Off I ran, and soon met them in reality; hurrah for old England!! they had come from the Victoria N'yanza, from which the Nile springs....*
>
> SAMUEL WHITE BAKER
> ***The Albert N'yanza: Great Basin of the Nile***

Speke was thrilled to see his old friend, and he and Baker were soon deep in conversation. But although Baker's pleasure in the meeting was genuine, he could hardly ignore the fact that he might have made the trip for nothing. The Bakers had travelled up the Nile and through the Sudd, a hideously difficult journey. Now they learned that Speke had seen Ripon Falls and decided that the problem of the Nile was settled once and for all. Baker had to hide his disappointment that his journey might have been in vain.

Speke threw Baker a crumb, however, and the Bakers' trip took on an entirely new meaning.

> *At the first blush on meeting them I had considered my expedition as terminated by having met them, and by their having accomplished the discovery of the Nile source; but upon my congratulating them with all my heart, upon the honour they had so nobly earned, Speke and Grant with characteristic candour and generosity gave me a map of their route, showing that they had been unable to complete the*

actual exploration of the Nile, and that a most important portion still remained to be determined.... I had been much disheartened at the idea that the great work was accomplished, and that nothing remained for exploration; I even said to Speke, "Does not one leaf of the laurel remain for me?"

SAMUEL WHITE BAKER
The Albert N'yanza: Great Basin of the Nile

With renewed vigour, the Bakers now prepared to resume their travels southward. But before they could set out from Gondokoro they were faced with a mutiny by their porters, of whom only two remained faithful, Richarn, a servant who had become attached to their party in Abyssinia, and Saat, a boy who had been abandoned in Khartoum and whom they had adopted. They also faced growing unrest to the south. The depredations of the slave traders operating out of Gondokoro had ensured that anyone travelling into the lake region from the north would face great hostility from the local population.

Eventually, on the morning of March 26, 1863, the Bakers set out, intent on staying ahead of the Turkish slaver and ivory-trader Ibrahim. But when Ibrahim overtook them, they negotiated with him and agreed to travel together. Their pace was now set by the trader — faster in travel, but slower during periods of business. They stayed in the land of the Lutakas until June. Then they moved on to Obbo, where they stayed until January 5, 1864. They passed through Shua, and reached the Nile on January 22 at the town of Atada, near the Karuma Falls where, fourteen months earlier, Speke and Grant had begun their overland journey from the Nile to Gondokoro.

It took the Bakers ten months to get as far as Speke and Grant had travelled in the reverse direction in only three months. At that point they

Baker on his riding-bullock, 1863.

were less than halfway through their eventual journey from Gondokoro to Lake Albert and back. The treachery of their porters, which had begun even before they set out, continued unabated. Malaria plagued them throughout their journey, and they dosed themselves liberally with quinine to help battle the symptoms of the fever.

But there was startling adventure, too, adventure that was to hold Baker's readers spellbound when he later wrote about his travels.

The Englishman and his fair wife were a constant source of amazement to the natives, and Baker was clever in taking advantage of this. At Atada, they at last made useful contact with Kamrasi's men. Interestingly, the natural boundary of the Nile itself — rather than some arbitrary and artificial line — was the actual border of Kamrasi's kingdom. In order to be allowed to cross it, Baker made himself look as much like Speke as possible and called himself Speke's brother:

> *"Let us look at him," cried the headman in the boat; having prepared for the introduction by changing my clothes in a grove of plantains for my dressing-room, and altering my costume to a tweed suit, something similar to that worn by Speke, I climbed up a high and almost perpendicular rock that formed a natural pinnacle on the face of the cliff, and, waving my cap to the crowd on the opposite side, I looked almost as imposing as Nelson in Trafalgar Square.*
>
> SAMUEL WHITE BAKER
> ***The Albert N'yanza: Great Basin of the Nile***

They reached M'ruli, Kamrasi's capital, on February 6, but Florence was very ill with fever. The Bakers were then quite close to Lake Albert, but could not reach it without the cooperation of Kamrasi, who was irascible and greedy for gifts. He was also distrustful. He openly voiced his opinion that he thought Baker was lying about wanting only to see the lake. In Kamrasi's mind, no man would ever leave his own country and his own people merely to gaze on a body of water.

The time spent trapped in Kamrasi's court was a miserable experience, made worse by rain and frequent attacks of malaria. At times the normally exuberant Baker showed signs of becoming completely despondent: "I am thoroughly sick of this expedition. I shall plod along with dogged obstinacy, but God only knows the end.... white ants and rats, robbers and small pox, these are my companions and neighbours."

Then, on February 22, 1864, Kamrasi offered Baker a surprising deal: He would give Baker passage to the lake, men to escort him there, and a virgin to amuse himself with. In exchange, Kamrasi wanted the loan of Florence while Baker was out on his lake mission. Both the Bakers at once attacked Kamrasi — Samuel with a gun and Florence with an enraged speech in Arabic. The gun was not fired and the Arabic was not understood, but Kamrasi let them go.

They left the next day, following the Kafu River westward. Florence suffered a severe case of sunstroke. Thinking — with good reason — that she was indeed about to die, Baker asked himself: "Is so terrible a sacrifice to be the result of my selfish exile?" Florence appeared to be near death for a week. There was almost no food, and Baker himself collapsed. Miraculously, they both rallied. Following the course of the Kafu River, they soon neared the great lake. Baker spent a sleepless night, thinking about the years he had spent preparing for and travelling to achieve the moment in which he might drink "at the mysterious fountain ... at that great reservoir of Nature that ever since creation had baffled all discovery."

They were up before dawn the next day.

> *The day broke beautifully clear, and having crossed a deep valley between the hills, we toiled up the opposite slope. I hurried to the summit. The glory of our prize burst suddenly upon me! There, like a sea of quicksilver, lay far beneath the grand expanse of water — a boundless sea horizon on the south and south-west, glittering in the noonday sun, and on the west, at fifty or sixty miles' distance, blue mountains rose from the bosom of the lake to a height of about 7,000 feet above its level.*
>
> *It is impossible to describe the triumph of that moment.... I felt too serious to vent my feelings in vain cheers for victory, and I sincerely thanked God for having guided and supported us through all dangers to the good end.*
>
> SAMUEL WHITE BAKER
> *The Albert N'yanza: Great Basin of the Nile*

Baker gazed upon "that vast reservoir ... that source of bounty and of blessings to millions of human beings," and named it the Albert Nyanza — Lake Albert. "The Victoria and the Albert lakes," he declared, "are the two sources of the Nile."

There is little doubt now that Baker was right about the two lakes being the great reservoirs of the Nile, though it could be argued that they are not, strictly speaking, the sources of the Nile. Baker and Florence, however, had no doubts on March 14, 1864, when they struggled down the steep path to the lake and, "with a heart full of gratitude ... drank deeply from the sources of the Nile."

On March 15, Baker surveyed the lake from the top of the escarpment with the aid of a telescope. From the edge of the 460-metre-high escarpment at the edge of the lake, in clear air, would he not have been able to see the southern shore? Probably not. Perhaps he was too far north, or his illness affected his eyesight, or there was mist to the south, or all of these. It does not matter. For whatever reason, he reached the conclusion that the lake stretched far to the south. The Nkusi River flows west into Lake Albert from the same swamp that the Kafu River flows out of to the east. If the Bakers

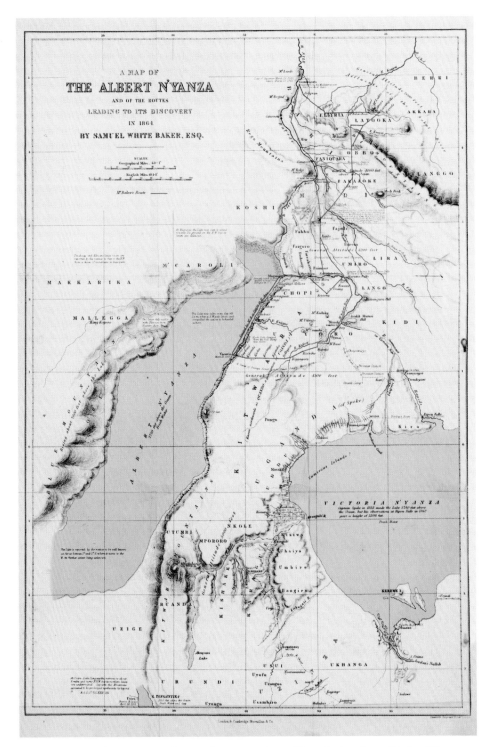

Baker's extraordinary map, showing his estimation of the relative sizes of Lake Albert (which he reached in 1864) and Lake Victoria.

had actually followed the Kafu from M'ruli, and then, in crossing the swamp, picked up the stream of the Nkusi, they should have arrived on the lake's shore only 20 kilometres from its southern end, and only 60 kilometres north of the Ruwenzori Mountains. The mouth of the Nkusi is about 150 kilometres from the north end of the lake.

Having reached his goal and prize, Baker, like most explorers, wanted desperately to get home and report what he had discovered. He sent most of the party north along the escarpment to Magungo at the north end of the lake, but he and Florence had to wait eight more days in the fishing village of Vakovia before Kamrasi sent the canoes he had promised them.

They set out on about March 22, but their boatmen deserted them that night and Baker had to train his irregulars for the job. On March 24 they survived a violent storm as they were crossing a large bay. Throughout the rest of the voyage northward, the weather was fine, but they had to get fresh boatmen at each village as none was willing to go farther than the next village. On about April 3, on the thirteenth day of their voyage, they reached Magungo on the eastern shore of the lake, just south of the mouth of the river they assumed was Speke's Somerset River, the Victoria Nile.

Baker was tempted by the nearness of the mouth of the White Nile less than twenty kilometres away. If they could sail down the river, even part-way, there was a chance that they could reach Gondokoro before the end of April and accompany the last traders of the season in their boats to Khartoum. Otherwise, they would have to wait another six months.

At the northern end of the lake, both the appearance of the terrain and Baker's calculations of Lake Victoria's elevation above sea level as compared with that of Lake Albert told him there must be a large waterfall on the Victoria Nile above Lake Albert. Despite their eagerness to return to Gondokoro, the Bakers set out to find the cataract. Nearly fifty kilometres upriver, they heard the unmistakable distant roar of the falls and knew they had been successful.

Just before reaching the falls, Baker wrote that he felt he might have "lain down to sleep in contentment in this spot, with the consolation that, if the body had been vanquished, we died with the prize in our grasp."

In fact, they were the first Europeans to see one of nature's most dramatic waterfalls — a violent explosion of water through a narrow gorge. Baker described it as: "a grand stream ... pent up in a narrow gorge scarcely 50 yards in width; roaring furiously through the rock-bound pass ... [plunging] in one leap of about 120 feet perpendicular into a dark abyss below ... the greatest waterfall of the Nile...." He named the falls after the president of the Royal Geographical Society, Sir Roderick Murchison, and his description of it was to inspire countless visitors to follow in his footsteps, among them General Gordon, Emin Pasha, Theodore Roosevelt, and Winston Churchill.

✲ ✲ ✲

The lake was known to extend as far south as Karagwé.... [F]rom the last point, which could not be less than two degrees south latitude, the lake was reported to turn suddenly to the west, and to continue in that direction for an unknown distance.

SAMUEL WHITE BAKER
The Albert N'yanza: Great Basin of the Nile

One thing is evident to me, and I believe to the Doctor, that Sir Samuel Baker will have to curtail the Albert N'yanza by one, if not two degrees of latitude. That well-known traveller has drawn his lake far into the territory of the Warundi, while Ruanda had been placed on the eastern side; whereas a large portion of it, if not all, should be placed north of what he has designated on his map as Usige.

HENRY M. STANLEY
How I Found Livingstone

* * *

Before going to Africa, I had read that the Nile above Murchison Falls rushes turbulently forward, while below it carries on peacefully towards the north end of Lake Albert only a little way from the start of the White Nile itself. My research had led me to expect something unique. But nothing could have prepared me for the power and the beauty of the sight itself.

Murchison Falls is now in Murchison Falls National Park, a 3,840-square-kilometre area bisected by a 115-kilometre stretch of the Nile. Abundant game and flora, tracts of pristine savanna, and unspoiled woodlands are attractions that have brought thousands of tourists, although for decades civil unrest has marred the peace of the park. The park was established when a huge tract of north-western Uganda was evacuated in an attempt to stop the spread of an epidemic of sleeping sickness.

As we entered the park from the east through the Kichumbanyobo Gate, I considered how it had taken the Bakers two years to cover as much territory as I could cover in a day. I found it appropriate that the renowned falls are now part of a park. The park at Murchison Falls is a beautiful drawing card, and its existence protects animals at a time when game hunting in Africa is big business, and hunters pay huge amounts of money for their trophies.

The fall of water was snow-white, which had a superb effect as it contrasted with the dark cliffs that walled the river, while the graceful palms of the tropics and wild plantains perfected the beauty of the view. This was the greatest waterfall of the Nile, and in honour of the distinguished President of the Royal Geographical Society, I named it the Murchison Falls, as the most important object throughout the entire course of the river.

SAMUEL WHITE BAKER
The Albert N'yanza: Great Basin of the Nile

A more natural replacement for our ingenious shower device.

These vast tracts set aside as parks prevent the aimless slaughter of animals and also protect important wildlife habitats from brutal deforestation. As a director of the World Wildlife Fund (WWF) in Canada, I am often asked why we need national parks and what the future holds for the concept of enormous reserves. The WWF advocates increasing the size of national parks to protect not just endangered species, but also endangered spaces. I am very much in favour of this. I believe, too, that good fences make good neighbours. The best fences in the world are natural boundaries: rivers, mountains, forests. When selected areas are made into parks, particularly along borders, potential antagonists may find peaceful coexistence easier.

Protected natural areas can be effectively policed. They can also bring tourists and hard currency into a region. The creation of vast stretches of parkland can garner the support of wealthy countries, businesses, and individuals. The payoff for everyone — and for the environment — is well worth the investment.

Our plan had been to drive north by north-west from Kampala to Murchison Falls and then west to the tip of Lake Albert. I was eagerly looking forward to learning more about the Nile at first hand, following stretches of the great river and camping on its banks. I was beginning to feel a sense of connection with the Nile by now, and it was a marvellous feeling. But with the experience at Murchison Falls, I entered a new phase, of deepening enjoyment and pleasure — almost as though I were rediscovering favourite familiar places instead of seeing them for the first time.

We asked about the danger from terrorists before we entered the park, and again were told that camping would be safe above the falls as long as we kept to the south side of the river. Although the park is in Uganda, the area north of the river is now almost totally controlled by Sudanese rebels. Everything north of the Nile was dangerous, particularly at the north end of Lake Albert. This was practically a no man's land. The area was heavily policed and people tended to leave other people alone. By late afternoon we had crossed more than half the length of the park. As we approached the falls on a winding game track through woodland and scrub, even over the noise of the Land Rovers' engines we could hear a faint sound in the distance. We drove on as the sun, on our left, sank over a west-flowing tributary of the Nile called the Sambaiya. Through the grass and the trees, as we drove, we caught glimpses of the Nile, glistening as it flowed through a landscape of small rounded hills. Three minutes later, we stopped again in a little clearing. And then we saw it — one of the most spectacular sights of my life. Its billowing spray filled the air. The cataract is not large, but it is a fierce, ferocious explosion of water, and the roar is stunning. I was too overwhelmed to speak, but I could not have made myself heard anyway. It was wonderfully exhilarating, the more so because I had not expected anything so spectacular.

We set up camp above the falls, with the great Nile thundering through the rocks and past us not five metres away — a mighty force heedless of everything and everybody. We could not talk. It drowned out all conversation except for an occasional, brief, high-pitched chatter of Swahili. Our efforts to communicate were somewhat comical.

I spent the last hour before dark photographing the falls — into the sun downriver, and then upstream towards the narrow gorge with the sun behind us. Later, clouds appeared on the horizon, so there was no sunset. But we waited around until, just before 7:00 p.m., thousands upon thousands of bats poured out of the sheer cliff face east of the falls, filling the sky above the high bank of the river. Falcons, kites, and other hawks soon gathered, swooping down to feast on their prey. There were a few successful strikes, but then the bats increased in number, and the birds disappeared, as if intimidated by sheer numbers. An amazing sight, in an extraordinary setting.

Back at the camp, Pollangyo stripped and washed himself only a few feet from the great river, using water from a canvas basin. The campfire's glow reflected against his glistening body. Ali blew on the coals to rekindle the fire for cooking our simple dinner of chicken and potatoes. A kerosene lantern lit his preparations in the now pitch-black night. Thad was under his tent, setting out his mosquito net, a circular green funnel that billowed to the floor. It was not mosquitoes he would have to worry about that night, but tsetse flies. I saw a line of bottles silhouetted against another kerosene lamp on the table in the big tent. Now and again a torch flashed on, someone going somewhere for something. The star-spangled sky arched endlessly above us. A firefly flickered across the dark horizon. And unceasingly, inescapably, the Nile thundered just a few metres away, its power palpable, awe-inspiring. The savanna surrounded us. The night enveloped us, safe beside the fire, managing a little chatter against the din.

I studied an excellent park brochure by the dim light and confirmed that Murchison Falls National Park, in north-western Uganda, is the country's biggest animal reserve. The Nile flows through the park from Karuma Falls in the east to Lake Albert in the west. An area called Acholiland lies north of the river, and to the south lies Bunyoro. Karuma Game Reserve (713 square kilometres) borders the park on the east and Bugungu Game Reserve (748 square kilometres) on the south.

The river rushes between Karuma Falls and Murchison Falls for a total drop of three hundred metres. The prehistoric rock wall of the western rift valley barely manages to contain this torrent until it blasts through the narrow gorge, then spills into what fishermen call the Devil's Cauldron at the bottom. Below Murchison Falls, the Nile is slower and wider, flowing fifty kilometres farther until it reaches Lake Albert.

I also dipped into an interesting guidebook to Murchison Falls, written by Shaun Mann. The Victoria Nile, he informed me, is considered by geologists to be young, having been created after the formation, about 500,000 years ago, of the Great Rift Valley system. It appears from the evidence of fossils that, about 300,000 years ago, a much larger lake, Semliki, incorporated Lake Albert, Lake Edward, and Lake George. Geologists believe a river flowed north from Lake Semliki, but whether it was a precursor of the Albertine Nile and where it originated remain a mystery. When the land rose to form the Ruwenzori Mountains, the large lake was split into three. A river called the Semliki links the lakes, carrying water from the mountains to the Nile. When one considers that the Alps were formed 30 million years ago, it's easy to see why geologists consider the Ruwenzoris young. This mountain system — as well as other parts of East Africa — are still prone to earthquakes and volcanoes.

Prehistoric tools have been found in Murchison Falls National Park. The tribes which were evacuated when the park was established had lived there for generations of unrecorded time. I knew that the European explorers who had first stood in the place I was standing were not the discoverers of the falls — except, perhaps, in the sense that any uniquely thrilling experience represents a discovery of a sort. In that sense, simply as a source of awe and wonder, Murchison Falls will always be a discovery well worth pursuing.

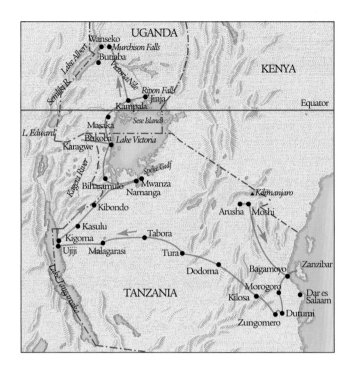

The Glory of Our Prize:
Murchison Falls to Lake Albert

I had traced the river to its great Albert source, and as the mighty stream glided before me, the mystery that had ever shrouded its origin was dissolved. I no longer looked upon its waters with a feeling approaching to awe for I knew its home, and had visited its cradle.

Samuel White Baker
The Albert N'yanza: Great Basin of the Nile

9

THE GLORY OF OUR PRIZE: MURCHISON FALLS TO LAKE ALBERT

Morning on the river Nile — after quite a night. Although I was asleep before 10:00 p.m., I awoke shortly after midnight to what sounded like an enormous downpour all around me. Of course, what it really was, was the Nile, pounding furiously along barely three metres from my tent. The night was balmy, but I had trouble getting back to sleep. I tossed and turned and slapped at invisible, hungry mosquitoes. I also dwelt on certain discomforting facts: for example, in a turbulent lagoon just below the falls, a hippopotamus bull had charged the Bakers' boat, lifting it half out of the water and nearly toppling the occupants into a part of the river that was — and still is — home to hungry crocodiles. I then thought about the track above the falls on which hippos must travel to the river and half convinced myself that our tents were pitched right on it.

There were pancakes and sausages for breakfast and strong coffee, which I needed badly. There was not much of a sunrise, again because of clouds, but it did not matter. There was nowhere else I would rather be. I took another sip of the scorching black brew.

En route to Paraa, we drove through the western end of the park, which was almost devoid of game — obliterated under Idi Amin. At Paraa, we set out to motor up the Nile in the riverboat *Kiboko*, which in Swahili means, appropriately, "hippopotamus." An antique launch, ten metres long, with

Upon rounding the corner, a magnificent sight burst suddenly upon us. On either side the river were beautifully wooded cliffs rising abruptly to a height of about 300 feet; rocks were jutting out from the intensely green foliage; and rushing through a gap that cleft the rock exactly before us, the river, contracted from a grand stream, was pent up in a narrow gorge of scarcely fifty yards in width; roaring furiously through the rock-bound pass, it plunged in one leap of about 120 feet perpendicular into a dark abyss below.

SAMUEL WHITE BAKER
The Albert N'yanza: Great Basin of the Nile

The Devil's Cauldron at the foot of Murchison Falls.

[B]oys are very ingenious little fellows, and have several games....

DR. DAVID LIVINGSTONE
Final journal, 1872

Previous page: Boys playing on the shores of Lake Albert.

metal struts holding up the roof, a few seats inside, and an engine in front, it was manned by the captain and one crew member. It made a distinctive chugging sound as we proceeded up the river close to the banks. The wildlife was amazingly abundant and varied. This one little strip of the Nile between Paraa and Murchison Falls seemed idyllic, a perfect habitat for wildlife: malachite kingfishers, red-throated bee-eaters, African jacanas, African darters, great white egrets, little egrets, cattle egrets, purple herons, African skimmers, long-toed lapwings, spur-winged plovers, a black-headed weaver, a Goliath heron, a purple gallinule (possibly Allen's gallinule), eastern grey plantain-eaters, spur-winged geese, Egyptian geese. We spotted several African fish eagles motionless on their perches — waiting, waiting ... and then suddenly the dive. But these joys were tempered by the clouds of tsetse flies that swarmed around us whenever we got near the bank. The Bakers' riding oxen had finally succumbed to tsetse-fly bites along this same stretch of the river.

The Nile was about four hundred metres wide at this point, about three kilometres below the falls. We were seeing the Nile exactly as Samuel Baker had seen it just over 130 years before us. Savanna and forest land stretched away on either side of the river. Once in a while, we saw an illegal fishing line tied on the bank, dipping into the river. They would have been trying for Nile perch, tiger fish, tilapia, and catfish. A Nile perch weighing eighty-six kilograms — the record — was caught here in 1995, by Francis Bella, a German.

Baker wrote that he, Florence, and their men managed to capture one half of a Nile perch from a crocodile, who had eaten the other half. The Bakers' half weighed 68 kilograms. Nile perch have become one of the best game fish of East Africa, and people go there just for this sport. The fish are enormous, obviously a different species from the little perch one gets in North America or England. *Lates niloticus* is a freshwater fish found throughout the Nile system, and also in the Congo, the Niger, the Volta, and Lake Chad. A related species, *Lates albertainus*, is found in Lake Albert and the Nile near Murchison Falls, but nowhere else. This species grows to nearly two metres in length and can weigh well over 135 kilograms. One of the reasons sport fishers value Nile perch so much is that they break water and put up quite a fight before being landed. They feed on other fish, so fishermen use smaller fish as bait.

Nile perch are sometimes speared after dark, and their eyes are rumoured to glow red in the lights used to attract them. They were known to the ancient Egyptians, and mummified remains of the fish have been found. There is some evidence that Nile perch may once have been the object of cult worship.

We gazed out over the river, a huge expanse of water. Silhouettes of acacia trees broke the line of the horizon — several shades of green against the light brown earth. It took two hours to get from Paraa to the falls, a trip that had taken the Bakers two days. Our guide was George Nube. He had been in

Hippos on the Nile below Murchison Falls.

Murchison Falls National Park for twenty years — a dedicated man who knew practically everything about the local wildlife. He had keen eyesight and seemed to see everything, far and near. He was confident, smiling, interested, readily asking and answering questions. He wore a green beret, an olive-green uniform, and ankle-high leather boots. He generally perched like a heron on the rail of the *Kiboko*, his back to the sun.

Quite suddenly, we rounded a curve in the river and saw the falls in the distance — a white spume boiling down a forty-eight-metre cliff between steep green banks. The chugging of the motor still masked the roar of the water being battered to foam on the rocks at the base of the falls. When I turned to look behind us, the sun's reflection seemed to drift on the surface of the river. Hippos wallowed near both banks, and large numbers of basking crocodiles lay about. A pied kingfisher hovered for a few seconds above the water, then speared downwards to catch its midday meal.

We went as far as we could go, up to the big rock about eight hundred metres from the falls. With the engines off it was peaceful, the boom of the falls the only sound. A pillar of spray rose into the air, dazzlingly white in the morning sun. In the distance, small clouds sailed against a hazy, light-blue sky. Swallows flitted. Pied kingfishers hovered, and in the distance, again and again, rang the mocking call of a fish eagle. To the right were the cliffs where, the night before, bats in their thousands had blackened the evening sky. The river flowed past us and away. Source of life. Source of plenty.

Bajao is the name the local Luo people give to the falls. *Bajao* means "devil's place," our guide told us. But it seemed like a paradise to me. Turbulent but dramatically satisfying. An end and a beginning.

At last, we turned about and headed back downstream. The sun rose higher in the sky, gleaming through the mist from the falls as we slipped through the narrows. Where the river widened out, half-submerged hippos stared glassy-eyed at us. A family of warthogs watched our progress from the northern bank. We passed the crocodiles again — still basking in the sun, their jaws open to help them stay cool, like dogs panting. Everyone was silent again. Silenced by the majesty of the falls. An hour downriver from the falls we reached Paraa again, then drove back to camp for a late lunch.

African fish eagle.

* * *

At 6:10 p.m., we watched the sunset over the Nile at Murchison Falls, first from the top of the escarpment and then from immediately above the falls, looking down through the gorge. The billowing spray blurred the golden horizon. I got soaked photographing. My most ambitious shot was from the very edge of the rock cliff looking down to the swirling waters below. The local park warden held my belt while I leaned over the abyss. Terrifying, but I got the shot. Drenched, I got back to camp by 6:38 p.m.

I showered under an acacia tree. What an ingenious contraption that plastic shower was. My God, but it was hot that day! Sweat had run down my body in rivulets. It was all washed away now with the cooling shower. I loved standing naked in the bush, water forming little pools around my feet in the mud amid thorns and stones. I sipped a cold Tanzanian Safari beer, then ate dried vegetables and rice for dinner. Thad had caught a catfish in the Nile that afternoon, and the guide had caught some carplike fish that was much larger. They said there was too much water, that the water was too high and the fish did not seem to be biting on their lures at all. The fish, it seemed, only wanted *ugali*!

It was a clear, cool, starry night. There were fireflies all over the place but, for a change, not many mosquitoes. We were silent around the campfire after dinner, just listening to the roar of the river only a few metres away. It was almost part of us now. Tomorrow we would head downstream to Lake Albert.

* * *

We left our idyllic spot above Murchison Falls as the sun rose over streaked clouds upstream to the east. No golden glow lit the sky, but the scene was magical all the same. I learned that the local name for the carplike fish the guide had caught the night before was *kasinga*. It was almost four kilograms and very scaly. We had to leave it behind with the guide, who was preserving it by smoking as we left.

After we broke camp we headed first for the Bugungu Gate of Murchison Falls National Park. Almost an hour later, we turned off and saw leopard scat on the road and leopard paw prints in the soil. We left the park about 9:30 a.m. and drove to the Bugungu Reserve, stopping briefly to buy two pineapples at a roadside stall. I also bought two handmade Wanyoro tribe knives and gave one to Thad.

We drove west for a while, then turned north onto a road running parallel to the north-east shore of Lake Albert. Across the water lay strife-torn Zaïre. At Wanseko, a fishing village situated right where the Nile enters the lake at its north-eastern corner, we got our first sight of Lake Albert. The town of Magungo, of Baker's time, must have been close to this northern shore of the lake.

This was the well-policed no man's land we had been told about earlier. Wanseko is a busy fishing village — we saw lots of boats, children, and dogs. From the shore we saw motor boats making their way down-channel to the Albert Nile — the White Nile — going north into rebel country. Almost certainly these were gunboats.

We turned south again, skirting the east shore of Lake Albert. Our route took us through flat land. After a police checkpoint, we entered the Bugungu Game Reserve. Just across the lake, in Zaïre, the terrain was quite mountainous. Ugandan guards were numerous. Lake Albert is a water highway used to transport all kinds of goods — provisions, certainly, but also vehicles and guns — carrying them north into Uganda and west into Zaïre. Wanseko is a key point — hence the heavy police presence.

Police apart, the eastern shore of the lake is a haven of tranquillity, well wooded and dotted with little fishing villages. We crossed the Waiga River — small, brown, not much more than a stream — flowing west into the lake. We saw baboons on the road — they are common around all human settlements outside the cities. They can become quite aggressive in their demands for food. Experienced travellers know enough to be wary of them, but tourists always have to be warned not to take them for granted.

At the turn-off to the fishing village of Butiaba, we picked up a hitch-hiker, a man of the Wanyoro tribe. He was carrying a bag of maize, fishing floats, chains, rock weights, and a clothes bag. We piled all this on the Land Rovers and drove the eight kilometres into town. He told us about the local drink, *waragi*, a strong beer made from bananas, and also about the *Robert Calendon*, a boat that used to ferry people the length of Lake Albert until it sank in 1961.

Butiaba was a typical fishing village, with the usual assortment of boats and birds, among them marabou storks, sacred ibis, and terns. Palmyra palms and the lakeshore bounded the village on the west, the hills of the

The north end of Lake Albert, with the Victoria Nile in the distance entering the lake.

escarpment on the south and east. On the shore, Wanyoro men, women, and children mended nets and bought, sold, and filleted fish. A cooling breeze blew from the lake. To me, this busy but peaceful village seemed like a little Eden. We decided to spend the night here. After lunch, we met the chief of the village, Mulinda Seremosi of the Wagungu — a subtribe of the Wanyoro. He invited us to stay in his compound, saying that it was safer this way and would give us some privacy away from the village crowds. We accepted gratefully and drove the Land Rovers right inside the compound. This inner court was about forty-six metres square, with the chief's thatched, mud-walled hut right in the centre. His wife, Nyamuhu, sat on a mat in front of the house, knitting — definitely the most important woman in the compound. She was in charge of everything — food, money, and all matters of protocol.

After some haggling, Thad and I hired a wooden boat for an afternoon's fishing on Lake Albert. The deal included an outboard motor and two villagers as guides. It did not look as if the vessel would stay afloat, or even

hold together for long, but we managed. We left at about 2:30 p.m. and returned after 6:00 p.m., just as the sun was setting. It was a wonderful afternoon. Thad and I each had several strikes of Nile perch, but the fish just took the line out and broke it, and that was the end of that. At least we had the thrill of having one of these huge monsters on for a moment, and also the pleasure of just being out fishing.

✳ ✳ ✳

In the 1960s, the Nile perch was introduced to the upper Nile as an additional food source, but has produced an ecological disaster. As the largest predator, it has destroyed other species and created a virtual monoculture in Lakes Victoria and Albert. Lake Edward has escaped because the fish have not been able to travel upstream past the cataracts between Lakes Albert and Edward. Interestingly, the people near Lake Albert seem to have their own theories as to why the thing is out of balance in Lake Victoria. They believe there were experiments on the western bank, and, during the rains, fish from a hatchery were washed into the lake.

Fish drying at Butiaba.

Another version is that in 1954 seven Nile perch were imported into the waters above Murchison Falls in a bathtub carried up the escarpment by a game warden. More fish were introduced during the next four years, but then it was discovered that the Nile perch could get into Lake Victoria through the turbines of the dam at Owen Falls. By the time scientists became aware of the detrimental environmental impact of the fish on Lake Victoria, it was too late. Now the species makes up an estimated 80 per cent of the lake's fish population.

* * *

When we were out fishing, we talked freely with our two guides. They told us that, in the morning, fishermen from the Uganda side go out into the middle of Lake Albert and meet fishermen from Zaïre. They are all quite friendly, and discuss politics and current events, and get first-hand information that way. They are far better informed than the general public, who have to get their distorted news second- or third-hand in the newspapers. Theirs is a simple life. They know what is going on, but keep to their daily routine and to themselves, hoping that the crazy world will leave them alone. The area remains relatively unspoiled because it is off the beaten track for tourists. The villagers make money from the fish, which are regularly trucked to the cities for sale to hotels and restaurants. The perch are a huge source of revenue, the mainstay of the local economy.

At sunset, we returned to the serenity of the village. Near the shore, fishing boats came in and went out. Children and women washed. Fishermen tended their boats and mended their nets. In the village, people chattered, cocks crowed, children laughed, and everyone seemed quite

Fisherman and Nile perch catch from Lake Albert.

relaxed and happy. In the distance, some Zaïrean music blared from a radio, but even that did not spoil the magic of the moment. It was wonderful to be there, and I remembered the tranquil and contented moments the early explorers treasured despite their discomforts and anxieties.

Of course, for the Bakers, any thought of lingering in an idyllic spot would have been offset by their anxious desire to return to civilization in order to report their findings as quickly as possible — just in case somebody else got back first and beat them to the prize.

*　✳ ✳ ✳*

In the chief's compound, we pitched our tents almost in a straight line on a small rectangle of grass in front of the wooden reed fence. They did not look too incongruous. The main tent was about the same height as the thatched huts in the compound. The villagers seemed extremely relaxed about our being there. Of course, as the honoured guests of the chief we were treated with some respect. The children, always curious, peered into the compound. If we stared at them long enough, they giggled and ran away with shrieks of embarrassed laughter.

Pollangyo and I looked across the silent lake at the mountains of Zaïre on the other side. "Do you think we should go there?" I asked him.

"Only if you want to die," he answered.

Like so many African nations, Zaïre has had different names under different regimes. The exploration of the area by Stanley was financed by King Leopold II of Belgium (1835-1909). Leopold founded the Congo Free State in 1885. He ruled it directly until 1908, plundering the territory, and increasing his own wealth exponentially. In 1908, the country's status changed to that of a colony of Belgium, and it was renamed Belgian Congo. In 1960, it gained its independence and became known as the Democratic Republic of the Congo. Years of civil unrest followed. In 1971, United Nations intervention stopped the hostilities. However, this still did not bring peace to the country. When I was there in late 1996, the current leader was Mobutu Sese Seko, another tyrant who plundered Zaïre in much the same way that Leopold had. Since 1965, when he came to power, he had supposedly siphoned $6 billion of the country's money into his private overseas bank accounts. In 1971, as part of his clash with the Roman Catholic Church, he declared a policy of "Africanization." He changed his name from Joseph Désiré Mobutu to Mobutu Sese Seko Kuru Ngebendu Wa Za Banga; the name of the country to Zaïre (the Portuguese transliteration of the native name "big river"); and the name of Lake Albert to Lake Mobutu Sese Seko. He was overthrown soon after I completed my journey and has since died. Zaïre is now called the Democratic Republic of the Congo again.

Before I reached Lake Albert, Zaïre was always "over there" — some distance west of Lake Victoria and beyond Lake Tanganyika and the Ruwenzoris. So I thought that whatever was happening there did not really affect me. But suddenly I was looking right at Zaïre, and Mobutu was in the very process of being overthrown. We could not ignore the political tension in the area. It was caused by the process and effects of colonization that had shaped East and Central Africa. The British explorers in whose steps I walked were part of the colonial system and had helped Britain extend its power into the area. We were very aware that we were witnessing first-hand some of the fall-out from colonialism.

* * *

Dinner that night was relaxed and happy. Joshua and Ali cooked up the most incredible meal: Nile perch prepared two separate ways, one fried, the other in a marvellous African Creole sauce. The sauce tasted like a mixture of coconut milk (of which there was none), white wine (again, none there), garlic, and tomato. We had several helpings, plus sweet potato and cabbage — all washed down with Nile beer. Everyone seemed quite high, and not just from alcohol. I thought they must be smoking something — *bhang*, perhaps. Even the chief's wife seemed to be walking on air — coming and going into the compound with a flashing torch and walking arm in arm with her lady-in-waiting. Around us were the sounds of village life — high-pitched, excited chatter, Zaïrean music, a cow mooing. The music of the night.

* * *

Unexpectedly, just after 5:00 a.m., it rained — at first a few rain drops pattering on my tent, and then a heavier downpour. Thunder rolled in the distance — a different sound from the rush and roar of the mighty Nile, to which I had awoken the day before. An hour later, the cocks began to crow. It sounded as though they were right in the compound, and all around it. The cows began mooing again, and almost immediately the village burst into life, as if in a great hurry. I could see a few streaks of light across the sky through the opening of my tent. The rain stopped, leaving the air clean and fresh.

Outside the compound the villagers washed at the edge of the lake, beside the boats hauled up on the beach. The villagers use open boats with high bows. They are flimsy wooden constructions held together by struts and a few nails. There were as many as thirty boats in this small village alone. Three boats headed out early onto the lake, getting a head start on the day's fishing. Two marabou storks glided down onto the soft, sandy beach. A flock of white cattle egrets flew across the horizon in formation, and twelve metres from shore a single grey heron stood regally on a post sticking out of the water. Dark clouds sat on the eastern horizon, hiding the sunrise. But across the lake the mountains of Zaïre were clearly visible, and off to the south the Ruwenzoris waited.

As I got ready for the day, women swept the sand inside the compound with reed brushes. They were so industrious that within minutes the square was clear and pristine. I was reluctant to walk on it in my boots. Everybody else was in bare feet. Chickens pecked away at the newly swept sand, looking for a morning morsel. The chief's wife stood outside her large thatched hut, surveying the scene and looking stern and disapproving. She gave us a perfunctory nod. We were intruders, but not unwelcome. The grey clouds threatening more rain seemed to put a damper on the day's affairs.

As I thought about how to say goodbye to the chief and his wife and their lovely village, I knew also that I had finished following the Bakers' journey. After their discovery of Lake Albert and Murchison Falls, weary, short of quinine and other supplies, they again found themselves in Kamrasi's court. Baker successfully strove to impress him by wearing Highland garb. It was not until September 1864 that a caravan of Arab slavers arrived from Gondokoro with mail and stores. The Bakers joined the slavers and travelled north, reaching Gondokoro in February 1865, two years almost to the day since they had left it. They then made the difficult way down to Khartoum, which they reached on May 15 and where they were shattered to learn of Speke's accidental death. They were in Suez by the end of August, and set out at last for England. Baker's wife, whom he described as "the devoted companion of my pilgrimage to whom I owed success and life," was with him. Her face, "still young, but bronzed ... with years of exposure to a burning sun; haggard and worn with toil and sickness, and shaded with cares," bore witness to the trials they had endured in their five-year struggle to see for themselves the sources of the Nile.

The Bakers soon became Sir Samuel and Lady Baker, acclaimed by all for their adventures. In 1866, Baker published *The Albert N'yanza: Great Basin of the Nile*, and the next year, *The Nile Tributaries of Abyssinia*. He eventually came to be known by the popular sobriquet "Baker of the Nile."

But if Baker managed to illustrate the marvels of the everyday life of the Africa he had seen, he did not actually shed much light on the mysteries of the Nile. All he really confirmed was that there was yet another lake with a river draining out of it to the north. He had no real proof of the relationship between what he had seen and what Speke had discovered. Of course, if Lake Albert were fed by an as-yet-undiscovered stream, the possibility existed that Speke's discovery at Ripon Falls was not so very important after all. Moreover, there still lingered the confusing possibility that a feeder stream for the Nile flowed out of Lake Tanganyika.

This was, apparently, Sir Roderick Murchison's analysis. On May 22, 1865, he delivered a eulogy of Speke to a meeting of the Royal Geographical Society. He then announced that the Society was about to send England's most renowned explorer, Dr. David Livingstone, to the lake district of Central Africa to straighten out the Nile issue. Livingstone's instructions were to carefully examine Lake Tanganyika to determine whether the Ruzizi River flowed into or out of the lake. If the Ruzizi could be proved to flow out of Lake Tanganyika and into Lake Albert, and if the river flowing north out of Lake Albert was the Nile, then Burton and Baker were the discoverers of the Nile source, and Speke and Grant were not.

James Grant clearly understood the threat that Baker presented, and when he found out that Baker had been knighted, he was enraged. He wrote, "By God! I never heard of anything more disgusting to us! The information about his woman too is not fair, for you know very well from poor Speke and myself the position she was in...." Apparently the irregular relationship with Florence rankled Grant nearly as much as Baker's growing fame.

Nevertheless, Baker was the archetypal Victorian explorer. The Bakers were the first Europeans to gaze upon Lake Albert. And there is little doubt that Lake Victoria and Lake Albert are the two great reservoirs of the Nile. Baker certainly made the whole Nile controversy more interesting, in part because of his own character, in part because of his relationship with Florence, and also because of his good relationship with Speke. He seems to be the only person who got anything out of Speke. It was generous of Speke to tell Baker that there was another great body of water to the south-west. This did not, however, allow Baker to solve all the riddles. On the contrary, it opened up further questions. The discoveries of Lake Albert and Murchison Falls, taken by themselves, were not as significant as the discovery of Lake Victoria and Ripon Falls.

Baker did not really provide an enormous amount of geographical data, as Speke had done. Nor did he provide anthropological data, as Burton did. Nevertheless, he was at the right place at the right time. He provided one more link in the chain — and, uniquely, added drama, glamour, and spice.

The process of pressing is managed by pounding the grain dry in a huge mortar....
RICHARD F. BURTON
The Lake Regions of Central Africa

More than anyone else he completely fulfilled the Victorian audience's expectations of what an explorer should be.

But what fascinates me most about Baker of the Nile is not what he actually discovered, but what he just missed discovering. Had Baker gone to the southern end of Lake Albert, he would have found the Semliki River, and possibly the Ruwenzori Mountains. He might well have asked himself where the Semliki came from and where it eventually went. He would have observed it winding its way into Lake Albert's southern end, and would certainly have developed a whole new set of theories about its role in the Nile system.

History is full of such near-misses. It is easy to speculate in the safety of one's study on what might have been. The truth of this was soon to become powerfully evident to me.

Women retain the power of suckling their children to a late age .... Until the child can walk without danger, it is carried by the mother, not on the hip, as in Asia, but on the bare back for warmth, a sheet or skin being passed over it and fastened at the parent's breast.

RICHARD F. BURTON
The Lake Regions of Central Africa

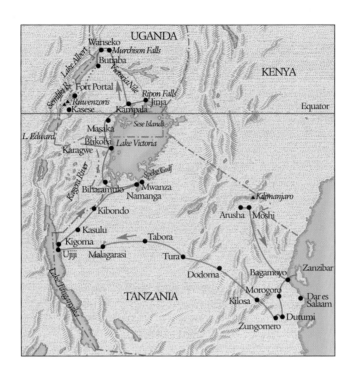

The Mountains of the Moon: The Ruwenzori Mountains and the Semliki River

[O]n the 25th of May, 1888, when scarcely two hours march from the Lake [Albert] beach, lo! a stupendous snowy mountain appeared ... an almost square-browed central mass — about thirty miles in length, and quite covered with snow; situate between two great ridges of about 5,000 feet less elevation, which extended to about thirty miles on either side of it. On that day it was visible for hours. On surmounting the table-land, the next day or so, it had disappeared....

[I]n January, 1889,... it was unseen, until suddenly casting our eyes, as usual, towards that point where it ought to be visible, the entire length of the range burst out of the cloudy darkness, and gratified over a thousand pairs of anxious eyes that fixed their gaze upon the singular and magnificent scene.

HENRY MORTON STANLEY
In Darkest Africa; or the Quest, Rescue, and Retreat of Emin, Governor of Equatoria

10

THE MOUNTAINS OF THE MOON: THE RUWENZORI MOUNTAINS AND THE SEMLIKI RIVER

D r. David Livingstone was fifty-two years old when, in 1865, he left England for his third and final journey to Africa. He was by that time a famous explorer and anti-slavery crusader whose writings and exploits had made him a household name in Britain. He had begun as a missionary in southern Africa in 1840, criss-crossing the continent, from Angola on the west coast to the mouth of the Zambezi River on the east coast, and happening upon the Victoria Falls along the way. His account of his years in Africa between 1840 and 1856, *Missionary Travels and Researches in South Africa*, published in England in 1857, made him a celebrity. His second expedition, from 1858 to 1864, took him back to the Zambezi, which he explored more fully. His third and final trip was sponsored by the Royal Geographical Society, and its purpose was to resolve the dispute over the sources of the Nile. However, his mandate from the Society probably interested him less than the anti-slavery crusade of which he was now the great spokesman and leader.

In 1833, slavery had become illegal throughout the British Empire, but enforcement of the law was very slow. The rationale for slavery was, of course, economic, based on the demand in many countries for cheap agricultural labour. Even after slavery was abolished, the demand for cheap labour continued, and produced forms of employment that were not very different from it. I recall the workers on the tea estates in the former Ceylon (Sri Lanka), where I grew up. These employees were mainly the descendants of indentured Tamil labourers conscripted by the British from south India in the mid-nineteenth century. The Tamils were transported to Ceylon because Ceylon's indigenous Singhalese had little inclination or aptitude

An old man, with white hair, and too feeble to flee ....

HENRY MORTON STANLEY
In Darkest Africa

Previous page: Flanking the path were familiar features, such as several camps of pigmies, who were here called Watwa .... The distance from the Semliki to these villages wherein we were now encamped is 15$\frac{1}{2}$ English miles, which we had taken three days to travel, and two days' halt in consequence.

HENRY MORTON STANLEY
In Darkest Africa

Men picking tea on the Uganda highland.

for manual labour. It was beneath their dignity to work in the fields, plucking shoots of tea leaves to fill a basket hanging from their shoulder. A wonderful word used in Ceylon — *nambuwa* — means "the way in which other people see you." For the Singhalese, picking tea leaves in the estates would destroy their *nambuwa*.

The Tamils were very industrious, though their living conditions were very poor. Even as a youth I could see that the Tamil workers on the tea estate were really only marginally better off than slaves. They were housed in the "lines" — long rows of one-roomed huts built of concrete and roofed with tin. The so-called plumbing was managed by building the dwellings with floors that sloped down to a communal drain. Families lived their whole lives — birth, death, and everything in between — in one room, eking out a meagre living picking tea for the British estate owners.

These workers were not slaves, of course, because the employers did not actually own the people. Nevertheless, they were virtual prisoners, since they had almost no hope of leaving for a better life somewhere else. Even today, although the estates are now managed by Singhalese (and by some Tamils), and the workers are unionized, it is still a desperately poor existence — a hangover from colonialism that threatens further escalation in the current ethnic strife in Sri Lanka.

As a boy I used to slip down to the lines to talk to the tea workers and see how they lived, though I risked punishment for doing so. Their lives fascinated me then, and I have never been able to suppress this side of my nature for long. I love meeting people in many different environments — on the road, on tea estates, in fishing villages in Africa, in jungles, on dhows in Zanzibar. I love mixing with crowds in Eastern markets. I love camping — cutting down to the bare essentials — and finding out about the lives of the people I encounter in out-of-the-way places. I struggle continually to balance this side of my nature with the comfort-loving side. Eventually, it always seems, the wanderlust wins, and I set out on my travels again.

Though I would not presume to compare myself to Livingstone, it is this side of my nature that gives me some sense of why Africa — both its people and its landscape — became so important to him. Livingstone felt at home in Africa and grew to love that land and its people — not simply as a stepping stone to fame and fortune in Britain, but for their own sake.

✳ ✳ ✳

Livingstone's third expedition was not a success. For six years, from 1865 to 1871, he explored portions of Lake Tanganyika and the Lualaba River, but was not able to clarify further the relationship, if any, between Lake Tanganyika and Lakes Victoria and Albert. Indeed, by 1871, sickened by a massacre he witnessed on the Lualaba River, he had given up any idea of following the Lualaba's course and returned, dejected, to Ujiji. It was there, on November 10, 1871, that one of the best-known events in the history of British exploration in Africa occurred: the historic meeting between Livingstone and Henry Morton Stanley.

Livingstone's role in the Nile story was not a large one, but he was important to a degree because it was his predicament that brought Stanley to Africa, and initiated the next important phase in the search for the Nile's source.

✳ ✳ ✳

Having followed Burton and Speke, Speke and Grant, and then the Bakers, I now began a part of my journey in which I could not exactly follow the routes of the explorers. I had already, of course, been to Ujiji, and I would soon complete my circuit of Lake Victoria as Stanley had done. But next on my itinerary was an area that Livingstone never reached: the Ruwenzori Mountains, Lake Edward, and whatever lay between. The itinerary I planned was one that I felt would incorporate Stanley's explorations, follow some paths that the Bakers had to leave unexplored, and, perhaps, add a few new twists to the tale.

We left our compound in Butiaba at 8:00 a.m., but were stopped as we entered the town centre and informed that there had been a murder during the night. When we reported to the police, as we had to do before leaving, we were ordered to drive one of the local policemen to Biso, ten kilometres east, so he could make radio contact with police headquarters in Masindi. People lined the street outside the police station, consternation in their faces. A

woman named Pasko, who had been accused of witchcraft, had been tortured and eventually beaten to death by a mob. A sick child had lapsed into a coma, and the villagers blamed the woman. Ironically, that morning the child seemed to have recovered. Seven other villagers were arrested, also apparently for practising witchcraft.

The assaulting of witches, sometimes resulting in their death, flares up from time to time in parts of Africa. Burton mentions that, in one country where burial was usual after death, the bodies of witches and wizards were left unburied. In 1962, a series of seven "witch-murders" near Mwanza was studied by the sociologist Ralph E.S. Tanner. He concluded that colonialism — with the introduction of the European adversarial system of justice, and the changes in the authority and responsibility of the native chiefs — had eliminated the traditional methods of discussion and compromise with which pressures used to be handled. Perhaps in Burton's time it had been the slavers' predations that drove some people to act in the same ancient, superstitious way.

After dropping the police officer at Biso, we drove south by south-west, heading towards Fort Portal, the biggest town in the Ruwenzori area. The road took us high up onto the eastern escarpment of the rift valley and gave us wonderful views of Lake Albert and Butiaba. We kept along the escarpment through lush woodlands and open fields planted with crops of bananas, papayas, and maize. We also noticed cane grass, used for fences and houses.

On the road to Fort Portal, we saw plenty to pique our interest. We crossed the Kafu River again — or, rather, the sister of the Kafu, the Nkusi, which springs from the same swamp but flows west into Lake Albert. Several times a contingent of prisoners guarded by uniformed men carrying machine-guns moved to the side of the road to let us pass. At Katoosa, we saw a shrine made of piled-up rocks which was dedicated to the twenty-two Catholic martyrs burnt by King Mwanga in 1886. The shrine was similar to one we had seen outside Kampala.

By mid-afternoon we were travelling through an area of vast tea planta-tions — low, green bushes on sloping hills along the escarpment road. Owned, or at least managed, by Ruwenzori Tea Commodities, they appeared to be in good condition, well tended. In Uganda, men seem to do the picking (in Sri Lanka and southern India this task is done by women). This was beautiful country, graced with tall eucalyptus trees, flame trees, and mango trees. The view across the plains below the ridge seemed endless. Then, about fifty kilometres ahead, we caught our first sight of the Ruwenzoris,

The office of Uganga includes many duties. The same man is a physician by natural and supernatural means, a mystagogue or medicine-man, a detector of sorcery, by means of the Judicium Dei or ordeal, a rain-maker, a conjuror, an augur, and a prophet.

RICHARD F. BURTON
The Lake Regions of Central Africa

Busy morning market in Fort Portal.

their peaks hidden in the clouds.

In the busy Fort Portal market place we bought garlic, onions, and other locally grown vegetables. As in so many of the African markets, there were all sorts of things for sale, including used clothing, leather goods, utensils, and hardware. After Ali had bought what he needed, we got back onto the main road and drove south to the town of Kasese, seventy-four kilometres farther on, passing through four police checkpoints along the way. As we travelled, we could see Lake George in the distance ahead of us. We passed a cement factory billowing smoke — an ugly blot on the horizon. We crossed the Mobuku River, which flows eastward to Lake George, and also passed the turn-off to Ruwenzori National Park.

* * *

It was Henry Morton Stanley who first brought back to England useful information about the Ruwenzoris, the Mountains of the Moon. Everything about Stanley's life was exceptional, perhaps because he possessed a verve and determination that turned everything he encountered into some kind of good luck. It was in 1869 that he received his fateful assignment from the publisher of *The New York Herald*, James Gordon Bennett, Jr. He was to attend the opening of the Suez Canal, make an extensive tour of the Crimea and the Middle East, head overland as far as India, and then return to "start looking round for Livingstone. If he is dead bring back every possible proof of his death."

Livingstone, though deeply dispirited, was of course still alive, and on

November 10, 1871, Stanley found him in Ujiji and recorded his version of their famous meeting:

> *... I did that which I thought was most dignified. I pushed back the crowds, and, passing from the rear, walked down a living avenue of people, until I came in front of the semicircle of Arabs, before which stood the "white man with the grey beard."*
>
> *As I advanced slowly towards him I noticed he was pale, that he looked wearied and wan, that he had grey whiskers and moustache, that he wore a bluish cloth cap with a faded gold band on a red ground round it, and that he had on a red-sleeved waistcoat, and a pair of grey tweed trousers.*
>
> *I would have run to him, only I was a coward in the presence of such a mob — would have embraced him, but that I did not know how he would receive me; so I did what moral cowardice and false pride suggested was the best thing — walked deliberately to him, took off my hat, and said:*
>
> *"Dr. Livingstone, I presume?"*
>
> HENRY MORTON STANLEY
How I Found Livingstone

Despite the enormous differences between them, Livingstone and Stanley became friends immediately. In one fateful meeting, both men got what they needed most. In Stanley, Livingstone had met the man to whom he could pass the baton, who could finish his work and make some sense of his explorations.

However, Livingstone did as much for Stanley as Stanley did for

Livingstone. To have his own name connected irrevocably with one of the most eminent men of the age gave Stanley a cachet that raised him from the status of renegade American journalist to that of legend.

What Livingstone had been unable to accomplish alone in nearly seven years he was able to accomplish with Stanley in less than a month. On November 16, 1871, Stanley and Livingstone set out from Ujiji for the north end of Lake Tanganyika. On November 28, they found proof that the Ruzizi River flows into, not out of, Lake Tanganyika. There were seven inlets in the mass of reeds and none showed a current, but, by penetrating up the centre channel, they came to a point where they observed a stream of discoloured water flowing towards the lake.

Plaque in Ujiji commemorating Stanley's 1871 historic meeting with Livingstone.

Further investigation showed that this stream had other channels flowing into the other inlets they had seen. This forced Livingstone to revise his theory that Lake Tanganyika drained north into Lake Edward. He now wrote: "The outlet of the Lake is probably by the Logumba [Lukugu] River into Lualaba ... but this as yet must be set down as a 'theoretical discovery.'" This theory was correct. On December 13, he and Stanley returned to Ujiji.

Together, Livingstone and Stanley then walked to Tabora, where Stanley had stockpiled some stores. Here Stanley gave Livingstone all that he could spare, enough for perhaps four years. Promising to send back porters and more supplies from the coast as soon as he reached Zanzibar, Stanley left Livingstone on March 14, 1872. He kept his promise, but he never saw Livingstone alive again.

Attended by his faithful servants Susi and Chuma, Livingstone waited at Tabora for the porters that Stanley had promised to send. During these long frustrating months, he lived a life of quiet piety. Then, when the porters arrived in August 1872, he set out for Lake Bangweolo, still trying to trace a Nile watershed based on the Lualaba River. His health by this time was very frail, and he never completed this last task he had set himself. On May 1, 1873, Dr. Livingstone was found dead, kneeling, still in a position of prayer. He then made his most astonishing journey. His body was gutted, salted, and dried in the sun for two weeks, then sheathed in bark and carried the 2,400 kilometres to Bagamoyo by his two faithful followers. From there, the body was shipped to London and examined at the Royal Geographical Society at its offices in Savile Row. Livingstone was eventually buried in Westminister Abbey in 1874, after lying in state in the map room of the Royal Geographical Society. His heart, however, remained behind — buried in Africa.

✳ ✳ ✳

The town of Kasese was very busy and very wet. This seemed to be a land of constant rain. The Ruwenzori Mountains loomed up in the west, dominating the landscape, their upper reaches disappearing into the dark grey clouds.

At 6:15 p.m. we signed into the Margherita Hotel, named after the taller of the twin peaks of Mt. Stanley, three kilometres outside the town. We had come to Kasese because it is the usual base for expeditions up the Ruwenzoris, though no expeditions were scheduled when we were there. Kasese is the westernmost terminus of the Ugandan railway and was once an important centre for the export of copper and cobalt mined at nearby Kilembe. However, the mines are no longer in operation.

In Idi Amin's time, visitors were required to register with the police when they arrived and even submit all their currency for scrutiny. Hotels were regularly raided then, too, and tourists detained for minor transgressions. Things are now more relaxed, but, because of the refugee situation, which we were soon to witness in a very dramatic way, Kasese is still a dangerous town.

Exhausted, thirsty, and extremely hungry, we relaxed over some Nile beer before dinner. Dinner was a very hot goat curry. Too hot. We discussed the Ruwenzori Mountains at length. Our initial plan was to spend six to eight days climbing some of the eastern slopes. I hoped to get at least above the cloud line to see the major peaks, and then view and make whatever conclusions I could about the drainage system from that elevated position.

The Ruwenzori Mountains extend for 100 kilometres along the border between Uganda and Zaïre. The local name for them is *Gambalagala*, "My eyes smart," referring to the dazzling effect of the glaciers. The highest, snow-covered peaks are Margherita at 5,119 metres on Mt. Stanley, followed by the peaks of Mt. Speke, Mt. Baker, Mt. Gessi, Mt. Emin, and Mt. Luigi di Savoia. We had been told that Mt. Speke was the safest choice for non-expert climbers. We were also warned that the mountains are always extremely wet and cold.

In his book *In Darkest Africa*, published in 1890, Stanley gives what must be the earliest extensive documentation of the Ruwenzoris. He even photographed them and printed an etching taken from one of the photographs. Stanley's research is remarkable and includes a series of maps of the Nile sources from ancient times collected by Judge Charles P. Daly of the American Geographical Society. Stanley presents maps made by Europeans beginning with Homer and continuing to the early nineteenth century. He also includes an Arab map from the eleventh century. He compares where the different map-makers placed the Mountains of the Moon and concludes that the ancient map-makers were closer to the truth than his own contemporaries.

On January 11, 1876, during his second expedition, Stanley camped on the escarpment, about 460 metres above the surface of Lake George. The Ruwenzoris could have been as close as 20 kilometres west of him, or as far away as 40 kilometres north-west of him. Did he see them? Most commentators seem to think not. Perhaps they were swathed in clouds for the short time he was there. On a later journey, the Emin Pasha Rescue Expedition, he saw the Ruwenzoris twice. The first time was on May 25, 1888. The second was the next year, around January 22, 1889, while conveying Emin Pasha to Zanzibar. At that time, he glimpsed them several times, occasionally free of clouds. Later sightings were made by naturalists G.F. Scott-Elliott and J.E.S. Moore, the geologist T.J. David, and other explorers, such as Dr. Franz Stuhlmann and the renowned Duke of Abruzzi, Prince Luigi Amadeo di Savoia, who in 1906 brought with him a skilled team of surveyors who mapped the mountains. The summit was reached for the first time in 1913.

I had been longing for a sight of the Ruwenzoris, so it was immensely disappointing to find that the mountain peaks are seldom visible in the wet season. The cloud cover is always there. One can feel the water in the air. It is damp, dank, grey, and cold. Of course, we could see the foothills, but the clouds seldom clear so the upper slopes remained veiled. Still, we were constantly aware of them, a powerful presence brooding over the surrounding countryside.

> *If we consider these circumstances as occurring periodically since the upheaval of the great range, and that mighty subsidence which created the wide and deep gulf now embraced by the Albert Edward Nyanza, the Semliki Valley, and Lake Albert, we need not greatly wonder that Ruwenzori now is but the skeleton of what it was originally....*
>
> *Another emotion is that inspired by the thought that in one of the darkest corners of the earth, shrouded by perpetual mist, brooding under the eternal storm-clouds, surrounded by darkness and mystery, there has been hidden to this day a giant among the mountains, the melting snow of whose tops has been for some fifty centuries most vital to the peoples of Egypt.*
>
> HENRY MORTON STANLEY
> *In Darkest Africa*

I asked endless questions about when the clouds might clear. Maybe in the evening, I was told — about 6:00 p.m. Or perhaps in the morning, about 6:00 a.m. But there was always the regretful warning that in the rainy season we might not see them at all.

The next day, well before 6:00 a.m., I waited for nearly an hour hoping to catch a glimpse of the Margherita Peak. However, the upper part of the range remained hidden. I enjoyed the early-morning silence. Swallows flitted on the shadowy horizon; grey pelicans swooped over the lush, green valley at the foot of the range; and pied crows simply hung around the hotel, as I did. It had rained heavily the night before so there was no rain that morning.

✴ ✴ ✴

Bakonjo, accustomed to the altitude, served as porters for Ruwenzori mountain expeditions.
1905 photograph courtesy of the Royal Geographical Society.

Kasese was in semi-chaos. Rebels — possibly from Zaïre — had crossed over the border only ten kilometres west of the town and were moving down to the Kazinga Channel, which runs between Lake George and Lake Edward. The previously deserted streets of the town were now suddenly crowded with Ugandans fleeing their villages along the border with Zaïre. We saw guns everywhere. In small groups, people were being herded first to one part of town, then to another. Families sat on doorsteps along the narrow main street, guarding their meagre possessions. There were armed men everywhere, some in uniform, but many not. It was difficult to tell who was in charge. Even without understanding a word of the language, we could tell that conversations were tinged with alarm.

We had wanted to start up the mountains as early as possible, but we had to wait until 9:00 a.m., when the Mountaineering Services offices opened. We asked about the possibility of hiking into the rainy highlands, and also about the drainage from the mountains into the Mbuku and the Rwimi Rivers. Both of these flow eastward, while on the west side of the Ruwenzori range, the Butawu, the Luusilubi, the Rualoni, and the Lamya Rivers flow into the Semliki River. We wanted to see for ourselves that the Semliki River drained out of Lake Edward into Lake Albert, and also that the east-flowing rivers drained into Lake George and then into Lake Edward.

As we discussed our plans, I began to change my mind about our course of action. Even though the visibility was terrible and the conditions miserably wet and cold, it would still have been a great experience to climb the mountains. However, I felt that the six to eight days it would take to get high

Ruwenzori Mountains in the distance, almost perpetually covered in cloud.

enough to see the peaks would be a poor use of our time. I was beginning to get a gut feeling that we should take a different tack. The journey down the east side of Lake Albert, up to Fort Portal and the Ruwenzoris, and then along the high escarpment had told me that there was more to the story than the mountains. It would have been easy to climb the Ruwenzoris and declare: "This is the true source of the Nile because all the water catchment is here. The forests are here. All the rivers run down into the lakes, and there down below is the Semliki Valley, with the Semliki River flowing north along the border of Zaïre into Lake Albert. The Semliki is a very important river." We would then make the short journey down to Lake Edward. But a question was forming in my mind and I began to suspect that the answer to it lay in the deep valley on the western side of the Ruwenzori Mountains.

It is easy to see why the early explorers overlooked the Semliki River. It would have been a major decision to go off the beaten track all the way around the foot of the Ruwenzoris down into the Semliki Valley. But for me, although climbing the Ruwenzoris would have been a tremendous physical achievement, it was one that many others had done before me. I now realized that what I really wanted to do was to explore all the ramifications of the source waterways that eventually come together to create the Nile. To do this, I would have to round the southernmost tip of the Ruwenzori range until I reached the Semliki River on the Zaïre border. I sensed that the reward for doing this would far surpass anything I might accomplish by climbing the mountains. Few people ventured into the region. We would be

Mount Stanley, the Ruwenzoris' highest peak.
1905 photograph courtesy of the Royal Geographical Society.

almost totally alone. As we were soon to find out, we would be in equatorial forest: dense, muggy, luxuriant, mosquito- and fly-infested swamp land.

When I announced my decision, it was clear that the others did not relish the idea at all. It was a relatively unknown and dangerous area. It might also take us a few days to travel into the Semliki Valley and around to the other side of the mountains. Why? Just so that we could see for ourselves that the Semliki River flowed north into Lake Albert from Lake Edward, and that it was fed by the many mountain streams that flow down the western slopes of the Ruwenzoris? However, although they were initially quite disappointed that we were not going to climb the mountains, my companions sensed my determination and eventually trusted my judgement.

By the time we had packed and were ready to leave, Kasese was in complete turmoil, thronged with refugees from the border towns of both Zaïre and Uganda. It took us nearly two hours to inch our way along the

Between this point and the Ruwenzori range lies the deep sunken valley of the Semliki, from twelve to twenty-five miles wide. From a point abreast of Mboga to the edge of the Lake, the first glance of it suggests a lake. Indeed, the officers supposed it to be the Albert Lake,... but a binocular revealed pale brown grass in its sere, with tiny bushes dotting the plain.

HENRY MORTON STANLEY
In Darkest Africa

Overleaf: The Semliki Valley between the Ruwenzori Mountains and Lake Albert.

Ankole cattle on the floodplains of the Semliki River.

main street of Kasese, but we knew that it was in our best interests to be patient. There was no gunfire, which seemed quite amazing, considering the number of guns clearly visible and the high level of tension.

While we were there, it was difficult to find out what was happening. But certainly Kasese was a logical destination in the region. It could be reached from the west, the south, or the north. Many roads also lead to Fort Portal, which is an important town. Too important, perhaps, for people who are wary of officialdom. Kasese is just a little, insignificant mountain town — and a much more obvious candidate for a rebel headquarters. The morning we left, there were more than five thousand people there. Quite obviously the town was not big enough to hold this crowd. Months later, watching the news on television in England, I saw the decimation of huge refugee camps that had grown up on the outskirts of Kasese. The camps must have been created soon after we were there, to provide shelter for thousands and thousands of homeless people: Zaïreans, fleeing the conflict between Mobutu's forces and Kabila's; tribal people from the Ruwenzori mountain slopes and from the border villages. Hutus from Rwanda, and from the refugee camps in Zaïre.

Aggression followed the mass movement of people into Kasese. The television clips I later saw told the awful story. The area through which we had travelled became a gruesome scene of carnage, with thousands slaughtered — or uprooted again and forced to move on.

I later found out that another source of conflict in Uganda stems from the fact that fourteen years ago the mountain people of the Ruwenzoris created their own kingdom, which did not recognize the suzerainty of Uganda's central government. The Ugandan government therefore keeps a wary eye on border developments and, when tensions mount too high, the troops are sent in.

Clearly, while we were there, the area was not yet the powder keg it later became. It was quite tense enough for my taste, however. After we left Kasese, we were stopped several times at roadblocks and closely questioned. There were troops all over the place. In retrospect, I am amazed that we never ran into real trouble. We seemed to be living a charmed life.

✳ ✳ ✳

> *There is no reason, save a fancy, why I should have expected those mountaineers familiar with mountain altitudes to be lighter in complexion than the people in the Semliki and Ituri Valley forests; but the truth is, they are much darker than even the Zanzibaris.... [T]hese dark-complexioned people ... sought shelter in the hills, and recesses of the Equatorial Alps, and round about them ebbed and flowed the paler tribes, and so the Wakonju were confined to their mountains.*
>
> HENRY MORTON STANLEY
> *In Darkest Africa*

The Bakonjo people, who, with the Bamba, inhabit the Ruwenzori Mountains, have been struggling for their independence throughout this century. Their traditional rivals are the Batoro who live around the northern side of the mountains. However, in the 1890s, the Bakonjo rescued the heir to the Toro throne from the hands of the Acholi invading from the north and delivered him to Colonel Lugard at Kampala. Under the Germans, the Batoro, but not the mountain peoples, received some of the benefits of colonialism, including formal education, roads, and a part in the administration of this territory. The Batoro discriminated against the Bakonjo, despite what the latter had done to save the king.

After the First World War, this part of German East Africa was transferred to the British Protectorate of Tanganyika. The British followed the German lead and decided to place the Ruwenzoris and their inhabitants under the administration of the Batoro. For this reason, as much as anything, the Bakonjo rebelled in 1919 under the leadership of Tibamwenda. The rebellion was not put down until 1921, after all the leaders were hanged.

Batoro continued to discriminate against the Bakonjo, especially in the education system, and tried to force the use of the Kitoro language on them. Unrest grew into rebellion. In 1965, Uganda's first high commissioner to London, Timothy Bazarrabusa, although himself a Mukonjo (that is, a member of the Bakonjo) asked the British journalist Tom Stacey if he would act as an intermediary between the Ugandan government and the rebels. Stacey tells the story of why he was chosen, and what he did, in his fascinating book *Summons to Ruwenzori*. He travelled into the Ruwenzoris and met with several of the Bakonjo, including the Rwenzururu independence movement's charismatic leader, his former friend, Isaya Mukirane. During this period of their dispute with the central Ugandan government, the rebels would slip across the border into the then Belgian Congo, by simply crossing some of the mountain streams. This raised the stakes, forcing Uganda to decide whether it wanted to risk an international incident by having their military, the East African Rifles (African troops with British officers), pursue the rebels into a foreign country.

The same sort of thing happened in the early 1980, and it is happening again. A new generation of Bakonjo rebels seems to have seized the opportunity to reassert their claims. They still use the tactics of slipping across the border into Zaïre, but they now have access to modern military weapons which were unavailable to the rebels of the 1960s.

✳ ✳ ✳

From Kasese, we headed first to Fort Portal, where we stocked up on provisions. Then we set out for the Semliki Valley, at the foot of the Ruwenzoris near the border of Zaïre. We drove along a spectacular, winding mountain road overhung by steep-sided cliffs, dropping at least 1,500 metres. We passed thatched houses clinging to the sides of the mountains, and banana and cassava plantations isolated high above the world. The road sometimes curved agonizingly around hairpin bends. It seemed to me that Thad was driving much too fast. Joshua clung to the edge of his seat in the back. Once in a while there was a bit of a landslide; rocks skittered behind us while goats grazed nonchalantly on the roadside grass. We saw Ankole cattle with their enormous horns. I glanced out of the window and caught a glimpse of Zaïre to the west.

We descended from the cloudy, damp atmosphere. There were hot springs in the flood plains below us, and steam rose glistening in the afternoon sun, a reminder of the volcanic activity that still occurs here from time to time. As we descended, it grew much hotter and drier. We were making our way out of the clouds. The vegetation also changed dramatically, its lush, deep greens giving way to the paler greens of the arid savanna. Below us stretched a huge valley, and we caught glimpses of the sun sparkling on a meandering ox-bowed river — the Semliki. Again I wondered why none of the early explorers had made this journey. If Baker had continued all the way around to the south end of Lake Albert and found the river, he might well have argued that the Semliki was the source of the Nile. Had he seen the Ruwenzoris he would certainly have claimed for himself, with some justification, a more significant place in the pantheon of British explorers. In the end, however, we had to wait for Stanley, with his exhaustive research and explanation, and his own claims of discovery.

As we descended into the Semliki Valley, I noticed that the lower we got, the shorter the people at the side of the road seemed to be. I mentioned this to Thad Peterson. "My God, you're right!" he agreed.

Deeper into the valley, we began to see people carrying spears, then people with bows and arrows, then men with long beards. Eventually, almost at the foot of the mountains, we found ourselves in an equatorial jungle, very humid and hot and dense, with massive trees soaring to great heights. We were right at the edge of Semliki Forest Park.

After we had introduced ourselves to the park staff, Joshua and Ali set up camp, while Thad, Pollangyo, and I headed farther into the jungle. We looked for pygmies and we eventually found a small group. It was getting late, however, and soon we had to head back to camp.

We ate dinner and settled in for the night. A guard had been assigned to us. Although he was quite short — he came up to my waist — he was very insistent that he was not a pygmy.

The plight of the pygmies is sad. Opium smoking and drunkenness are common among the men, and both men and women live mainly by begging, capitalizing on their curiosity value, I suppose. The pygmies we saw were on the Uganda side of the Semliki River. Stanley mentioned them, writing on his map, "This is where the pygmies are." They are the original inhabitants of this forest. Few travellers ever reach this part of Africa; it is like taking a step back in history.

The pygmy settlement is near the village of Ntandi, three kilometres outside the park entrance. On our way to the park we passed road-side stands at which they were selling home-made pipes, bows and arrows, and their own special type of castanets.

With our diminutive guard outside the Semliki Forest Park.

* * *

301

For a few coins I bought a handwritten sheet, in English, listing a few facts about pygmy history and culture. The pygmies claim to be the original people of Zaïre, having descended from a man called Twa. The Bantu call them *abatwa* for this reason. Twa is believed to have come from a deep hole in Mahoyo Forest, accompanied by his wife, Nguya, which is the word for pig. Twa fathered two sons, Kujerume and Agamio.

Handwritten sheet in English about pygmy history and culture.

According to the legends, one day the brothers went out to hunt in Mahoyo Forest and killed an elephant. When Agamio, the younger, claimed the slain animal's heart, the older brother felt insulted and decided to kill him. Agamio, however, escaped, fleeing to Ituri Forest, now in Zaïre, where he camped at Bhongabuliki, which means "a camp of exile."

Having lost his brother, Kujerume, the older boy, returned home. On the way, he met a beautiful girl, whom he called Amabhuhigi (a gift from hunting). He took her as his wife. Meanwhile, in Ituri, Agamio also took a wife, Nkumabhenda (queen of the forest).

Time passed and Twa died. Agamio returned to Mahoyo for the funeral. When Kujerume saw him coming, he rallied his family to fight Agamio, who fled back to Ituri. The brothers' offspring spread to different parts of the forest, and as time went on, the two branches of the family began to intermarry.

These pygmies believe that they came to Uganda in the sixteenth century, when Kujerume's family, who had migrated to Ituri Forest, were driven out by Agamio. They then crossed the Semliki River to Semliki Forest in Uganda and camped at a place called Kyanzoki, where Kujerume befriended Metibhu, the god of the Semliki Forest. Migration from Mahoyo Forest was necessary for Kujerume's people because the wild fruits and roots that they used for food had become depleted, as had the animals in that part of the forest. Kujerume had also lost most of his children, and he felt this meant the god of Mahoyo was displeased with him. Some of his remaining children, however, eventually returned to Mahoyo Forest.

The document I bought from the pygmies briefly described some of their customs. It said, for instance, that they marry by bartering sisters. If a pygmy wants two wives, he has to build the hut of the first wife on the right side of the family home and the hut of the second wife on the left side of the family home. In a dwindling tribe, it's not surprising that twins are highly prized. A woman who has twins names the first Amgbekua and the second Ambusa, regardless of gender. She has the right to carry two empty bags, one on each side, to collect food and money from anyone passing by.

As in many cultures, the onset of menstruation is cause for celebration, in this case for the women of the girl's family. It is the duty of the girl's mother to break the news to the girl's father. All males are circumcised between the ages of five and ten, and this event is celebrated by a feast at which the men dance the "Luma" and the women dance the "Muredhu."

Belief in the afterlife is expressed by the pygmies in two ways. When a family member dies, the family moves to a different place so that the spirit of the dead one will not invite other spirits to come and kill them as they sleep. They also name the first child who comes into the family after the dead person in order to appease the dead one's spirit.

The pygmies eke out a meagre living by hunting. They use spears, and arrows tipped with a poison called *mitali* made from the roots of certain plants. They also make animal traps, and they fish by pouring pulverized leaves of a poisonous plant called *bhapi* into the stream to kill the fish. In former times, they would sacrifice a rat to Kalisia, the god of the hunt, and also wash their bodies with *nsamba*, a special potion used to give good fortune in the hunt.

In 1966, in an effort at self-government, the pygmies appointed a man named Aurangama as their first tribal chief. Autu, the son of Aurangama, became the second chief, on the death of his father in 1976. Autu died in 1983 and was succeeded by his younger brother, Costa Kijabange. After Costa's death, in 1994, his son, Njito Geofrey, became the chief. In 1993, a number of pygmies converted to Christianity, and received as a gift from the church iron sheets to construct better homes.

✳ ✳ ✳

After seeing the pygmies, we returned to camp just outside the Semliki Forest Park. It was completely surrounded by tall cane grass, a clearing about forty-five metres square. My diminutive guard, whose name was Seth, told me that the minute insects that were biting us were called *bukukuni*. They were an awful nuisance, but came out only before 10:00 a.m. (after which time the heat of the day dispelled them), returning for about an hour and a half at 5:00 p.m., just before the sun went down. The bites left awful welts — particularly around the eyes and ears.

Seth, who said he was a Christian, kept on insisting that he was not a pygmy, despite his small stature. He said, "My real name is Bitabakoli. I was born in Bundibugyo — not in the forest. Pygmies are born in the forest!"

According to Seth and other local tribesmen, the correct spelling of the river is "Semuliki," although the correct pronunciation is "Sem liki." Thad agreed with me that it really did seem remarkable that the river was not given its due importance in any discussion about the Nile's source: "All the rivers starting in the Ruwenzoris would have to drain into the Semliki River sooner or later."

He made another comment about the area that spurred my curiosity. "Another interesting point," he said, "is that anthropologists studying the origins of man now have evidence showing that the development of the rift valley may have been a critical point in determining the divergence of early man from the chimpanzee and the great apes. The creation of the rift valley set up an environmental barrier between the land to the east, which became drier, and the land to the west, which remained tropical — the original environment for the chimpanzees and the great apes. The western inhabitants were not forced to change much. But those in the east had to adapt to a new environment of fewer trees and a less abundant food supply. The theory has it that as they ceased to be tree dwellers they developed bipedal locomotion and became hunters. The use of tools followed and the development of a different behaviour structure."

Thad's comments came as an eye-opener. It was intriguing to think that the land movements over the last few million years that had created the headwaters of the Nile might also have played a crucial role in the development of the human species.

There were more disturbing radio reports before we went to bed that night. Seventy thousand people — a mind-boggling number — both Ugandans and refugees from Zaïre, had moved or were being moved into the Kasese area. We had seen only a few thousand on the streets of Kasese when we had left that morning. The reports implied that the Ugandan army had either taken control of Kasese or was about to.

✳ ✳ ✳

I was up early the next morning, greeted by a strident avian chorus: the "kraark-kraark-kraark-ak-ak-ak" of a roller, the "keep-keep-keep-keep, ark-ark-ark" of a hornbill, the chattering of weaver-birds, the scolding of a yellow-vented bulbul, the cooing of doves — quite a cacophony. I lay on my back in my tent for a while, delaying getting up. It had been a peaceful night, and I had slept well, cradled in this unique corner of Africa just a few kilometres from the mouth of the Semliki River.

The previous night we had decided to start our walk early, heading through the marshes to the river. We struck out west, bumping our way through tall cane grass and past cocoa plantations, the first we had seen. At about 9:00 a.m., we left the two Land Rovers and set out on a five-kilometre trek through deep swamps, the water sometimes up to our waists. We trudged through marshes and stands of papyrus, forded streams, and eventually found ourselves crossing open fields. On the flood plain, we came upon a number of small villages, encampments of people who, while not actually pygmies, are nevertheless relatively short. The tallest were about

The canoes here were of one log of timber hollowed out, fifteen feet long .... They were propelled by poles through a winding channel closely shut in by the papyrus, and by paddles when in the stream, a man at each end holding one about five feet long.

JAMES AUGUSTUS GRANT
A Long Walk across Africa

165 centimetres — but most were much shorter. Like the pygmies, these tribespeople still hunt with bows and arrows and blowpipes and poisoned darts. All their settlements were in very lush, well-cultivated areas.

We went through thick, luxuriant jungle, crossed a deep tributary by dugout canoe, trekked through an acacia grove, and eventually reached the Semliki River. It was about fifty metres wide, turbulent, full of silt, and flowing north at a swift rate. I looked up towards the Ruwenzoris to the south, covered in cloud, an amazing mountain range with peaks rising to five thousand metres. From the valley it felt as though the great mountains began at your ankles and swooped up to the clouds. The Mountains of the Moon. In this spot Samuel Baker would surely have said, "This has to be the source of the Nile." It was as stunning in its way as the first sight of Lake Victoria. A huge geographical fact. The Ruwenzoris are the beginning of something enormous.

To begin with, in the Ruwenzoris, you cannot help noticing that there is so much water. It is everywhere. Our trip had taken us from the arid plains of Tanzania, west through Uganda — up to where all the water is — and then down to this river valley, the first destination of that water on its long journey to the sea. It was exhilarating to be here, but also frustrating, because we knew the snow-covered peaks were there, and the water from them was all around us, but we could not actually see them.

And then, quite suddenly, as we stood by the river, the clouds cleared, revealing the three northern peaks. We could see a glacier and the snowcaps. To have this sight now, after our long trek through that hot, humid, insect-infested swamp, was an incredible, unlooked-for gift. In that one brief moment, we saw the sun shining on the peaks, the sun of Africa glistening on the snow. Then, even as we marvelled at the mountains' grandeur and immensity, the clouds closed again and the sight was gone. It was as if the mountains did it just to tantalize us, as if to say, "This is not for you. Stay where you belong, down in the valley. Down there is where the water ends up, but up here is another world."

After our single brief glimpse of the mountains, we began our trek back, through the swamps and network of water channels. At one point, where the water was deep and muddy, one of the Africans who were with us carried me. There was a practical reason for this. I had cameras and all sorts of other equipment on me that he did not want to get wet. I was in a mess, up to my waist in mud. Most of the time I carried my equipment over my head, but this time, he said, "Don't worry, I'll carry you." He was the same height as me, but much stronger.

As we journeyed towards the south-west ... we observed that in the same manner as a change had come over the character of the Semliki Valley the slopes of Ruwenzori had also undergone a similar change.

HENRY MORTON STANLEY
In Darkest Africa

The long trek to the shore of the Semliki River.

It was an emotional gesture, as well as a practical one, and it had an enormous effect on me. He carried me because he wanted to. It was an act of generosity of one man to another.

However, after he had put me down on dry land, he was troubled by the echoes of the past — a slave carrying a boss — an African carrying a foreign explorer. This was an extremely sensitive, intelligent person, but the symbolism that might have been attached to his act embarrassed him. He made me promise that I would not write about him in person or include any photographs of the event. Later, I begged him to let me include a photograph of the incident in my book but he refused to let me.

To me, this story reveals so much about the legacy of European colonization of Africa. Because of the long history of exploitation of black Africans by white Europeans, this kind man knew that this generous, brotherly act was open to misinterpretation that might lessen his dignity in the eyes of other people.

We made our way out of the floor of the valley back to the Land Rover, did what we could to clean up, and drove through the plantations again. Along the way, I bought a *muhoro* — a long-handled *panga*, a knife used for multiple purposes by the Bamba tribe. An extraordinary weapon. A detour of only a few minutes found us deep in the equatorial forest looking at the high, slender thread of the Mungiro waterfall.

When we reached the town of Bundibugyo, where we bought some *waragi*, the locally made banana brew, we were warned by the police not to take any photos, for security reasons. The Bamaga people, the Bundibugyo townspeople, were more concerned about our ability to handle the *waragi*. As we were leaving, a man laughed, pointed, and said, "That's called 'Kill me quick!'"

The tribespeople also told us a riddle: A Bamba man has one leopard, one goat, and one bundle of grass. If left alone the leopard will eat the goat; and the goat will eat the grass. How does the Bamba tribesman get the leopard, the goat, and the bundle of grass across the Semliki River? He can take only one animal or the bundle of grass on any single journey across the river. Answer: First he takes the goat across the river and leaves him. Then he goes back alone in the canoe. Then he takes the leopard across, but brings the goat back to the first shore and leaves it there while he takes the bundle of grass across. Then he returns and takes the goat across to join the leopard and the bundle of grass.

✳ ✳ ✳

At the fourth hour it was quite a thin forest on the left side of the Semliki, while to the right it was a thick impervious and umbrageous tropic forest, and suddenly we were on the bank of the Semliki. At the point we touched the river it was sixty yards wide, with between a four and five-knot current.

HENRY MORTON STANLEY
In Darkest Africa

✳ ✳ ✳

Finally, on the bank of the Semliki River.

Just before 1:00 p.m., we left the Semliki Forest to return to Fort Portal. We stopped for lunch on the winding road overlooking the flood plains and the Semliki River — now no longer a mystery to me. Something had clicked into place.

The Ruwenzoris are a key element in the whole system of waterways. The prevailing winds have three opportunities to drop their moisture: the western escarpment, the Ruwenzoris, and the eastern escarpment. Precipitation on the western side of the Ruwenzoris and on the east face of the western escarpment has to run into the Semliki; precipitation on the eastern side of the Ruwenzoris and the face of the eastern escarpment has to drain either northward directly into Lake Albert, or east and south into Lake George, or directly south into Lake Edward. Thus, all this water ends up in Lake Albert, most of it via the Semliki River. Although Lake Albert is a lot smaller than Lake Victoria, it still plays a crucial role in the Nile's mysterious beginnings.

For me — for most people, I suppose — there is a huge difference between knowing intellectually that something is true and knowing something is true because I have been there, have seen and heard the power of the rushing waters, have felt the sun's heat or the river's spray on my skin, and have breathed the air of the rain-washed jungle. It is the immediate experience itself that proves things for me and triggers the feeling of discovery.

At the Semliki River, I knew I had made a lucky choice. My instincts had told me that the trek to the river could make things fall into place for me in a way that climbing the mountains would not. Only by putting myself in the landscape, rather than looking down on it from a mountain, could I get the sense I wanted of how all the pieces of the puzzle were connected — mountains, rivers, and lakes, all bound together in an intricate harmony that at last I could trace and understand. It was sheer chance and good fortune that the mountains, too — the last piece of the puzzle — had been unveiled for one breathtaking moment.

Of course, it may have seemed a richer, more significant experience because it came after hours of trudging through filthy, mosquito-infested swamps, sometimes up to our necks in bog, making our way across impossible waterways in dugout canoes, hacking through reeds and thickets of matted vegetation. On and on, with mud caking our legs, mud in our hair, between our fingers, on our equipment. It was a sweeter victory, perhaps, for being so hard won.

* * *

To get back to Fort Portal, we had to negotiate the winding inclined track we had descended so rapidly two days before. It was very muddy in parts. The four-wheel drive was a terrific boon here. Without it we would never have made it to the higher ground. It was a clear day, with only a few clouds and no rain, at least not at the low altitudes.

If the Bakers had not had to contend with illness and mutiny and lack of provisions, would they have gone the extra distance around the south-east corner of Lake Albert to the Semliki River? If they had done so, and followed it to Lake Edward and the Ruwenzoris, they could have won the great prize geographers had speculated about from the earliest days of recorded history. What seems a small omission robbed Baker of the big prize. Had Baker returned to England with the news that he had seen for himself the Mountains of the Moon and that they were indeed a source for the Nile, he would have resolved the argument begun by Speke and Burton. Livingstone might never have been sent on his final trip; Stanley would not have been sent to find Livingstone. History would have been different.

* * *

Of all the explorers whose paths I had retraced, in a way Livingstone's contribution is the hardest to assess. In his day, Livingstone was regarded as one of Britain's greatest explorers. He added significantly to understanding of the geography of southern Africa, although his explorations did little to advance knowledge of the sources of the Nile. His reputation today rests on a triple foundation: explorer, missionary, and — perhaps most important of all — anti-slavery crusader. Though his personal contribution to Nile exploration was slight, his celebrity helped focus attention on the problem, and was the catalyst for Stanley's involvement in African exploration. And Stanley's explorations, of both the Nile sources and the Congo, filled in many blanks on European maps of Africa.

I suspect that Livingstone cared little about his position in history. He kept going back to Africa, and to his life there of service and exploration, because of a deep sense of connection to the place and its peoples. He was also a restless person who found some relief for that restlessness in his travels. This is something I understand. It is during the exertions and privations and sensations of the journey that I feel most at ease with myself, and know I am where I want to be. It satisfies a part of my nature. I do it both because I want to see for myself and because I want to share the experience with others — perhaps as a way of creating something to leave behind.

Livingstone's destiny was bound up with Africa. It was his love of Africa that renewed his sense of purpose. In many ways he paid a terrible price for that love. His health was ruined. His family life was a tragedy. And yet not to heed the call of Africa would have diminished him.

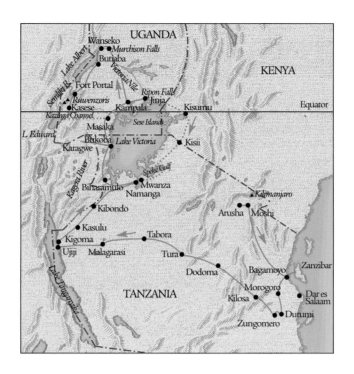

In Darkest Africa: Lake Edward and Circling Lake Victoria

The trip to the Albert Nyanza [Lake Edward] was not unsuccessful.... We reached the Lake, saw it, drank of its waters, and took an astronomical position of it.... We had explored the land lying between the two Lakes, discovered the snow mountain of Gambaragara [Mount Gordon-Bennett] ... and made the interesting discovery that a low hilly ridge about a mile and a half [long] forms the water-shed of rivers flowing into the Albert [Lake Edward] and Victoria Nyanza, besides obtaining much interesting information of the countries bordering the route ....

HENRY MORTON STANLEY
The Exploration Diaries of H. M. Stanley

11

IN DARKEST AFRICA: LAKE EDWARD AND CIRCLING LAKE VICTORIA

Pulling away from the valley of the Semliki, we drove straight through Fort Portal and continued south towards the Kazinga Channel. Once we found the channel, we would have completed all of the trip I had planned except for Stanley's trek around Lake Victoria.

As we headed south, we passed a truck full of Ugandan soldiers, armed and in full battle dress. We were only a stone's throw from the border of Zaïre, so we assumed they were expecting another influx of refugees. As the soldiers approached, we got out of the way. We came to our own conclusions and did not need to be told not to hang around anywhere near the Zaïre border. It began to feel normal to be taking the danger into consideration each time we reviewed our itinerary.

We passed through Fort Portal and Kasese without stopping. We saw men with sub-machine guns silhouetted against the cotton fields. All the small rivers we crossed came down the eastern slopes of the mountains and flowed into Lake George. We crossed the equator again, this time going south. The equator runs right through the area where all the drama of the early explorations took place. We went back and forth across it many times, and each time it felt like a significant event. There was usually a sign that read, "You are crossing the equator."

After a couple of hours we got to the Kazinga Channel, the clouded Ruwenzoris still visible behind us to the north. It was, of course, Stanley who claimed to be the first modern European to see the Ruwenzoris and he saw them from Lake Edward. I imagined how wonderful it would be if the clouds

It would be difficult to tell what dishes we did not make there ... fowl in every form ....

JOHN HANNING SPEKE
What Led to the Discovery of the Source of the Nile

Its shores and waters are favourite haunts of birds, from cranes, herons, and pelicans to the small Parra Africana, egrets and waders, which find excellent feeding over the large spaces near the extremities and shore line of bays,... hippos abound, and, unfortunately, armies of mosquitoes.

HENRY MORTON STANLEY
In Darkest Africa

Previous page: Sunrise over the Kazinga Channel.

cleared. I hoped we would get to see them as Stanley had seen them. But the mountains remained shrouded. It was a gorgeous evening nonetheless, with a brilliant blue sky above and around the cloud-wrapped mountains.

The Kazinga Channel connecting Lake George to Lake Edward is a remarkable body of water, exceptionally rich in animal and bird life. One often sees leopards and elephants, and, in the mornings and evenings, an astonishing variety of birds. There are not many other places in the world where one can see, as we did, sixty different bird species in a matter of two hours.

We passed Lake Nyamunuka, a salt lake, to our north, and sighted elephant and buffalo grazing not far off the road. We reached the Kabatoro Gate of the Queen Elizabeth National Park just before closing time at 6:00 p.m. Every guard there was armed with a sub-machine gun. We signed in, registered our vehicles, and drove on into a dramatic sunset over Lake Edward.

At our campsite on the edge of the Kazinga Channel, it was almost too dark to pitch tents, though the sunset created a wide golden glow behind us. *Euphorbia candelabra* were silhouetted against the burning sky. Mosquitoes hummed insistently. We disturbed a bushbuck on the site and listened to hippos grunting below us in the channel.

By 8:15 p.m. the camp was set up, with Ali cooking over the fire under an enormous candelabra tree. We cracked open the *waragi* we had bought in Bundibugyo. Even mixed with mango juice, it was strong. We toasted the Semliki River and the Ruwenzori Mountains several times with the cool, clear banana spirit. Two strong tumblers of *waragi* were quite enough for a dangerous buzz. We remembered the warning just before we left Bundibugyo: "Kill me quick!" You could easily go blind on this stuff. No wonder it is distilled again before being officially sold to the public.

With bravado, I put two ounces of the clear spirit in my plastic beaker, got everyone's attention, and said, "Look what we're drinking." With that, I threw the liquid on the open fire. Immediately, it exploded into a bright sheet of flame extending over the fire, cooking pots, and other paraphernalia, and briefly lighting up the entire camp. This cooled our enthusiasm for the spirit and gave the term "fire water" new meaning.

We ate chicken with cooked bananas and cabbage for dinner. There was no more *waragi*, so we washed everything down with Nile beer instead. Nile beer is fantastic. When we were lucky enough to get it cold, it was the most thirst-quenching thing ever. That day in the field was hot and dry and we were parched and dehydrated. Even up in the Ruwenzoris, whenever we worked hard and were thirsty we really looked forward to Nile beer. It is full-bodied, stronger than most other beers in Africa; you can taste the hops. It is a commercial beer, of course — not one of the village brews. I felt I was drinking the drink I should be drinking in this place. The Nile was all around us. It was in our heads, in our bodies, under the wheels of our cars; we were hitting it, looking for it. What else should we be drinking but Nile beer?

The evening was cool, perfect for sleeping. We heard hyenas in the distance, and the hippos continued to grunt in the channel. In the morning, we saw that they had grazed all over our campsite in the night. There were tracks everywhere. They had probably chosen the site for the same reason we had — a narrow strip of land between the Kazinga Channel to the east of us and an inlet of Lake Edward to the west.

* * *

We decided to have a rest day, a break from travel in the intense heat. After coffee at 7:00 a.m., we meandered off on a game drive. Just as suddenly as the first time, the clouds cleared for a few seconds, giving us another glimpse of the snow-capped Ruwenzori peaks — this time from the south. Seeing them this close to Lake Edward brought Stanley vividly to my mind and got me thinking about him. Before I got to the Ruwenzoris, Stanley was little more than a name to me. But now I was there and practically standing in the footprints of the man who claimed to be the first white man to have seen the Mountains of the Moon. Of course, I realized that at this point, we were actually following Stanley's route in reverse.

Queen Elizabeth National Park is in the west of Uganda, cradled between the Ruwenzoris on the north and the eastern escarpment of the western rift valley on the east. We looked forward to the chance of seeing leopards and chimpanzees and other wildlife. The area is noted for the richness of its fauna, which is rumoured to include blue- and red-tailed monkeys and tree-climbing lions.

We explored some of the craters and salt lakes formed at the north-east end of Lake Edward by volcanic activity about ten thousand years ago. This area seemed bereft of wildlife. We saw no sign of animals at all — except for the odd buffalo track and one isolated herd of elephants. Poaching, as well as butchery to feed the Amin army in the 1970s, almost completely eradicated wild game. But there are still beautiful grasslands, dramatic craters, and incredible views of Lake George and Lake Edward, with the Ruwenzoris always hovering behind the clouds. We saw rain in the distance, falling beyond the Kazinga Channel. Later the same afternoon, we were hit with a heavy downpour and strong winds. We drove down to the lowlands, where, despite the rain and mist, we sighted some game: buffalo, kob, warthog, reed-buck, bushbuck, and a whole array of bird life. I saw a Verreaux's eagle-owl for the first time.

The rain persisted into a cold, dark evening. What a change in temperature! We put on extra clothes and huddled around the fire, after moving it in under the overhang of the big tent. Our dinner of red beans, cooked bananas, and rice also generated some warmth, but we did not linger very long afterwards. We went to bed to enjoy sliding into the extra warmth and comfort of our sleeping bags. As I lay down to sleep, I could hear the deep, throaty communications of lions in the distance — somewhere down by the water. And, closer, some hyenas' excited laughter. They were all too far away to be of any real interest. Doing their own thing. Starting their own evening.

* * *

We explored the thirty-six-kilometre-long Kazinga Channel in a boat the next morning, following it all the way to the entrance to Lake Albert. The channel flows sluggishly from east to west — that is, from Lake George to Lake Edward. Then the Semliki River flows out of Lake Edward from Zaïre northward to Lake Albert. Zaïre was still only a little distance away across the lake. We saw little except reeds on the northern bank, but the south bank of the Kazinga Channel was alive with fantastic bird life. It was here that we identified no fewer than sixty different species, including the usual array of pelicans, egrets, yellow-billed storks, herons, terns, kingfishers, and fish eagles. Thad and our very knowledgeable guide recorded the sightings with the help of our birding book. As well, we also saw more buffalo, kob, hippopotami, warthog, bushbuck, and crocodile — a very full

Pin-tailed whydah, near the Kazinga channel.

day. At a tiny fishing village on the south bank of the Kazinga Channel, almost at the entrance to Lake Edward, we bought some tilapia fish for dinner.

There are no Nile perch in Lake Edward and Lake George, even though there are plenty in Lake Albert. According to Henry Busulwa of the Uganda Institute of Ecology, although the Semliki River flows from Lake Edward to Lake Albert, several constrictions, rapids, and waterfalls between the two lakes make it impossible for the fish to travel upriver to Lake Edward. At one time, Mr. Busulwa said, there probably were Nile perch in Lake Edward and Lake George. But after the most recent earth shift or perhaps during the last glaciation when so much water was locked up in ice, the two lakes dried up, which killed off the fish. Lake Albert, which is three hundred metres lower than Lake Edward and much deeper, did not dry up and the Nile perch survived there. In Mr. Busulwa's opinion, the alarming increase in the Nile perch of Lake Victoria was the result of a badly managed experiment. There is now a law in Uganda that you cannot introduce fish into protected areas.

* * *

On our evening explorations, the Kazinga Channel seemed under a benign enchantment. Everything was bathed in a beautiful golden light. Animals and birds, too, seemed to enjoy the tranquil scene. Hippos yawned; bushbuck stood motionless; terns and swallows swooped low over the water, feeding on the insects; pelicans and cormorants took leisurely flight against the evening sky. As we returned to camp, we practically ran over a spotted hyena — the first we had seen so far in the area.

The next day, I learned that in 1990 a census counted no fewer than eight thousand hippos in the Kazinga Channel. This number did not include

On the banks of the Kazinga Channel, a mother and newborn hippo.

those in Lake George and Lake Edward.

Our breakfast of fried cabbage and leftover rice pancakes was not really very appetizing, but we were in a hurry to get going. We broke camp at 8:30 a.m. under a cloudy sky and hit the main road south toward Katumguru where we crossed the Kazinga Channel by means of a narrow bridge guarded by three men with machine-guns. We were back in the banana belt now, travelling diagonally up the eastern escarpment of the rift valley, heading south away from the Ruwenzoris. Below us we could see craters filled with banana plantations, a spectacular sight.

With our exploration of the Kazinga Channel, we realized that now we had at least seen all the major elements of the great central water system: Lake Victoria, the outlet of Lake Victoria at Ripon Falls, the Nile at Murchison Falls, Lake Albert, the Semliki River between Lakes Albert and Edward, and the Kazinga Channel between Lakes Edward and George. Our ambition now was to get back east as quickly as possible, because we wanted to follow Stanley's route circling Lake Victoria for a while. So we made straight for the western shore of Lake Victoria, planning to make our way north again to where we could see the Sese Islands. After rounding the north end of the lake, we would head south, skirting the eastern shore, through Kenya and into Tanzania, arriving at last, we hoped, in Mwanza, where we had started out, and where Speke had seen Lake Victoria for the first time. I hoped by doing this to follow both Stanley and Speke, and perhaps to tie their experiences together.

As we travelled, we saw armed guards everywhere. The reason became clear as we read the day's news. Border rebels infiltrating Uganda had prepared to attack Kasese with the presumed intention of advancing all the way to Kampala. They were stealing supplies and had displaced about 100,000 people along the way. The rebels had attempted to cross the Queen Elizabeth Park where we had just camped, making for Kasinga, but had been stopped by Ugandan troops. Once again, we had unwittingly been in the midst of conflict. It was always very difficult to find out what various signs of trouble meant. Sometimes we heard radio news about events as they happened, but more often we heard explanations only much later. And we could never be sure that what we heard was accurate.

At that time I had no idea that the ongoing conflict in Zaïre would eventually result in the overthrow of the dictator Mobutu Sese Seko. But there was little doubt that the border skirmishes in western Uganda were inspired by the Muslim fundamentalists. They had already made considerable inroads in the north of Uganda, and were switching their focus to the area bordering Zaïre. Yoweri Museveni, the president of Uganda, was away in Europe at the time, and it is possible that they were making an opportunistic push to take over key inland territory while he was out of the country. Whatever the explanation, the fighting seemed to be concentrated in the west where we were, and it was only by chance that it missed us. We saw the armed guards, fortified bridges, machine-guns, and lorries full of troops being shunted to and fro — but our movements were never restricted. We were extremely fortunate to get out of Kasese before fighting actually broke out. We were equally lucky that the invasion did not take place in Bundibugyo while we were trying to find the mouth of the Semliki River.

✳ ✳ ✳

As we drove down from the highlands into the bowl of the Lake Victoria basin, we saw bright sunshine again and once more travelled on a tarred road stretching between seemingly endless banana plantations springing up out of the red earth. When we reached the university town of Mbarara, we saw more signs of settlement. Mbarara is a busy town with much new construction. New houses sported red-tiled roofs, tin roofs, blue roofs, green roofs, grey roofs. There were stores on both sides of the road again and telephone wires criss-crossing the skyline. Nearer the centre of town, shade trees divided the highway — a clear sign of British influence. We saw no more of the police checks that had slowed us up for miles after we left the Kazinga Channel that morning.

We sped back towards Lake Victoria through rolling country, past workers on bicycles carrying big, unsteady loads of bananas and charcoal; past cattle and herds of goats, old English milestones, and, again, churches, schools, and clinics with religious names unfamiliar to me: New Hope Clinic, Bright Angel Nursery School, St. Charles Wanga Church, Uganda Martyrs University, St. Peter Nanziga Church School.

In the middle of the afternoon, we crossed the equator again, this time going north. Late in the afternoon — after five hundred kilometres non-stop — we were battling the rush-hour traffic of Kampala on our way to Jinja, where we finally called a halt. Now, for a second time, we were back on the shores of Lake Victoria where the Victoria Nile starts its turbulent journey down to Lake Albert.

⁂ ⁂ ⁂

By May 1872, Stanley had reached Zanzibar, leaving Livingstone to continue his explorations in what later proved to be the watershed of the Congo. Stanley published *How I Found Livingstone* in 1872, and honours were heaped upon him. In 1873, the Royal Geographical Society awarded him its Patron's Medal. Queen Victoria gave him a gold snuffbox. But Stanley felt that Livingstone's work had been left unfinished at the great missionary's death in 1873. Stanley was determined to finish that work himself.

In 1874, Stanley set out to make a complete circuit of Lake Victoria. He was amply financed by *The New York Herald* and *The Daily Telegraph*. As travelling companions he chose younger men, Frederick Barker and the brothers Francis and Edward Pocock. The Pococks were a fisherman's sons and Barker was a clerk. He chose these working-class men for their abilities — and also, perhaps, because they were the sort of men least likely to compete with him or to claim the glory for themselves.

Stanley's expedition left Zanzibar in the middle of November 1874. It was completely equipped with every conceivable necessity, including the 12-metre *Lady Alice*, a boat that broke down into sections that could be carried by some of the 356 men who accompanied Stanley. They started out with 7,000 kilograms of supplies.

Slaves in Buganda, 1875.

The expedition took three and a half months to get to Lake Victoria. By then Edward Pocock, the younger of the Pocock brothers, was dead, and a hundred others had either died or deserted. Stanley was not afraid to meet violence with violence and did not hesitate to shoot at hostile tribesmen. His marches were quick and purposeful. He did not bother to ease his passage with persuasion and diplomacy, like Livingstone; nor to stop for geological and anthropological observations, like Burton; nor to amuse the natives, like Speke.

At Mwanza, Stanley had the *Lady Alice* assembled, then set out on March 8, 1875, being rowed northward along the eastern shore of Lake Victoria, intending to circumnavigate the lake. Along the way he encountered a man whom Speke had earlier had to contend with, King Mtesa of Buganda.

The frightening, violent, exuberant youth who had welcomed Speke was now almost forty years old, the commander of an army of 150,000 warriors. Gone were the days in which Mtesa was amazed by the shooting of cows. His soldiers were well armed. He now had 3 million subjects and ruled over an area extending for 240 kilometres along the lake. Mtesa was tall, clean-shaven, still "large-eyed," according to Stanley, and still possessed of great nervous energy, though his manner had grown suave with experience.

Stanley was considerably impressed with Mtesa, and thinking that instruction in Islam had been the moderating influence, even attempted to convert him to Christianity. Some commentators even feel that the meeting between the two men helped pave the way for future missionaries, who eventually made the establishment of a British protectorate much easier. Mtesa, who was far more interested in Islam than in Christianity, replied with polite interest. The years had taught him diplomacy. He now knew that there was much to gain by remaining calm in the presence of those whose goods and connections could benefit his kingdom. Mtesa's rule had brought progress and prosperity to his people, though he retained his callous disregard for human life. He had, for example, killed thirty people as a welcoming gift to another white visitor a few months before Stanley's visit. During our journey, I came across an article in a local newspaper honouring the contribution of Mtesa I to Christianity and the progress of technology in Uganda. The article quoted the U.S. ambassador to Uganda, who praised Mtesa for inviting missionaries to come to Buganda — missionaries who had helped to build the infrastructure of the country such as schools, roads, and hospitals. Others quoted in the article applauded Mtesa's religious tolerance and lamented that his important contribution to the development of Uganda has gone largely unrecognized. The article highlighted for me a key issue of exploration and colonization — that one can never really predict what will result from the meeting of two different cultures.

Stanley circled the entire lake — a trip of 1,600 kilometres — in fifty-seven days, re-entering Mwanza on May 6, 1875. This voyage proved exactly what Speke had said: that Victoria was indeed a single lake with its outlet at Ripon Falls. Stanley also noted that the Kagera River was the only significant

King Mtesa with his courtiers, 1875.

intake of Lake Victoria. As he wrote: "Speke has now the full glory of having discovered the largest inland sea on the continent of Africa, also its principal affluent as well as its outlet. I must also give him credit for having understood the geography of the countries we travelled through better than any of those who so persistently opposed his hypothesis...."

Stanley now set out on the next portion of his trek: to travel to and circumnavigate Lake Tanganyika, in order, again, to check the flow of the Ruzizi River and any other bodies of water, including Lake Albert, to which Lake Tanganyika might somehow be connected.

Tribal unrest in the area of Lake Albert threatened the safety of Stanley and his men. Although Mtesa had provided Stanley with a small escort to help him to explore the lakes, this plan fell through, and Stanley was thus not able to add to the knowledge of Lake Albert and Lake Edward as he had hoped. However, he did visit the kingdom of Karagwe, and there he met the ageing King Rumanika. Stanley was the last white man to see the genial king alive. Rumanika produced for Stanley a treasure he had safeguarded

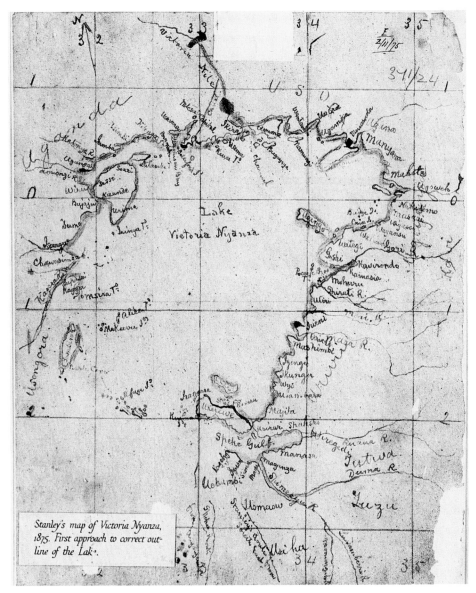

Stanley's map of Victoria Nyanza, 1875. First approach to correct outline of the Lake.

I knew what had been accomplished by the African Explorers, and I knew how much of the dark interior was still unknown to the world. Until late hours, I sat up, inventing and planning, sketching out routes, laying out lengthy lines of possible exploration, noting many suggestions which the continued study of my project created. I also drew up lists of instruments and other paraphernalia that would be required to map, lay out, and describe the new regions to be traversed.

HENRY MORTON STANLEY
Throught the Dark Continent

Map courtesy of the Royal Geographical Society.

for nearly two decades: a gun given to him by Speke. Sadly, time and tragedy overtook Rumanika. He killed himself not long after his meeting with Stanley.

It took Stanley until June 1876 to launch the *Lady Alice* from the shores of Lake Tanganyika at Ujiji. He travelled the entire circumference of the lake and reached the inescapable conclusion that no river flowed out of it that was connected to the Nile system. Burton's theories were thus finally, and conclusively, proved wrong.

Stanley had one more great task before him: to follow the Lualaba wherever it might lead. This journey, which eventually brought him to the mouth of the Congo, is not part of my story, but it is one of the most remarkable adventures in the history of African exploration. As recounted by Stanley in *Through the Dark Continent*, it is the tale of a harrowing journey down a river to an unknown destination. During the journey, the expedition faced starvation, hostile tribes, shipwreck, and the ever-present threat of drowning and disease. Frank Pocock, the older of the two brothers, the last white man left with Stanley, drowned on the voyage. Of the 356 people who had set out with Stanley, only 114 remained alive at the journey's end.

* * *

We left Jinja and headed east along the northern shore of Lake Victoria to the Kenyan border. We travelled through fields of sugar cane and past crowds of schoolchildren in uniforms of pink and blue. Cyclists in white negotiated their tricky way through clouds of black diesel smoke from buses. Signs advertising Nile beer vied for attention with the ever-present ecclesiastical signs: Queen of Apostles Philosophy Centre, Bulanga Elm Church, Bishop Willis Teachers' College.

The border between Uganda and Kenya is at the Sio River, about fifty kilometres east of Jinja. A battalion of taxi cyclists was crossing at the same time — every one of them sporting a pink shirt. We were again besieged by money changers offering a ridiculously poor rate of exchange, and by boys hustling Coke, Pepsi, Fanta, and Sprite. Pandemonium!

It took us one and a half hours of the usual hassles to get through Kenyan Immigration. During the wait, one of the thieves who abound in the area tried to steal the shovel off the back of our Land Rover. Ali chased him and caught him.

Police checks were numerous: along one stretch of our journey south, parallel to the lake, we encountered a police check every three or four kilometres. At the checkpoints the road was barricaded by a heavily spiked metal gate. At some checkpoints, we were stopped and questioned about ourselves and the Land Rovers, before the centre section of the spiked gate was pulled aside by the guards to let us through. At others, we were just waved through without having to stop.

The roads in Kenya are rough compared to those in Uganda. There were huge troughs in the road where you would least expect them, and the potholes were bad — tough even on Land Rovers.

The road took us over several small rivers, and we crossed the equator yet

Crossing south into Kenya from Uganda.

again on our way to Kisumu, Kenya's third-largest city, after Nairobi and Mombasa. We followed the railway line into this peninsula town set on flat land on the edge of the lake, passing brown-paper shacks on the outskirts, ugly telephone posts and lines, and then an avenue of flame trees. We stopped at the Kisumu market to bargain. I felt an absurd sense of triumph at having haggled and won — walking off with a vintage denim shirt and a leather belt that cost me the equivalent of six U.S. dollars.

From Kisumu, we pressed on towards the big bustling town of Kisii, only thirty kilometres straight south but farther by road around Kavirondo Gulf. A sign along the way read: "AIDS is not witchcraft. AIDS is real." At Kisii there was another lively market, but we soon continued south, through field after field of sugar cane — until we got stuck behind some sugar-cane trucks. It was quite impossible to pass them. The canes protruded almost a metre on each side, and the road was narrow and winding with no shoulders or passing lanes. At the roadsides, clusters of schoolchildren, still in uniform, watched us pass in slow cavalcade. Joshua had to drive very carefully to avoid hitting them — and to keep from knocking down the ever-present cyclists.

At last, however, we reached the town of Isebania, on the Kenya–Tanzania border, and at sunset left the Kenyan Immigration offices and walked across the border to Sirari. We were back in Tanzania.

We ended our day's journey in the town of Tarime less than ten kilometres from the border. We found a small roadhouse, where we were given a bed and a primitive kind of shower. We needed it. After a dinner of curried chicken and rice, Tanzania style, I settled in for an evening of research and writing.

✳ ✳ ✳

I awoke at 5:30 a.m. to the sound of children singing. Then a little later I heard grown-ups' voices. Then they all sang together. I could not figure out what was going on, but it was an inspired way to start the day. Across the street from the roadhouse was a teachers' training school. I learned later that the singing was an early wake-up exercise. All this before the birds' morning chorus or any other human chattering.

We got on the road by 7:30 a.m. and headed for Mwanza, 256 kilometres south. We soon found ourselves on slightly rolling plains interrupted only by settlements of small, round, mud houses with thatched roofs. Rock outcroppings, called *kopjes*, varied the landscape. We crossed the Mara River — the first that we had come to that flowed into Lake Victoria from the east.

We drove on towards Speke Gulf, and were soon very close to the lake, moving through wide stretches of flat, sandy terrain without many trees or shrubs. The air seemed hazy as we crossed the Grumeti River, another that flows into Lake Victoria from the east but that almost disappears in the dry season.

We arrived at Speke's Bay Lodge, a cluster of thatched buildings owned by a Danish couple and a Dutchman. It was not officially open yet, but they allowed us to stay in their tent campsite. We dropped our kit and almost immediately set off south for Mwanza and the final leg of our journey around Lake Victoria. In a sense, Stanley was interested in what flowed out of Lake Victoria, whereas I was more interested in what flowed into it because I was still compelled by the idea that the Kagera River was the significant Nile feeder, via Lake Victoria. This conviction had only grown stronger now that I knew that the Semliki was a significant feeder of Lake Albert. Two feeder rivers. Two lakes. Two reservoirs of the Nile.

The flat coastal road runs through thatched village settlements, past herds of cattle grazing, goats, chickens, and ploughed fields waiting to be planted with cassava or maize. We crossed the Magu River — a small river which also flows into Victoria, at Speke Gulf. The land was mostly very flat and dry, but interrupted by rock outcroppings at frequent intervals.

We veered west along Speke Gulf, once in a while passing small banana plantations. These were nothing like the lush plantations in Uganda. We noticed black-and-white Abdim's storks, and white cattle egrets. Women in colourful *kangas* carried bundles of maize, firewood, and sugar cane. In contrast to the women wearing native dress, all the men wore Western-style trousers and shirts. In spots, the relatively good road gave way to appalling stretches where ruts, bumps, and potholes jarred the Land Rovers and threw

There was a bellicose activity about their movements, an emphasis in their gestures, and a determined wrathful fury about the motion of the head and pose of body that were unmistakable.

HENRY MORTON STANLEY
Through the Dark Continent

Overleaf: Militant schoolchildren in Uganda.

Tanzania market scene.

us all over the place. We found it easiest to drive on the shoulders — although this was sometimes impossible. The road outside Mwanza was in such horrendous shape that I wondered why anyone would worry about this city being invaded. It would have been almost impossible to drive any troops or equipment over that road. Eventually, it took its toll by giving us a flat tire.

> [T]he banana plant will supply a peasant ... *with bread, potatoes, dessert, wine, beer, medicine, house and fence, bed, cloth, cooking-pot, table-cloth, parcel-wrapper, thread, cord, rope, sponge, bath, shield, sun-hat, even a canoe — in fact almost everything but meat and iron. With the banana-plant, he is happy, fat, and thriving; without it, he is a famished, discontented, woe-begone wretch, hourly expecting death.*
>
> HENRY MORTON STANLEY
> **Through the Dark Continent**

When we eventually got into Mwanza we drove to the police station to retrieve our guns, then to Forté's Safaris to pick up the radios we had left with them, then to the petrol station to fix the tire, and last to the Indian supermarket to get provisions. Mwanza is a hot, dusty town — full of smells and bad vibrations. Not my favourite city, but, still, important to me as the site of Speke's great moment of revelation.

After the shopping, and fixing the flat tire, and a quick meal of greasy chicken, Thad and I set out from the Speke commemorative plaque to walk the last mile, to the top of Isamilo Hill. We approached the crest of the hill through rough terrain, encountering as we went the stinking carcass of a dead dog. Despite this unpromising beginning, we knew that something extraordinary lay ahead and we were not disappointed. Before us lay a vast expanse of water — a spectacular vista. The view is so compelling it is not hard to see why Speke leaped to his bold conclusion that this was the source of the Nile. Behind us the bay to the west of Mwanza glistened in the

Pollangyo scouting our route south to Speke Gulf.

afternoon sun. I felt an enormous sense of accomplishment.

We had driven more than seven thousand kilometres and had completely circled Lake Victoria. For the second time we stood on the spot where the first European set eyes on the vast lake.

On our way to the peak of Isamilo Hill, Thad asked a group of schoolboys whether we would actually see the lake from the crest of the hill ahead of us.

"Oh yes," they said.

"Do you know who discovered the great lake?" Thad asked.

"Yes — some German wasn't it?"

Thad explained that it wasn't, and that it was actually John Hanning Speke — an Englishman.

"Ah yes, now we remember."

Then Thad asked, "This lake is the source of a great river. Do you know what the name of that river is?"

"Yes," one of the boys replied, stunning us with his answer, "the Kagera."

Had he got the facts muddled? Had he, like Speke's Arab informants,

forgotten the river's direction of flow? Perhaps. Or perhaps in his own mind, the Kagera and the Nile were the selfsame river.

* * *

As I stood in this historic spot, I thought not only of Speke, but also of Stanley — one of the best organized and highest achievers among the Victorian explorers. He was methodical and determined. He set out on a mission and completed it. I wondered, not for the first time, what the relationship is between a man's urge to be an explorer and the same man's urge to be a writer. Burton's output as a writer was enormous, but until his only significant commercial success, *The Arabian Nights*, first published in 1886–88, he was really only a recorder of the wonders he had seen in his travels. Speke, too, was a recorder, and much of the interest of his narrative comes from his own lively interaction with the people he met. Speke's relations with the Africans were full of warmth and humour, and even though his skills as a writer were limited he somehow managed to make his narrative live.

Journalism was Stanley's career. He went to Africa for a scoop. And he got the story of the century. It was really Livingstone who made Stanley the writer into Stanley the explorer. And although my own efforts have convinced me that it is not easy to make an explorer into a writer, it is a much more significant accomplishment to make a writer into an explorer.

Stanley's contributions to knowledge about the geography of Africa and the source of the Nile were enormous. He was the first to realize just how confused the issue of the Nile source had become. Before Stanley, people certainly "discovered" things and made enthusiastic claims: Speke came back with Lake Victoria, guessing correctly that it was the source of the Nile. Baker brought back Lake Albert as a source and a reservoir. Livingstone was fixated on the Lualaba, and Burton clung tenaciously to his speculations about Lake Tanganyika.

Stanley simply garnered the necessary support, then went out and found out the facts for himself. Years of drama and controversy were set aside in the face of undeniable proof.

As I delved into Stanley's research, and the descriptions of his work, I got a clearer picture of the man as well as his methods. He was an organized, practical achiever. And in the end, practical achievers almost always have to complete the work of thinkers and dreamers.

✷ ✷ ✷

One hundred and forty years after Speke's visionary prediction that Lake Victoria would prove to be the source of the Nile, I had come to Africa to see for myself. I arrived laden with a great store of knowledge about the Nile — all the lore and learning amassed since Speke's great discovery. I had all the facts, but I was not satisfied.

The early explorers had struggled to fill in the blank spaces on the map. And my trip, in its turn, was a struggle to translate the lines on the map and the words on the page back into living, breathing experience as vivid and powerful as the experiences of the Victorian explorers.

I now felt I had done that — and more. Nothing I had done had added new lines to the map, or even changed the lines that were there. But I felt differently about the map now that I had seen what structures and forces lay behind the features so cryptically sketched on the page. I saw the map differently; I interpreted it differently. I remembered a statement from Alan Moorehead's book: "For ordinary purposes it would seem most sensible to accept the site of the Ripon Falls as the source, since it is only from there that the mighty river confines itself to a definite course...." I had now seen for myself what the explorers had written about, and I felt an instinctive resistance to that "sensible" conclusion. I now believed that much of what had been written too narrowly defined the term "source." It allowed Lake Victoria and the Ripon Falls to claim the lion's share of a fame that should

Lake Victoria from Isamilo Hill.

really be divided among a wider group of claimants.

My trip had given me the ability to interpret both the map and the explorers' stories in a new way. I felt I had, in a sense, discovered the truth behind the facts. And I had proved once again that, for me at least, though the knowledge that comes from books is not to be scorned, the knowledge that comes from experience is more solidly satisfying.

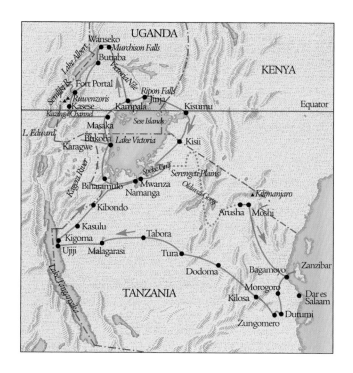

The Return Journey

Happy are we that, — after completing our mission, after the hurry and worry of the march, after the anxiety and vexation suffered from fractious tribes, after tramping ... through mire and Stygian marsh, — we near Beulah's peace and rest!

HENRY MORTON STANLEY
How I Found Livingstone

12

THE RETURN JOURNEY

Exhilarated, we walked down from the crest of Isamilo Hill, past the dead dog, past the palatial houses and the warren of streets around the central square, back to the plaque commemorating Speke's achievement. There were only a few, small, scattered villages in the area when Speke arrived in 1858. Now, Mwanza is Tanzania's third-largest city and growing at an astounding rate.

Driving east out of Mwanza, we made a rough return journey along the questionable coastal road to find ourselves back at Speke's Bay Lodge just before sunset. The lodge, a small, picturesque complex on the shores of Lake Victoria, comprises a number of round, white, plaster buildings with thatched roofs and seven or eight covered tents. Guests have access to a bar, a dining room, and washing facilities. The very friendly owners and managers are Kurt W. Jorgensen and Ann Mette Erno, both Danish, and Jan Willem Fhalfwerk, who is Dutch. We had showers, dinner, and a relatively good night's sleep in the small green tents.

During dinner, the invasion of western Uganda from Zaïre, as reported on the radio, had been one of our main topics of conversation. While we were in Kasese, I had not known that the conflict was primarily a case of civil strife among tribes of north-western Uganda who refused to acknowledge the current government. Among these are the Acholi, the Bunyoro, the Batoro, and the Bakonjo. The Bakonjo people, who live in the foothills of the Ruwenzori Mountains, have been fighting almost continuously against the central government for over thirty years. In the long, chaotic aftermath of the ouster of Idi Amin in 1979, they managed to set up their own kingdom for a short while. In Stanley's *In Darkest Africa*, he described his first encounter with the people he called the Wakonju: "Wherever we looked there were villages, and if courage aided numbers the people were capable of an obstinate resistance. So we pressed bands of armed men up to the mountains, and the skirmishing was brisk...." His force made peace with the Wakonju (Bakonjo) and received a great deal of geographical information from them, including their name for the mountains.

...various fruits, plantains, limes, and pawpaws; and of vegetables, brinjalls, cucumbers, and tomatoes, which relieve the indigenous holcus and maize, manioc and sweet-potato, millet and phaseoli, sesamum and groud-nuts.

RICHARD F. BURTON
The Lake Regions of Central Africa

Previous page: The Loliondo highlands, where the "doming" of East Africa is most apparent.

"Ruwenzori, called [various names] by the forest tribes, became now known as the Ruwenzu-ru-ru," which is the Bakonjos' name for their country. These people are fiercely independent and expert at escaping up the mountains and across the border into Zaïre when pursued by armies sent to find and fight them.

Again and again we were told, "Don't believe what you read in the papers. What else can the government say but that there has been an invasion by Zaïre? The trouble is not over, nor will it be over for some time. This is a dangerous area — and eventually will be just as troublesome as the border along the north of the Nile."

⋆ ⋆ ⋆

Just before dawn, the fish eagles' mocking cries woke me up. The bird life was plentiful on the waterfront. We saw malachite and pied kingfishers, stilts, pied wagtails, Cordon-bleus, black-headed weavers, sparrows, and the ever-present marabou storks. After the usual exchange of addresses and cards, we left the lodge at 8:30 a.m. and headed for the Ndabaka Gate of Serengeti National Park, just a few kilometres to the east. Serengeti National Park was the first such park in Tanzania, and it is the largest, consisting of almost 14,500 square kilometres of rolling plains. Visitors and staff are expected to conform to the environment, not the other way around.

I thought of this whole journey as having two parts. The first part, the exploratory journey in which I was trying to replicate parts of the trips of the Victorian explorers, ended when we got back to Mwanza and I had a chance to stand on Isamilo Hill. The second part, a sort of "journey of summation," began when we left Mwanza and headed east through the Serengeti towards Kilimanjaro.

Like the explorers before me, I was now faced with the long trek back to my starting place. But I would not have to face a journey of many months with dwindling supplies and exhausted workers. In contrast, I was looking forward to resting, collecting my thoughts, writing, researching, and generally piecing together everything I had learned and observed.

The journey so far had a somewhat rushed quality to it because there had been so much ground to cover in a specific amount of time. But now the rush was over, and I relished the thought of having more time to talk to Thad Peterson. I wanted to learn more about his own thoughts on modern East Africa and the effect the early Victorian explorers had on this part of the continent.

I had been to the Serengeti twice before. I love the Serengeti; I feel at home there. Out in the savanna, under an open sky, beside my tent, sitting in front of a fire, whittling a stick, chatting about experiences of the past and plans for the future, I nurture the notion that I am most myself. I also feel when I am there that I am doing something worthwhile — trying to see all the sides of a big, complex question. On this particular journey I was trying to develop a detailed picture that would make the Nile's drainage system clear to me — and to others. As we headed slowly eastward, I felt that Kilimanjaro, Ernest Hemingway's great mountain of mystery, was a fitting destination. After all, people had once thought that Kilimanjaro was itself the source of the Nile, although that myth has long since been dispelled.

I also relished the time I would now have to talk to Joshua, Pollangyo, and Ali. We had done the journey together, and they, too, had first-hand experience of the Nile's secrets. We had all contributed towards getting where we needed to be in the most efficient manner possible. Now, however, we could ease up a little. I probably accomplished more in the ten days between Lake Victoria and Kilimanjaro than I could possibly have done in two months after leaving Africa. Everything was fresh in our minds, and we could try to put it all in context.

Heading east, away from Mwanza, we travelled down the western corridor of the Serengeti, camping first at Kiramira on the crocodile-infested Grumeti River. The Grumeti shrinks every year during the peak dry season, leaving behind only isolated pools of water. These are much sought-after by the resident game, and the crocodiles lie patiently in wait for their prey.

We heard on the radio that there was more fighting in Kasese, and that the Hutu and Zaïrean refugees who had been pouring into Kigoma were being sent back to Zaïre after fighting broke out in the Tanzanian refugee camps. It was not that surprising that some refugees eventually had to return to Rwanda as well because of the violent and overcrowded conditions in the camps. There had also been further reports of brutal killings of these refugees by the Rwandan Tutsis — more reprisals for the 1994 massacres. Rwanda officially claimed that all its refugees were back in Rwanda, that there was no longer a refugee problem, and that international intervention was no longer required. On the other hand, the United Nations High Commission for Refugees argued that there were several hundred thousand to a million refugees who were still homeless, unaccounted for, and in need of international assistance. Nothing was very clear.

Then on Thursday, November 28, we heard radio reports that many tribes, including the Bakonjo and the Batoro, in and around the town of Kasese had banded together to fight against the Museveni government in Uganda. Reports further stated that the rebels were receiving funding and arms from within Uganda itself and that sometime in the near future they would invade and capture Kampala. I found this explanation of events suspect, because to me an invasion of Kampala seemed much more likely to be perpetrated and influenced by external powers, those, for example, from Zaïre or the Sudan. We never quite knew what to believe.

Though disturbed by the news, we continued on our way to the Loliondo highlands, where we camped for two nights, enduring heavy rain. This is Maasai country, with its own distinctive sights and sounds: *bomas* (brushwood fences), cattle, mud, and red *rubegas* (the Maasai's toga-like clothing). Thad got into deep conversations in Swahili with the Maasai

Crocodiles on the banks of the Grumeti River.

about contracts with his company, to set up exclusive camping sites in a 650-square-kilometre section of the Loliondo highlands. It is indicative of just how much things have changed that tourists would consider visiting this northern land of the Maasai. The Maasai had so strong a reputation for being a dangerous people that Burton, despite his curiosity about them, assiduously avoided going near them. He chose to travel by the more southerly caravan route to the great lakes from Bagamoyo instead of the route from Mombasa through Maasailand. He may never have met a single Maasai, but at one point the expedition was harassed by people his guides claimed were the Wahumba or Wahumpa, "one of the terrible pastoral nations," who "from their dialect [were] a tribe or sub-tribe of the great Masai race." They were and are the warriors of the great savanna, and they remain an impressive people. We certainly did not find them dangerous, but they are imposingly tall, and apparently fearless. They are, however, less nomadic than they once were.

While camping, we took the opportunity to do our game drives and game walks. The evenings in the Serengeti are blessed with a wonderful, tangerine-coloured light — tremendous for photography — a soft, warm glow. It is clearly the best light for photographing wildlife. However, although still a keen wildlife photographer, I am now just as interested in the drama and character of the human face.

In the evenings, we were able to see some nocturnal animals. We saw a huge variety — African wildcat, zorilla (striped African polecat), bat-eared fox, impala, Thompson's gazelle, elephant, baboon, buffalo, and many other species, including Grant's gazelles — a living reminder of the explorer.

Maasai boma.

We saw no leopards or lions — although we did hear their deep-throated sawing and grunting through the night.

Driving south from Loliondo across the great short-grass plains of the Serengeti, we passed through the Olduvai Gorge. Olduvai comes from the Maa word *ol-dupái* (wild sisal), which is very appropriate, because sansevieria (*Acacia mellifera*), or wild sisal, grows abundantly here. Also common in the gorge are umbrella thorns and "wait-a-bit" thorns, small, backward-curved thorns that have an uncanny ability to hook into clothing. The gorge, which runs roughly east–west, is fifty kilometres long and up to ninety metres deep. There is a side gorge running in from the south to join the main gorge about ten kilometres west of the Olbalbal Depression. At one time there was a lake here fed by streams from the slopes of Lemagrut, Ngorongoro, and Olmoti, the three volcanoes to the north and east. Sediments in Olduvai date back about 2 million years to a time when there was a large shallow lake here. This is known from the fossils of flamingoes, which need shallow water in order to feed. About 1.7 million years ago, several faults related to the Great Rift Valley cut across the Olduvai Gorge, allowing some of the water in the lake to find an outlet. The fossils of the area show that the fauna changed at about that time from swamp animals to riverine and savanna animals. In the last very active period of faulting, between 100,000 and 30,000 years ago, the north-west foothills of the Ngorongoro volcano subsided to become the Olbalbal Depression and released the last lake waters into the rift valley, encouraging the formation of the gorge as we know it.

The fossil record also shows that, between 2 million and 1.1 million years

Olduvai Gorge: "The place of the wild sisal."

ago, two hominids, *Australopithecus boisei*, a tool-user, and *Homo habilis*, a tool-maker, lived in this area, and that about 1.1 million years ago, a new hominid, *Homo erectus*, lived here.

The first European to see Olduvai Gorge was a Professor Kattwinkle, who came upon it in 1911 while hunting butterflies in what was then German East Africa. The geologist Professor Hans Reck led the first scientific expedition here in 1913 and found a number of fossils, including a human skeleton (dated in the 1970s as being about 17,000 years old). Reck also accompanied Louis Leakey's first expedition to the gorge in 1931. Leakey expected that stone tools would be found here, and his view was vindicated within an hour of the expedition's arrival at the campsite. Mary Leakey first came to the gorge with her husband in 1955, and in 1959 discovered the skull of a hominid called *Zinjanthropus* or *Australopithecus boisei*. Since then, Olduvai Gorge has been irrevocably linked to the search for the origins of humankind.

Anthropology and the study of genetics and evolution have advanced

greatly since then. For example, studies have shown that mitochondrial DNA, which can be inherited only from one's mother because it exists in eggs but not sperm, is identical for all human beings. This means that we all have one common female ancestor — and there are strong indications that she was African. Although early hominids have been found outside Africa, East Africa has had ideal conditions for the preservation of fossils, and study in several disciplines has not found anything that would disallow the evolution of *Homo sapiens* here. The stream of humanity may have a single source in this very part of Africa.

Why would this evolutionary incident have happened in East Africa? Because of natural-selection pressures in conjunction with new evolutionary opportunities resulting from environmental changes. And what caused the environmental changes? The formation of the Great Rift Valley — the very same process that changed the Nile and its sources. What I learned at Olduvai Gorge added an intriguing insight into the story of the events that created the Nile.

The Olduvai Gorge runs eastwards into the main rift, sometimes called the Gregory Rift in honour of John Walter Gregory, the first geologist to

Cheetahs on the Serengeti Plains.

study it (in 1893) and the person who coined the phrase "rift valley." In the last few decades, geologists and geophysicists have learned that about 15 million years ago, the area of Tanzania and Ethiopia underwent "doming," raising the surface as much as one thousand metres in some places. The process is similar to that of a large bubble raising the surface of a pool of thick mud. The area experienced lateral outward pressure, and the rift began to form between parallel faults. Tectonic forces have been shaping the Great Rift Valley ever since, with a great deal of activity in the last 2.5 million years. The process was not uniform, and is, of course, still going on.

The previous major rifting event to affect the African tectonic plate happened over a period of several million years and resulted, about 55 million years ago, in severing a "small" continental plate, now known as India, from the eastern side of Africa. This tectonic plate was then forced northward until it collided with the Asian plate. The collision raised, and

continues to raise, the Himalayan mountains. This affected the wind and weather patterns of the whole planet, and gave birth to the monsoons of the Indian Ocean.

In the latest rifting process in Africa (the ongoing current one), as tectonic forces reshaped the landscape of East Africa, they not only affected the flow

The Wagogo sell their fellow tribe-men only when convicted of magic .... The same is the case amongst their northern neighbours, the Wamasai, . . . who, however, are rarely in the market, and who, when there, though remarkable for strength and intelligence, are little prized, in consequence of their obstinate and untameable characters; — many of them would rather die under the stick than level themselves with women by using a hoe.

RICHARD F. BURTON
The Lake Regions of Central Africa

Overleaf: Maasai morani.

of the rivers, but also profoundly altered the climate of the region. The rising escarpments on the edges of the rift created a rain shadow. As well, the Earth experienced periods of global cooling. These combined to change the vegetation.

The area west of the rift valley remained forest. The area to the east became savanna. Because of these environmental changes, two precursors to *Homo sapiens* diverged. In the west, the Panidae continued to evolve in adaptation to their life in the humid forests of the region. But a smaller group, the Hominidae, who now found themselves on the savanna, were forced to devise new ways of surviving. They became scavengers, adding to their diet the remains of animal kills when they could find them. Over time, those who could walk upright — and were therefore able to scan the ground for carcasses — gained an evolutionary advantage. It was the discoveries of Mary Leakey in the Olduvai Gorge that led to this theory of the origins of humankind, a theory that views Africa as the cradle of the human race. In short, the evolution of our ancestors may well have been triggered by the very same geophysical events that formed the present headwaters of the Nile. Dr. Richard Leakey, Louis Leakey's son, and a noted anthropologist and conservationist in his own right, states unequivocally that up until 2 million years ago, the only forerunners of the human race existed in Africa alone. "How many of the world's population," he asks, "grow up knowing that it was in fact African people who first moved and settled in southern Europe, Central Asia and migrated to the Far East? How many know that Africa's principal contribution to the world is in fact humanity itself?" For Leakey, Africa is not a "laggard" in the development of the world as we know it, but is instead the progenitor. It was not "discovered" by Europeans. It created them.

In some ways, the search for our origins seems very removed from the geographical explorations of the nineteenth century. After all, the explorers were there primarily to chart unknown lands for the benefit of the countries from which they themselves came. But, on the other hand, to be involved in discoveries of such global significance as those of the Leakeys can be seen as a natural extension of all the earlier work — especially since modern science has begun to show just how integrated the Earth is in its physics, its peoples, and its future.

Once we were clear of the Olduvai Gorge, we continued south-west, first

[T] heir well-made limbs and athletic frames ... were displayed to advantage ... and were set off by opal-coloured eyeballs, teeth like pearls, and a profusion of broad massive rings of snowy ivory round their arms, and conical ornaments like dwarf marling-spikes of hippopotamus tooth suspended from their necks.
RICHARD F. BURTON
The Lake Regions of Central Africa

Young Maasai morani pausing after scooping well-water for cattle.

up into the Ngorongoro highlands, then past the mighty Ngorongoro Crater, down to the soda lakes of Eyasi and Manyara, and on to the dry scrub plains and wooded grasslands bordering the Tarangire National Park. From here we went south to the Loibor Serrit in South Maasailand, where we camped just outside the *boma* of Oleure Parmelo, a Maasai elder who boasts seven wives and thirty-one children.

* * *

I awoke to the sound of a ground hornbill drumming its deep notes. The Maasai say it announces the rain, and I could indeed feel the impending rain in the air.

From our campsite, we drove out into the Maasai Steppe on the eastern side of the rift valley. After five hours of driving through arid scrub land interspersed with wide open *mbuga* (grasslands), we reached Makami village in South Maasailand. There had been very little rain — particularly as we moved farther east — and there was plenty of red dust.

In Makami encampment, we met elders and visited two *bomas*. The Maasai elders, and the *morani* (warriors), women, and children were friendly and curious — as though from a different, unspoiled era.

We drove eight kilometres up to Tiakunini, near the base of the Ldigera Mountain, to another encampment of Maasai. There was a constant parade of Maasai while we pitched our tents. A young boy had just been bitten by a black-necked spitting cobra, and was being treated with the "black stone": a porous stone that sucks poison. It is boiled in milk to cleanse it for future use. Thad also "zapped" the bite with a strong electric charge. This is often used now for cobra and other snake bites. Whichever method did the trick, the boy soon seemed well on the way to recovery.

We visited the well, the main water source for the village, and watched naked young *morani* scoop up water for their cattle. This was a *morani* responsibility. The well was thirty metres deep. Rather than do it themselves, the Maasai pay the Chaggas and other tribes to dig these deep wells. The Chagga well-diggers charge 400,000 Tanzanian shillings (about $700 U.S.) to dig the well the first time, plus six steers and six gunnysacks full of corn for cleaning it.

* * *

We were told that three lions — a male, a female, and a young cub — had been snatching cattle and donkeys from the villages. When we were in Tiakunini, the Maasai warriors had not yet dealt with the marauders. Thick bush was the excuse. Rumour also had it that three leopards had been sighted in the

Watered cattle returning from the Maasai well-head, sixty metres below the level of the plain.

vicinity of our camp. Two days before we arrived, one had been disturbed by a young Maasai herdsman returning home and the leopard escaped up a tree. The leopards had given the Maasai little trouble, however, and the villagers felt that the animals treated them with respect. Ordinarily, the respect is mutual, though a leopard had been cornered and killed by three *morani* a few weeks earlier — but not before each warrior had been wounded by the beast.

✷ ✷ ✷

At 5:30 a.m. I woke to the sound of Maasai herdsmen and boys whistling to their herds of cattle and goats, getting them moving before sunrise. We broke camp, watched by several Maasai visitors, as curious about us as we were about them. As we left, they waved *kwa heri* (goodbye). The morning sun glistened on their bronze bodies enveloped in the traditional red cloaks.

We headed north from Makami through thick bush and acacia scrub — all Maasai grazing land. Herds of cattle and goats kicked up dust. Young Maasai herdsmen, following, prodded the cattle and directed the animals with the occasional blast on a whistle.

We passed the granite outcrop of Naibormui (White Neck) Mountain, through some agricultural land, then onto the open Simamtiro Plains — still Maasai country, but also grazing plains for zebra and wildebeest in the wet season.

Heading north, we descended from the Maasai Steppe to the valley just south of Mount Meru. Kilimanjaro was visible in the distance, mostly screened by cloud and haze. Once in a while, though, we caught a glimpse of the unique square-topped, snow-covered mountain peak.

We reached Arusha at 5:00 p.m., after an hour and a half of dreadful driving, over potholes and behind trucks, through clouds of black dust. Though still hot, it grew a little cooler as we reached the Peterson compound. Before dinner I had a most welcome hot shower, the first I had had since Kampala. Dinner was an unusual fondue of eland, wildebeest, topi, and Grant's gazelle — a wilderness feast. Then to bed in the guest house, where this time I slept undisturbed through the night. No thieves or marauders.

✷ ✷ ✷

The next day I spent alone with Joshua in the shadow of Kilimanjaro, first browsing around the town of Arusha, then driving slowly through Arusha National Park, talking, speculating, exchanging ideas, and looking at all sorts of game: buffaloes, dik-diks, water-bucks, bushbucks, colobus monkeys.

In the jungles quadrumana are numerous; lions and leopards ... haunt the forests.
RICHARD F. BURTON
The Lake Regions of Central Africa

Leopards had been sighted in the vicinity of our camp.

Kilimanjaro, at 5,895 metres, is the highest mountain in Africa. At its base it is about fifty kilometres from east to west and about thirty kilometres north to south. The first European known to have seen this mountain was Ernst Rebmann in 1849. The first European known to have reached its peak was Hans Meyer in 1889, forty years later. However, this mountain was probably seen two thousand years ago by Greek sailors who reached East Africa. Kilimanjaro is a dormant, not an extinct, volcano. One can still smell sulphur in certain areas of the mountain. In the late 1880s, Monsignor A. le Roy described his journey from Zanzibar to Kilimanjaro in his book *Au Kilima-Ndjaro (Afrique orientale)*. He wrote that *kilima* was a common word in many of the area's languages for "mountain," but he had trouble finding out what *ndjaro* meant. Some told him that is meant "big," others that it meant "whiteness." Still others told him that it derived from a Maasai word meaning "water" because of the many streams that came from the mountain.

Joshua has been on many safaris with me and has become a close friend. His tribe, the Chagga, are a mountain people. According to Chagga tradition, when the tribe's founding ancestors arrived on the slopes of Kilimanjaro, five centuries or more ago, they came upon the Wakonyingo or Wateremba pygmies, who ran away when they were approached. Only a few of them stayed and they now live by cultivating bananas. The Chagga came to control the southern and eastern sides of Kilimanjaro. It is not known exactly when the first settlements were established, but shards of pottery and stone bowls dating back to the time of Christ, and hence pre-Chagga, have been found on the western flank of the mountain. The chief of one Chagga clan has a staff with notches indicating that his people have been recording their existence in this way for forty generations, though most modern Chagga are aware of their genealogy for the past dozen or so generations — the past three centuries.

The fertile areas at the base of Kilimanjaro have sustained hunter-gatherers, shepherds, and farmers for countless generations. Many tribes settled in the plains around the mountain, including Maasai, Arusha, Pare, and Dorobo. The various tribes were able to pool their skills. Through hunting, agriculture, animal husbandry, metalworking, and other occupations, they prospered and extended their territory.

Their arms, which are ever hung up close at hand, are broad-headed spears of soft iron, long "Sine," or double-edged daggers, with ribbed wooden handles fastened to the blade by a strip of cow's tail shrunk on, and "Rungu," or wooden knob-kerries, with double bulges that weight the weapon as it whirls through the air. They ignore and apparently despise the bow and arrows, but in battle they carry the Pavoise, or large hide-shield, affected by the Kafirs of the Cape.

RICHARD F. BURTON
The Lake Regions of Central Africa

Maasai chief with hand-made panga.

Maasai maidens.

Before colonization, there were more than a hundred sovereign Chagga chieftancies on the lower slopes of Kilimanjaro. Orombo of the Keni region, Sina of Kibosho, Rindi of Moshi, Marealle of Marangu, Abdiel Shangali of Machame were some of the famous chiefs. By 1899, violent clashes had reduced the number of chieftancies to thirty-seven. When the slave and ivory trade was at its peak in the mid-nineteenth century, Kilimanjaro was a meeting place for caravans using the route across Maasailand from the coast to Victoria Nyanza. Coastal traders bought ivory from the Chagga rulers and obtained provisions from the Chagga markets. Chagga rulers provided safe campsites for the caravans and safe passage through their territory.

Colonization by the Germans between 1886 and 1916 brought rapid and far-reaching change to the world of the Chagga, introducing them to cash, Christianity, formal education, and the commercial cultivation of coffee. A cash-based economy came to replace the barter economy whose monetary units had been cattle, pigs, and iron hoes.

The British controlled Kilimanjaro from 1916 to 1961. The first British administrator of the area, Sir Charles Dundas, came to be admired by the Chagga for his efforts to protect and promote the interests of native coffee growers in the face of colonial plantation owners' objections. He felt that Kilimanjaro needed a cash crop, and coffee filled the bill. Many Chagga had grown coffee in their own gardens for their personal use, but Dundas promoted the formation of the Kilimanjaro Native Planters Association, later replaced by the Kilimanjaro Native Co-operative Union (KNCU), and instituted controls that protected the business rights of native growers. During their tenure in power, the British oversaw many political changes: in 1928, a Council of Chiefs representing the three major groupings of chieftancies was introduced and was further formalized in 1946. In 1960, the district's first president was elected.

The cultivation of coffee, the spread of Christianity, the establishment of school systems, political reorganization, the importation of goods, and the provision of medical care changed the tribal society of the Chagga forever. After Tanzanian independence in 1961, the Kilimanjaro region became a collection of seventeen municipal districts whose capital is Moshi. Kilimanjaro remains an important part of Tanzania, not least because it has supplied the country with a disproportionate number of administrators and business leaders.

The Chagga have traditionally thrived by combining agriculture with the rearing of animals, sometimes having had to protect their herds from the marauding Maasai. A complex irrigation system, developed over centuries, has improved banana and maize cultivation and has allowed the successful growing of other crops — manioc, sweet potatoes, kidney beans, and French beans — some of which are exported.

☆ ☆ ☆

In all of Africa, only two countries escaped the colonial domination that lasted from the 1880s to the 1960s and 1970s: Liberia and Ethiopia (if we ignore Italy's attempt to subjugate it, 1937–42). Many problems in African countries today are the inevitable result of colonialism. The explorers, especially Livingstone, but Speke and Stanley, too, were convinced that they were a force for good in the lands to which they came. They believed they were laying the groundwork for a magnificent enterprise. They would have been shocked and grieved to see the exploitation that followed their efforts.

As we made our journey, particularly when we travelled west of Lake Victoria into turbulent refugee territory, I knew that I was seeing at first hand one of the worst legacies of colonialism. The conflict between the Hutu and the Tutsi tribes in Rwanda is a perfect example of this. We may never know

Overleaf: Captain Burton bethought himself of gaining a little elementary training in East African travelling, by spending the remainder of the dry season in inspecting various places on the coast; and, if a favourable opportunity presented itself, he felt desirous of having a peep at the snowy Kilimandjaro Mountain, of which the Rev. Mr Rebmann, who first discovered it, had sent home reports, and which had excited such angry and unseemly contests amongst our usually sedate though speculative carpet-geographers in England as rendered a further inspection highly necessary.

JOHN HANNING SPEKE
What Led to the Discovery of the Source of the Nile

exactly what the relationship between the Hutu and Tutsi was before they were encountered by Europeans. They were first described by John Hanning Speke in his *Journal of the Discovery of the Source of the Nile*, and he and those who followed developed what we might now regard as naïve, romantic, and racist theories of the origins of and the relations between the two groups. The original inhabitants of Rwanda do seem to have been the Twa pygmies. First the Hutu, from the north, and then the Tutsi, from the Ethiopian Horn, do seem to have migrated into the area. Before the Europeans arrived, the Hutu and Tutsi had worked out a mutually beneficial relationship. The Hutu were primarily concerned with farming, and the Tutsi with herding (because they measured wealth in animals). When the Europeans arrived, the Tutsi monarch had beneath him three sorts of chiefs: those responsible for landholding (agriculture and taxation), for men (the army), and for pastures (grazing lands). Most of the chiefs were Tutsi, but many, especially those dealing with agriculture, were Hutu. First the Germans and then the Belgians encouraged the Tutsi to be junior administrators and civil servants and to assume other social roles of power over the Hutu, relegating them to a sort of peasant class — a form of societal organization that the Europeans were perhaps more familiar and comfortable with. The resentments, inequalities, and disruption caused by this imposition of European values is a direct antecedent of the Rwandan tragedy of racial prejudice, bloodshed, and vengeance which has been playing out for the last forty years.

We know that the tribal conflicts that force thousands of people to flee as refugees are not solely the result of colonialism, nor did colonialism result only in evil. Roads and education are but two proofs of the opposite. But I will never forget my first sight of the crowds of refugees on the shores of Lake Tanganyika. That sight jarred me as little else has in a lifetime of travel. The deeper into refugee territory we went, the more appalling the evidence of their plight became — so that some sights are permanently etched in my memory.

The central lake region of Africa has been opened to the rest of the world for only 140 years — a brief period in the history of a continent that may be the cradle of the human race. But the impact of that 140 years has been great. Less than 50 years after Burton and Speke, Africa was no longer the totally impenetrable, completely inscrutable, commercially unpromising "dark continent," but instead had been divided up among the European powers, who ruthlessly exploited its wealth at the same time as they established the beginnings of a modern infrastructure on the European pattern. The transition from colonial domination to independence was equally swift, as many parts of the continent became a laboratory for experiments in post-colonial government. The boundaries of Africa, created in the nineteenth century by the colonizers — primarily England, France, Belgium, and Germany — are European boundaries, not natural or tribal boundaries. There is little doubt now that these colonizers' boundaries will blur, giving way to natural geographical boundaries created by rivers like the Nile; mountains like the Ruwenzoris; and lakes like Tanganyika, Albert, and

Victoria. Tribal and religious boundaries, in part affected by the growth of Islam in Africa, will also begin to replace political boundaries. The rise of Islam will substantially affect the history of many African countries during the next century and will dramatically alter the artificial boundaries created in the nineteenth-century grab at Africa.

The rebirth of tribalism in Africa may also greatly affect the reorganization of the continent and the redrawing of borders and boundaries. It will be very interesting to see how the thrust towards democracy will meld with the re-establishment of tribal Africa. In countries where food production cannot keep pace with population growth, the struggle for scarce resources will also influence the movement of peoples across the current national boundaries. The migrations of people and the shifting of boundaries in many African countries are likely to continue for many years yet. But the turmoil is not a new phenomenon. Burton, Speke, Baker — the work of the explorers was constantly being affected by conflicts in the areas they visited. The delicate relations among the three kingdoms visited by Speke — the balance of power among Mtesa, Rumanika, and Kamrasi — added tension and drama to his journals. The indigenous conflicts of Africa — tribal and otherwise — were masked during colonial rule, just as many of the ethnic conflicts of Central Europe were masked during Communist rule. They are re-emerging now, and the way they are sorted out may not necessarily be to the liking or benefit of the Western nations.

As well, the attitude of most colonials was that all African history, culture, and tradition was perhaps colourful, but so primitive and unimportant as not to be worth study, respect, or preservation. As independence spread, so did the impulse to "Africanize." Africans felt the need to rediscover, and accept (and get others to accept) the worth of their rich past as equal in value to that of Europeans and other non-Africans.

Western aid and investment are undoubtedly important to many African countries, and the Western nations are adept at using economic leverage to promote the policies they favour. But the new forces of Islam, tribalism, and changing self-image are powerful, and economic leverage may no longer be enough. We are entering an era when partnerships will need to replace financial aid in the relations between African and Western nations. This is certainly possible in the campaign to preserve habitats and wildlife. It is possible in other areas, too, I believe, especially if Africa is welcomed into full participation in the global economy.

Such cooperation is possible, however, only if the attitudes of both parties change, and this cannot happen overnight. The generosity of donors will not achieve its aims if it is accompanied by behaviour and conditions that are humiliating to the recipients. And in our complex human nature, gratitude for help may be mixed with feelings of resentment, and even rage. Moreover, even though independence has been won, it is still difficult for many Africans to feel unequivocal goodwill towards "white" people who, until quite recently, were privileged members of a ruling minority. Given this context, even the benign — or at least neutral — actions of a non-African can be misunderstood.

It can be quite upsetting to be labelled an "exploiter" unjustly. I had to think long and hard to understand why I was so disturbed by the incident in which Pollangyo was accused of selling out because he helped me get some photographs I wanted. It was a paradoxical situation, because I was taking photographs of a Tanzanian school, the sort of fine school that the British set up in Africa. Such schools have launched many Africans into excellent careers both at home and abroad. That there should be anger at me and an accusation that I was showing "poor" Africa to the "rich" world seemed inappropriate. It was not poor people I was photographing. Those particular schoolchildren were extremely well looked-after. Yet the assumption was that I must be trying to take advantage of Africans in some way. If that did not reveal deep antagonism towards a man perceived as "white" then I misunderstood what was happening. The attitude seems to be: "What's past cannot be changed, but it will never be forgotten by us." This antagonism — a hangover from the days of colonialism — is probably inevitable, now and for some time to come.

* * *

I spent the last two days of my African journey with Joshua. With Joshua I did not need to worry about any hangovers from colonialism. Despite our different origins, Joshua and I are soulmates. We understand each other. We trust each other. This rapport and mutual trust grew out of several journeys, during which we shared some good times and some bad times. These last few days were an opportunity to cement those bonds further by talking together and clarifying what we had both experienced.

We talked about Kilimanjaro, fitting it into our story. In some ways, I knew more about Kilimanjaro and its tribal legends than Joshua did, and it was wonderful to be able to share with him some of what I had learned. He was clearly fascinated with the folklore I had unearthed. He was also delighted to learn more about the history and the former customs of his own people, the Chagga.

We had a great time together on the lower slopes of the mountain. And then a fantastic evening: our first full sighting, after six o'clock, of Kilimanjaro. The sun setting behind us cast a magical orange glow on the majestic snow-covered cone.

The next day we explored the mountain again, and I also had the great honour of being a guest in Joshua's home and having lunch with him and his wife and children. I felt then a bond not only with Joshua and his family, but also with the past — with Burton at ease among the caravan traders in Tabora, with Speke as he entertained the ladies of Mtesa's court, with Livingstone being attended by his faithful native servants even in death, and with Stanley who went to Africa as a newspaperman and left it a hero.

It was a convivial and appetizing meal. Bananas, which are harvested year round, are the staple food of the Chagga. Stewed with meat, they produce *ntori*, a very popular dish. Fermented and mixed with eleusine they produce *mbebe*, a local beer, consumption of which is traditionally limited to festive occasions. We ate and drank well. It was a festive occasion — a fitting end to our successful quest.

The hours and minutes ticked away. The closer I came to departure the more I felt that Africa will always be a mystery. The more one learns, the more there is to learn. At one time I really thought that I could offer some wisdom about Africa's past, some insight into its present and future. But in the end I felt that Africa always had and always would ultimately provide its own answers.

And the Nile, just when it seems to have revealed all of its mysteries, will suddenly find a way to puzzle us anew.

* * *

In terms of the time it took, our safari had been short, measured in months instead of years as it did for the Victorian explorers. In terms of distance travelled, however, we had done quite well. Right after I landed at Kilimanjaro Airport, I made a note of the odometer reading in Thad's Land Rover — 114,644 kilometres. Now, just as I was about to depart, it read 124,668 kilometres. Our journey had covered a total of 10,024 kilometres — roughly equivalent to one-fourth of the Earth's circumference at the equator — and one and a half times the length of the Nile.

Just a few hours earlier, at 6:00 p.m., in Machame I saw my final sunset on Kilimanjaro. The evening rays touched the peak for just a few, brief minutes; then the clouds swirled in, cutting short my last look at the legendary, square-topped mountain.

Two beers with Joshua and then a hazardous drive to the airport. Lights dimmed, oncoming cars flashing their high beams. Concentration. "A lot of accidents," Joshua said. I was not a bit surprised.

At 10:10 p.m. I was aboard a KLM flight for Amsterdam where I could catch a connecting flight to England. I wrote furiously in my diary, recording all I could remember of Joshua's final words. In his own simple, truthful way, he seemed to get it right and to put it all together.

"The Nile is the greatest river of Africa, and Lake Victoria is the great lake. When you see it you know it is really the start of the Nile. We have gone all the way around it, and have been in some very dangerous places. We were lucky. We were also lucky to understand the waters — not just Lake Victoria but the other lakes, Lake Albert and Lake George and Lake Edward. And also the two big rivers — the Kagera and the Semliki. Maybe the Kagera is the Nile. It should be called the Nile before Lake Victoria. And the Semliki is the Nile before Lake Albert. The two rivers give a lot of water to the two lakes. And also the Ruwenzori Mountains. All the lakes and rivers flow from the mountains into the Semliki. Incredible. Originally, they thought

Kilimanjaro was the source of the Nile. That would have been good —
because it is my home. But the Ruwenzori range is really the 'Mountains of
the Moon,' and also the source."

That was a pretty fair description of our geographical findings. But we
had gained so much more from the trip than mere geographical knowledge,
and I was delighted — and somewhat startled — by what he said next. It
seems right, somehow, to let Joshua have the last word.

"This has been the longest journey of my life. I have been to places where I
would never have gone. I have seen people I would never have seen. And I
have done things I would never have done. The Nile was our goal, and the
source was our challenge. But we found much more. We found ourselves. We

are stronger and have more understanding — of the world, of the people, of you, and me, and God too.

"You know, Christo, we are all children of God. The rains come, the rivers start, the lakes form, and bigger rivers flow. Like the Nile. Like the lakes. Like the clouds. And the world goes on. You know the true source of the Nile, Christo? Up there. In the heavens. God knows. That is the true source."

CHRONOLOGY

1813	Mar. 19	David Livingstone born, Blantyre, Scotland.
1821	Mar. 19	Richard Burton born, Torquay, Devon.
	June 8	Samuel White Baker born, London, England.
1827	Apr. 11	James Augustus Grant born, Nairn, Scotland.
	May 4	John Hanning Speke born, Bideford, Devon.
1831		Charles Darwin sails on *Beagle*, under Capt. Fitzroy.
1832		Sayyid Said, Sultan of Oman, moves capital from Muscat to Zanzibar.
1838	Sept. 5	Livingstone accepted as medical missionary to China by London Missionary Society.
1839		Livingstone meets Dr. Moffat; decides to work in Africa.
1840	Nov.	Livingstone completes medical Licentiate, is ordained missionary.
	Dec. 8	Livingstone sails for Africa (first trip, 1840 – 56).
1841	Jan. 28	Henry Morton Stanley born, Denbigh, Wales; baptized John Rowlands.
1843	Aug. 3	Baker marries Henrietta Martin.
1845	Jan. 2	Livingstone marries Mary Moffat.
1847		Speke meets Grant in India.

1848		Baker founds settlement of Nuwara Eliya, Ceylon.
	May 11	J. Rebmann sees Kilimanjaro near equator; snow cap suggests Nile source.
1849	Dec. 3	Johann Ludwig Krapf sees snow-capped Mt. Kenya.
1853	Nov.	Livingstone travels west to Angola (May 1854), then east to mouth of Zambezi (May, 1856); first European to cross Africa.
1854	May	Burton leaves England on Royal Geographical Society (RGS) expedition to Somaliland.
	Sept.	Baker and Speke meet on ship from Bombay to Aden, where Speke meets Burton.
1855	Apr. 19	Attack at Berbera ends Somaliland expedition; Burton and Speke wounded.
	Dec. 29	Henrietta Baker dies in Spain.
1856	Oct. 18	Sayyid Said dies at sea.
	Nov.	Burton and Speke arrive in Zanzibar to arrange Nile expedition.
		Sayyid Majid, son of Said, declared Sultan of Zanzibar.
	Dec. 9	Livingstone reaches England (end of first trip).
1857		Livingstone resigns from London Missionary Society. Stanley goes to United States as cabin-boy; jumps ship in New Orleans.
	Feb.	Indian Mutiny begins.
	June 16	Burton and Speke sail for Bagamoyo on *Artémise*.

Infancy gilds the fairy picture with its own lines and it is probably never forgotten …. They would go back to freedom and enjoyment as fast as would our own sons of toil, and be heedless to the charms of hard work and no play, which we think so much better for them, if not for us.

DR. DAVID LIVINGSTONE,
Letter, 1871

1857	June 27	Burton and Speke start march from Kaole.
	Nov. 7	Burton and Speke reach Kazeh.
	Dec. 4	Livingstone delivers Cambridge Lectures; formation of Universities Mission to Central Africa.
1858		Darwin and A.R. Wallace publish theories of evolution.
	Feb. 4	Burton and Speke cross Malagarasi River.
	Feb. 8	Livingstone appointed British consul at Quelimane; leads expedition to East and Central Africa (second trip, 1858 – 64).
	Feb. 14	Burton and Speke reach Ujiji on Lake Tanganyika.
	Apr.– May	Burton and Speke seek northern river said to flow into Lake Tanganyika.
	July 9	Speke leaves Tabora to find rumoured vast lake to the north (Lake Victoria).
	Aug. 3	Speke sights Victoria Nyanza at Mwanza.
	Sept. 26	Burton and Speke leave Tabora for return to coast.
1859		Building of Suez Canal begins. Darwin's *The Origin of Species* published. Livingstone explores Shiré River, a northern tributary of Zambezi.
	Feb. 2	Burton and Speke reach Indian Ocean coast near Kaole.
	May 8,9	Speke reaches England after expedition with Burton; tells Sir Roderick Murchison of finding Lake Victoria.
1860		Burton's *The Lake Regions of Central Africa* published.
	Sept. 21	Speke and Grant set out from Zanzibar.
1861	Apr. 12	American Civil War begins with shelling of Fort Sumter.
	Apr. 15	Samuel and Florence Baker start trip up Nile.
	June 23	Baker sees Atbara River in flood.
	Dec. 14	Prince Albert dies.
	Dec. 15	Rumanika presents Speke with sitatunga specimens.
1862		Stanley joins Confederate Army, and is captured by enemy.

1862	Jan. 15	Speke crosses Kitangulé River.
	Jan. 28	Speke sees Victoria Nyanza from hills north of Karagwe.
	Feb. 13	Speke crosses Mwerango River flowing north, indicating Nile watershed.
	Feb. 20	Speke reaches Mtesa's palace near present-day Kampala.
	Apr. 27	Livingstone's wife, Mary, dies in Shupanga on Zambezi River.
	May 27	Grant arrives at Mtesa's palace.
	June	Bakers reach Khartoum after year exploring Abyssinian rivers.
	July 7	Speke and Grant leave Mtesa, head for Kamrasi's court near present-day Masindi Port.
	July 16	Speke sends home specimens of Grant's zebra.
	July 19	Speke and Grant separate; Speke heads east to Nile.
	July 28	Speke reaches and names Ripon Falls.
	Aug. 15	Speke's attempt to boat down Nile thwarted by rapids; he continues overland.
	Sept. 9	Speke and Grant reach Kamrasi's court.
	Nov. 9	Speke and Grant attempt canoe trip down Kafu to Nile; go overland from Karuma Falls.
	Dec. 20	Bakers leave Khartoum for Gondokoro.
1863		Stanley enlists in Union Army to gain release from prison.
	Feb. 1	Bakers reach Gondokoro; Speke and Grant see Nile for first time in three months.
	Feb. 16	Speke and Grant reach Gondokoro and meet Bakers.
	Mar. 26	Bakers head east and south from Gonodokoro, seeking Luta Nzige Lake.
	June 22	Stanley discharged from Union Army.
	July 2	Livingstone receives dispatch from Earl Russell, recalling Zambezi expedition.
	Sept.	Speke's *Journal of the Discovery of the Source of the Nile* published.
1864		Speke's *What Led to the Discovery of the Source of the Nile* and Grant's *A Walk across Africa* published.
	Jan. 22	Bakers reach Nile near Karuma Falls on north edge of Bunyoro.

1864 Feb. 6 Bakers reach M'ruli, Kamrasi's capital.

Feb. 14 Livingstone sails for Bombay on return to England.

Feb. 22 Bakers leave Kamrasi's court for Luta Nzige.

Mar. 14 Bakers reach Luta Nzige; name it Albert Nyanza.

Mar. 22 Bakers canoe north from Vakovia, surviving storm on Lake Albert.

Apr. 3 Bakers reach Magungo at mouth of Somerset River (Victoria Nile).

Apr. 6 Baker sees and names Murchison Falls.

Apr. Bakers continue east along Victoria Nile on foot; wait two months on island during Kamrasi's war.

July 23 Livingstone arrives in London (end of second trip).

Sept. 15 Speke dies in shooting accident day before planned debate with Burton at British Association conference.

Sept. 19 Livingstone addresses British Association about slave trade.

Sept. Livingstone writes *Narrative of an Expedition to the Zambesi*....

1865 Feb. Bakers reach Gondokoro; sail for Khartoum.

mid-May Bakers reach Khartoum.

May 22 Murchison delivers Speke eulogy at RGS; assigns Livingstone to settle Burton/ Speke dispute.

Aug. Livingstone sails for Africa.

Aug. 31 Bakers reach Suez.

Oct. Bakers reach England.

1866 Baker knighted; his *The Albert N'yanza, Great Basin of the Nile* published.

Mar. 19 Livingstone sets out from Zanzibar on final expedition (1866 – 73).

Dec. False report of Livingstone's death reaches Zanzibar.

1867 Stanley becomes war correspondent during U.S. Indian wars.

Apr. 2 Livingstone reaches south end of Lake Tanganyika.

1868 Jan. 20 Stanley hired by *New York Herald*.

1869 Baker appointed Governor of Equatoria by Khedive of Egypt.

Mar. 14 Livingstone reaches Ujiji on Lake Tanganyika.

Apr. 5 Baker accepts command of Expedition for the Suppression of the Slave Trade.

July 12 Livingstone sets out to explore north-west of Lake Tanganyika.

Oct. 18 Stanley sent to find Livingstone.

Nov. 17 Official opening of Suez Canal: Stanley covers event for *Herald*; Bakers host Prince and Princess of Wales.

1870 Sayyid Majid dies; succeeded by his brother Bargash.

Dec. 31 Stanley arrives in Zanzibar on trip to find Livingstone.

1871 Mar. 21 Stanley leaves Bagamoyo for Lake Tanganyika.

July 15 Livingstone sees massacre by Arab slavers.

Nov. 5 Livingstone reaches Ujiji.

Nov. 10 Stanley finds Livingstone at Ujiji.

Nov. 28 Livingstone and Stanley find that Ruzizi River flows into Lake Tanganyika.

Dec. Stanley and Livingstone return to Ujiji; set out for Unyanyembe (Tabora).

1872 Mar. 14 Stanley leaves Livingstone at Unyanyembe with promise of re-supply.

May 6 Stanley reaches Bagamoyo.

May 29 Stanley leaves Zanzibar for England.

Aug. 1 Stanley reaches London.

Aug. 16 Stanley addresses Geographical Section of British Association.

Aug. 17 Stanley, in running battle with RGS, is accused of fraud.

Aug. 25 Livingstone leaves Unyanyembe for Lake Tanganyika.

Sept. Livingstone travels down east side of Lake Tanganyika.

Oct. 21 RGS gives Stanley its Gold Medal.

Nov. 15 Stanley's *How I Found Livingstone* published.

Dec. 3 Stanley lectures in New York about meeting Livingstone.

1873		Baker resigns as Governor of Equatoria; is replaced by Gen. "Chinese" Gordon.
	May 1	Livingstone dies near south shore of Lake Bangweolo.
	June	Britain and Sayyid Bargash sign treaty for suppression of slave trade in Zanzibar.
1874	Feb. 1	Livingstone's servants reach Bagamoyo, having carried his remains about 3000 kilometres.
	Feb. 25	Stanley, at Cape Verde, learns of Livingstone's death; decides to complete his explorations.
	Apr. 18	Livingstone buried in Westminster Abbey; Stanley is pallbearer.
	Nov.	*The Last Journals of David Livingstone* published; Stanley begins exploration from Zanzibar.
1875	Feb. 27	Stanley begins circumnavigation of Lake Victoria.
	Apr. 5	Stanley meets Mtesa at Rubaga (present-day Kampala).
	Aug.	Stanley confirms Ripon Falls as only northern effluent of Lake Victoria.
	Dec. 12	Stanley crosses Katonga River.
1876		Sayyid Bargash of Zanzibar outlaws slave trade in all his dominions; United Mission to Central Africa erects church on ruins of Zanzibar slave market.
	Feb. 19	Stanley crosses Kagera River on way to Rumanika's capital.
	Feb. 28	Stanley meets Rumanika, who promises assistance.
	May 27	Stanley reaches Ujiji; monsoons have advanced shore 220 metres from 1871 point.
	June 11	Stanley begins circumnavigation of Lake Tanganyika from Ujiji.
	July 15	Stanley proves Lukuga River flows out of Lake Tanganyika.
	July 27	Hostile locals end Stanley's hope of exploring Lakes Albert and Kivu.
	Nov.	Stanley follows Lualaba River westward down Zaïre River.
1877	Aug. 9	Stanley reaches west coast, 998 days after leaving Bagamoyo.

1878		Stanley's *Through the Dark Continent* published.
1884		Members of Church Missionary Society martyred in Uganda.
1886		Burton made Knight Commander of St. Michael and St. George.
1886 – 88		Burton's *Thousand Nights and a Night* published.
1887 – 89		Stanley leads Emin Pasha Rescue Expedition; sees Ruwenzoris.
1890		Stanley's *In Darkest Africa* published.
	Oct. 20	Burton dies while British consul at Trieste.
1891	July 12	Stanley marries Dorothy Tennant in Westminster Abbey.
1892		Stanley becomes British citizen; is elected to Parliament.
	Feb. 11	Grant dies, Nairn, Scotland.
1893		J.W. Gregory coins term "rift valley" after study of African Rift.
	Dec. 30	Baker dies of angina in Devon.
1897	Apr. 5	Sayyid Hamoud of Zanzibar abolishes legal status of slavery.
1899		Queen Victoria confers Grand Cross of the Bath (knighthood) on Stanley.
1904	May 10	Stanley dies of pleurisy in London.
	May 17	Stanley's funeral in Westminster Abbey; burial refused there; ashes buried in Pirbright village churchyard.
1959	July 17	Mary Leakey discovers skull of *Australopithecus boisei* in Olduvai Gorge.

BIBLIOGRAPHY

Explorers' Accounts of Nile Expeditions

Baker, Samuel White. *The Albert N'yanza, Great Basin of the Nile, and Explorations of the Nile Sources.* 2 vols. London: Macmillan and Co., 1866.

Burton, Richard F. *The Lake Regions of Central Africa: A Picture of Exploration.* 2 vols. London: Longman, Green, Longman & Roberts, 1860.

———. *The Nile Basin.* London: Tinsley Brothers, 1864. Reprint, London: Frank Cass & Co., 1967.

———. *Personal Narrative of a Pilgrimage to Al-Madinah & Meccah.* Memorial Edition. London: Tylston and Edwards, 1893. Reprint, New York: Dover, 1964.

———. *Zanzibar: City, Island & Coast.* 2 vols. London: Tinsley Brothers, 1872.

Grant, James Augustus. *A Walk across Africa or Domestic Scenes from my Nile Journal.* Edinburgh: William Blackwood & Sons, 1864.

Speke, J.H. *Journal of the Discovery of the Source of the Nile.* New York: Harper & Brothers, 1864.

———. *What Led to the Discovery of the Source of the Nile.* Edinburgh: William Blackwood & Sons, 1864. Reprint, London: Frank Cass & Co., 1967.

Stanley, Henry M. *How I Found Livingstone: Travels, Adventures and Discoveries in Central Africa.* London: Rea & Inchbould, 1873. Reprint, London: Sampson Low, Marston, Searle & Rivington, 1887.

———. *In Darkest Africa; or, The Quest, Rescue, and Retreat of Emin Governor of Equatoria.* 2 vols. London: Sampson Low, Marston and Company, 1890; new edition, 1893.

———. *The Life, Labours, Perilous Adventures and Discoveries of Dr. Livingstone....* Toronto: Maclear & Co., 1873.

———. *Through the Dark Continent.* 2 vols. London: Sampson Low, Marston and Co., 1878. Reprint, Toronto: Dover, 1988.

Stanley, Richard, and Alan Neame. *The Exploration Diaries of H.M. Stanley.* London: William Kimber & Co., 1961.

Explorers and Exploration

Bierman, John. *Dark Safari: The Life behind the Legend of Henry Morton Stanley.* New York: Alfred A. Knopf, 1990.

Bradnum, Frederick. *The Long Walks: Journeys to the Sources of the White Nile.* London: Victor Gollancz, 1969.

Brodie, Fawn M. *The Devil Drives: A Life of Sir Richard Burton.* London: Eyre & Spottiswoode, 1967. Reprint, London: Eland, 1986.

Carrington, Richard. *The Tears of Isis: The Story of a New Journey from the Mouth to the Source of the River Nile.* London: Chatto & Windus, 1959.

Ettinger, Nathalie, Elspeth Huxley, and Paul Hamilton. *Africa and Asia: Mapping Two Continents.* London: Aldus Books and Jupiter Books, 1973.

Hall, Richard. *Lovers on the Nile.* London: Quartet Books, 1981.

Hugon, Anne. *The Exploration of Africa from Cairo to the Cape.* Trans. Alexandra Campbell. London: Thames and Hudson, 1993.

Ludwig, Emil. *The Nile: The Life-Story of a River.* Trans. Mary H. Lindsay. New York: Viking Press, 1937.

Maitland, Alexander. *Speke and the Discovery of the Source of the Nile.* Newton Abbot: Victorian (and Modern History) Book Club, 1971.

McLynn, Frank. *Burton: Snow upon the Desert.* London: John Murray, 1990.

McLynn, Frank. *Stanley: The Making of an African Explorer*. London: Constable, 1989.

Middleton, Dorothy. *Baker of the Nile*. London: Falcon Press, 1949.

Moorehead, Alan. *The White Nile*. London: Hamish Hamilton, 1960.

Rice, Edward. *Captain Sir Richard Francis Burton*. New York: Charles Scribner's Sons, 1990.

Richards, Charles, ed. *Burton and Lake Tanganyika, 1857*. Early Travellers in East Africa series. Nairobi: East African Literature Bureau [1957?], printed 1965.

Royal Geographical Society. *The Sources of the Nile: Explorers' Maps A.D. 1856 – 1891*. Notes by G.R. Crone. London: Royal Geographical Society, 1964.

Seaver, George. *David Livingstone: His Life and Letters*. London: Lutterworth Press, 1957.

African History and Geology

Allegre, Claude. *The Behavior of the Earth*. Cambridge, Mass.: Harvard University Press, 1988.

Atlas of Exploration. Foreword by John Hemming, director of Royal Geographical Society. New York: Oxford University Press, 1977.

Bere, Rennie. *The Way to the Mountains of the Moon*. London: Arthur Barker, 1966.

Davidson, Basil, with J.E.F. Minha and Bethwell A. Ogot. *The Growth of African Civilisation: East and Central Africa to the Late Nineteenth Century*. Nairobi: Longmans of Kenya Ltd., 1967.

Elton J.F. *The Lakes and Mountains of Eastern and Central Africa*. London: John Murray, 1879. Reprint, London: Frank Cass & Co., Ltd., 1968.

Hurst, H.E. *The Lake Plateau Basin of the Nile*. Cairo: Ministry of Public Works, 1927.

Hyam, Ronald. *Empire and Sexuality: The British Experience*. Manchester and New York: Manchester University Press, 1992.

July, Robert W. *A History of the African People*, 2d ed. New York: Charles Scribner's Sons, 1974.

le Roy, Mgr. A. *Au Kilima-Ndjaro (Afrique Orientale)*. Paris: L. de Soye et fils, no date.

Leakey, Mary. *Olduvai Gorge: My Search for Early Man*. London: Collins, 1979.

Leakey, Richard. *The Origin of Humankind*. New York: Basic Books (Harper Collins), 1994.

Lloyd, B.W., ed. *Livingstone: 1873–1973*. Cape Town: C. Struik (Pty.) Ltd., 1973.

Mamdani, Mahmood. *Citizen and Subject: Contemporary Africa and the Legacy of Late Colonialism*. Kampala, Uganda: Fountain Publishers, 1996.

Martin, Phyllis M., and Patrick O'Meara. *Africa*, 3d ed. London: James Currey, 1995.

Odhiambo, E.S. Atieno, T.I. Ouso, and J.F.M. Williams. *A History of East Africa*. London: Longman, 1977.

Oliver, Roland, and Anthony Atmore. *Africa since 1800*, 4th ed. Cambridge: Cambridge University Press, 1994.

Pakenham, Thomas. *The Scramble for Africa: 1876–1912*. London: Abacus/George Weidenfeld & Nicolson, 1991.

Prunier, Gérard. *The Rwanda Crisis 1959–1994: History of a Genocide*. London: Hurst & Co., 1995.

Said, Rushdi. *The River Nile: Geology, Hydrology and Utilization*. Oxford: Pergamon Press, 1993.

Sheriff, Abdul, ed. *The History and Conservation of Zanzibar Stone Town*. London: James Currey (The Department of Archives, Museums & Antiquities, Zanzibar), 1995.

Stacey, Tom. *Summons to Ruwenzori*. London: Secker & Warburg, 1965.

Tanner, Ralph E.S. *The Witch Murders in Sukumaland*. Uppsala: Scandinavian Institute of African Studies, 1970.

INDEX

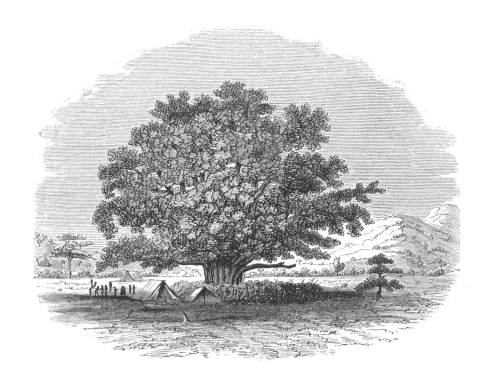